Wrongly Convicted

Wrongly Convicted

Perspectives on Failed Justice

Edited by
SAUNDRA D. WESTERVELT
JOHN A. HUMPHREY

With a Foreword by
MICHAEL L. RADELET

RUTGERS UNIVERSITY PRESS
New Brunswick, New Jersey, and London

Library of Congress Cataloging-in-Publication Data

Wrongly convicted : perspectives on failed justice / Saundra D. Westervelt and
John A. Humphrey ; with a foreword by Michael L. Radelet.
    p. cm
    Includes bibliographical references and index
    ISBN 0–8135–2951–4 (cloth: alk. paper)—ISBN 0–8135–2952–2 (pbk. : alk. paper)
    1. Trials—United States. 2. Judicial error—United States.   3. Criminal justice,
    Administration of—United States.   I. Westervelt, Saundra Davis, 1968–
    II. Humphrey, John A.

KF220 .W76 2001
364.973—dc21   00–045748

British Cataloging-in-Publication data for this book is available from the British Library.

Manufactured in the United States of America

*To the wrongly convicted, known
and unknown, and the advocates
and researchers who fight for the
exoneration of the innocent and for
safeguards against continued injustice*

Contents

MICHAEL L. RADELET

Foreword

Why are so many people making so much of a fuss about the possibility that innocent people are being convicted of crimes? After all, everyone probably agrees that most of those convicted and sentenced are guilty, and an occasional mistake is the price we must pay to ensure that as many criminals as possible are arrested, prosecuted, and convicted. And as the defenders of our current justice system so frequently claim, even if the defendant is innocent of this particular crime, she or he probably committed lots of other crimes for which no conviction was obtained.

Nevertheless, one can imagine other ways to respond to the question. For example, what if someone discovered a mechanical flaw in the space shuttle just minutes before the flaw would have caused a deadly explosion? In such a case, we would expect the people involved to learn from the mistake. Authorities would act quickly to study the problem, conducting endless reviews of procedures and interviews of personnel to learn how the flaw was made and how it was overlooked. Responsible parties might be sacked, and those in charge would develop procedures intended to prevent the same error from occurring again.

In contrast, consider what happened when Joseph Green ("Shabaka") Brown was released from custody in 1987, after serving fourteen years in prison for a crime he did not commit—and coming within fifteen hours of execution. As he recalled in early 2000, the releasing guard's exact words were "Hurry up and get the hell out of here." Brown's first act as a free man was to panhandle a quarter so he could call his attorney and ask for a ride because he feared that his jailers were setting him up to be shot as an escapee. No hearings were ever held to pinpoint the blame for his erroneous conviction. No heads rolled, no apologies were delivered, and no compensation was given. In essence, the only lesson that certain people learned was to take better precautions to avoid getting caught using questionable methods to secure convictions.

Learn from our mistakes? Students of the criminal justice system who read this unique book will discover many hazards to avoid, and they will learn about many errors that inevitably lead to the conviction of the innocent. In these pages, we see example after example of what goes wrong in American criminal investigations and prosecutions. Arguably, the biggest mistake of all is the one that our political and judicial authorities continually make: they deny the possibility of error and completely ignore it when it occurs. They show no interest in learning from their mistakes. In jurisdictions that still retain capital punishment, political leaders refuse to minimize the harm that results from erroneous convictions by replacing the death penalty with sentences of long imprisonment. In the face of such resistance, the researchers and legal practitioners featured in this book struggle to reveal flaws in the justice system in the hope that we can learn from these mistakes and provide remedies to reduce wrongful convictions in the future.

A miscarriage of justice is especially problematic in capital cases, where a wrongful conviction can result in the death of an innocent defendant. To be sure, no state has ever admitted that an innocent person has been executed in the twentieth century. Nevertheless, that claim is no reason for confidence. More than seven dozen prisoners were released from American death rows in the last three decades of the twentieth century because of doubts about guilt. Case studies of these blunders show only too clearly that luck was the main ingredient in these exonerations—a situation that gives us little faith that these cases were the only ones in which innocent people were sent to death rows.

But there is another, and more important, reason to examine erroneous convictions in capital cases: they provide us with a window through which we can view the shortcomings and limits of the criminal justice system. If our system cannot convict the correct perpetrator, we have no guarantee that the many other decisions of criminal justice officials who use the death penalty are made with the precision needed for life-and-death decisions.

Each year, some 20,000 homicides are reported to U.S. police, and roughly 250 perpetrators are sentenced to death. In effect, to decide who should be executed, one needs to arrange those 20,000 murderers into a hierarchy of culpability and sentence only the top 2 or 3 percent to death. Deciding who should die requires drawing lines on all sorts of continua. How much premeditation does the defendant have? How much criminal intent? How much is the defendant influenced by other participants? How old is the defendant? How crazy or mentally retarded is she or he? How dangerous will the defendant be if not sentenced to death? Has the race, ethnicity, gender, or sexual orientation of the defendant or victim affected our decisions? Are our decisions a function of the quality of the crime or the quality of the defense attorney or prosecutor? How much of the defendant's criminality is the result of bad parenting or the failure of a community to ask "what does he deserve" only after the abused child grows up and the capital offense is committed?

In reality (assuming one can agree on what makes a person more or less culpable), many of the 250 defendants at the top of the culpability hierarchy are not sentenced to death, and many of the bottom 19,750 are. If we fail to make the most important judgment correctly and convict an innocent person, how much confidence can we have that those found guilty of a capital homicide (as opposed to other degrees of homicide) and sentenced to death are in fact the worst of the bunch? This is why the issue of erroneous convictions is so important and why the friends of the executioner are so eager to deny that innocent people have been put to death. Convicting the innocent shows the fallibility of every other decision made by politicians and criminal justice personnel. It shows they make godlike decisions without godlike skills.

This book will make many readers feel acutely uncomfortable— a contribution that should give us some hope.

Acknowledgments

We are pleased to thank the people whose thoughtful suggestions, time, and hard work helped bring this manuscript to completion. First, we thank our colleagues at The University of North Carolina at Greensboro for supporting our efforts. In particular, Julie Capone, whose contributions far exceed a departmental secretary's, provided invaluable assistance in editing and preparing the manuscript. In addition, from the outset, graduate assistants Beth Hughes and Cindy Dollar enthusiastically helped develop the project. Finally, Allison Amick provided an excellent index. We also thank our editor at Rutgers University Press, David Myers, who responded to our endless questions with openness and good humor. The original anonymous manuscript reviewers provided several helpful suggestions at the outset of the project, all of which helped focus the book and added to clarity.

Our primary thanks, however, go to the individuals whose work appears in this book—a distinguished group of scholars, researchers, and practitioners who are widely known for their work on wrongful conviction. We have been impressed by their dedication to the project and their efforts to ensure its timely completion. Their original contributions, completed under considerable constraints of time and space, exceeded our expectations in every way.

Although we owe all the contributors a tremendous debt, we extend particular thanks to Richard Leo and Michael Radelet. Early in the development of the project, Richard was a constant source of ideas for both the manuscript and possible contributors. His generosity has been unbounded. In addition to agreeing to write the foreword to the book, Mike provided encouragement and advice early in the process. The book is substantially stronger for Richard's and Mike's insight and suggestions.

Finally, we thank our families for their patience, support, and willingness to share us for a brief time with these individuals whose impact on the process of justice affects us all.

Saundra D. Westervelt
John A. Humphrey

Wrongly Convicted

JOHN A. HUMPHREY

SAUNDRA D. WESTERVELT

Introduction

Arguably, the American system of criminal justice is armed with more safeguards against wrongful conviction than those of any other nation in the world. The Bill of Rights of the U.S. Constitution provides nineteen separate individual rights for the alleged criminal offender. Among these constitutional safeguards are the right to be free of unreasonable searches of person and place of residence; the right to the presumption of innocence; the right to effective legal representation; the right to a speedy trial with a jury present; and the right to be adjudicated without regard to race, gender, and religious preference. In sum, we are afforded the right to due process at each stage of the criminal justice process.

Despite these safeguards, however, national attention has recently focused on the repeated discovery of the factual innocence of convicted persons (Connors et al. 1996). Documented cases of wrongful convictions continue to accumulate. For example, Radelet et al. (1992) report on four hundred cases of wrong-person convictions involving Americans found guilty of crimes, many punishable by death. Twenty-three of these convicted persons were executed, while others spent several years in prison. More recently, a significant National Institute of Justice study (Connors et al. 1996) documented twenty-eight cases of individuals who since 1979 had been convicted of either murder or sexual assault, only to be exonerated by DNA evidence. Since the publication of this study, another thirty-six individuals have benefited from

DNA exonerations (Scheck et al. 2000). Some of these cases also appear on the Death Penalty Information Center's list of death row prisoners who have been fully exonerated and released (Dieter 1997). Furthermore, a recent FBI investigation finds that in approximately 25 percent of sexual assault cases under FBI review, DNA evidence excludes the primary suspect, hinting that without this new sophisticated technique many of these suspects would be formally adjudicated and quite possibly convicted (Connors et al. 1996).

In fact, the wrongful conviction issue has become the centerpoint of the current debate over the death penalty. For example, since the 1977 reinstatement of the death penalty in Illinois, thirteen inmates have been exonerated and released from death row, one more than the number of inmates actually executed during that time. Uncertainty over the actual guilt of persons condemned to death led the state's governor George Ryan to issue a moratorium on executions in January 2000. After announcing the moratorium, he called for the establishment of a special panel to study the processes involved in the imposition of capital punishment in Illinois. "Until I can be sure that everyone sentenced to death in Illinois is truly guilty," Governor Ryan observed, "no one will meet that fate" (Associated Press 2000).

Other states have also considered implementing a moratorium on executions in light of increasing concern over the accuracy and fairness of death penalty convictions and sentencing. The state legislatures of New Hampshire and Nebraska have voted for a moratorium, only to have their votes overridden by governors' vetoes. In March 2000, Indiana governor Frank O'Bannon called for a review of the capital punishment system in his state, although he did not impose a moratorium. Several local governments also have voted to suspend the death penalty, including Buffalo, New York; Atlanta, Georgia; Baltimore, Maryland; Chapel Hill, North Carolina; and San Francisco, California (Death Penalty Information Center 2000).

By March 2000, eighty-seven death row inmates in the United States had been exonerated, including the thirteen in Illinois, a situation prompting the establishment of the National Committee to Prevent Wrongful Executions. Headed by former Florida Supreme Court chief justice Gerald Kogan, the committee includes former FBI director William Sessions; former White House counsel Charles Ruff; former president of the International Chiefs of Police Charles Gruber; Laurie Robinson, a former assistant attorney general; and Mario Cuomo, former governor of New York. Judge Kogan considers the group's diversity a strength, describing its composition as "Republicans and Democrats, conservatives and liberals, pro- and anti-death penalty. What we share is a common abhorrence that innocent people are at risk of execution because of failures in the legal system" (Davies 2000).

Conviction of the innocent has also become a media focus, as evinced by the spotlight directed at the exoneration of Rubin "Hurricane" Carter, who was incarcerated for nineteen years for a 1966 triple murder that he did not commit. In 1976, the New Jersey Supreme Court ruled unanimously that the prosecution at the first trial withheld evidence favorable to the defense. Nevertheless, Carter was again convicted that year, when the prosecution was permitted to allege that the murders were racially motivated. In 1985, after nineteen years in prison, he was released. In his ruling, Judge H. Lee Sarokin of the Federal District Court in Newark, New Jersey, commented: "It would be naive not to recognize that some prejudice, bias and fear lurks in all of us. But to permit a conviction to be urged based upon such factors or to permit a conviction to stand having utilized such factors diminishes our fundamental constitutional rights" (*Carter v. Rafferty* 1985: 560). Three years later, the U.S. Supreme Court affirmed Judge Sarokin's ruling (*Rafferty v. Carter* 1988), and prosecutors decided not to seek a third trial. Today, Rubin Carter lives in Canada, where he has been active on behalf of the wrongly convicted through the Association in Defense of the Wrongly Convicted (AIDWYC), an organization he helped establish. In 1999, his life and his fight against the American criminal justice system were dramatized in the motion picture *The Hurricane*.

The case of Kerry Cook also has received considerable attention. Cook was released in 1999 after having been incarcerated for nearly twenty years in Texas's death house for sexual molestation and murder. He was tried three times. His original 1977 conviction was reversed in 1991, when the Court of Criminal Appeals, the court of last resort in Texas, ruled that a psychologist who interviewed him did not adequately inform Cook that his intent was to determine Cook's future dangerousness.

Two more trials ensued. In 1992, the jury could not reach a verdict, and the trial ended. In the 1994 trial, however, Cook was again convicted of sexual molestation and murder and sentenced to death. Two years later, the Court of Criminal Appeals ruled that the 1994 conviction was legally flawed and set aside the verdict. The court held that the prosecutor's office "allowed itself to gain a conviction based on fraud and ignored its own duty to seek the truth" (see McCloskey 1999). In addition, the court found that "the illicit manipulation of evidence on the part of the State permeated the entire investigation of the murder" (see McCloskey 1999).

In February 1999, Kerry Cook, freed on bond, was awaiting his fourth trial; but rather than face it, he chose to plead "no contest" to charges against him in exchange for his immediate unconditional release. (A no-contest plea is treated generally like a guilty plea within the criminal justice system, although it falls short of an actual admission of guilt.) Two months later, testing on newly submitted DNA evidence was completed, definitively excluding Cook as the offender. At present, he holds the dubious distinction of being the innocent person who has served the longest time on death row—almost twenty years—before being released.

The media report on these individual cases and others like them, and public and criminal justice officials note them. Rarely, however, are such cases understood as part of a larger pattern of failures and flaws within our criminal justice system. Many Americans and system officials view these cases as tragic but atypical, certainly not events that should prompt a reconsideration of the adjudicatory process as it is played out across the country. The criminal justice system— the adversarial method of arriving at the "truth" with regard to the accused's criminal liability—is judged to·be fundamentally sound, and justice is administered as usual. After all, we in the United States have numerous constitutional safeguards in place that are intended to protect the criminally accused. We pride ourselves on the due process guarantees that are supposed to ensure the conviction of the guilty, and only the guilty, beyond a reasonable doubt. These safeguards are supposed to protect the innocent from the unintentional mistakes and intentional abuses of police, prosecutors, and judges. From this point of view, cases of wrongful conviction may be viewed as anomalies— people who slipped through the cracks of the criminal justice system.

Such confidence in our criminal justice system assumes that constitutional protections are always paramount and safeguards always implemented. This may not, however, be the case. Over the past several decades, U.S. officials have embarked on a "war on crime," resulting in increases in arrests, convictions, and the use of severe penalties (Chen 2000). During this time, "justice" has become synonymous with "crime control." The pressure to arrest and convict created by this "war on crime" ideology increases the possibility that an innocent person will be rushed through the system and, despite constitutional safeguards, convicted to quiet the public's anxiety about community safety and answer calls that "justice be done." Thus, inherent in the administration of justice is a struggle between the protection of the due process rights of the accused and a response to the public's righteous, yet largely emotional, need for justice against criminal violators.

Systematic analyses of wrongful conviction cases, such as those in this book, reveal that this balance is difficult to maintain. Constitutional safeguards are, in some cases, inadequate to protect innocent people from the pressures that push police, prosecutors, and courts to convict at all costs. This book emphasizes that these cases are not anomalies that have slipped through the cracks but mistakes—both intentional and unintentional—that result from systemic failures and flaws in the operation of "justice." In short, justice should not continue to be administered as usual.

Studies consistently reveal a number of factors that can lead to the conviction of innocent people. For example, police mistakes and misconduct have caused wrongful convictions. The police have been found to focus on suspects prematurely and ignore evidence that does not support this selection, coerce false confessions, conduct poorly administered and biased lineups, focus on culturally or racially marginal groups, and withhold exculpatory evidence from prosecutors. Police, however, are not the only sources of wrongful convictions. Prosecutors have been known to ignore evidence counter to their case, misuse informants they know to be unreliable, and fail to report exculpatory evidence to the defense. Defense counsel have been found to be ill-prepared to argue their cases.

These are not problems found in only one or two wrongful conviction cases but are systemic problems that, either alone or in concert with each other, have produced wrongful convictions. Such problems are created when pressures to convict and process cases outweigh the safeguards intended to prevent mistakes and abuses. The chapters in this book reveal that the due process safeguards do not always protect the innocent and ensure that the guilty are brought to justice.

Overview of the Book

What makes certain criminal cases particularly vulnerable to wrongful conviction? What goes wrong during this process that overcomes all of the procedural safeguards built into our system that are intended to prevent the conviction of an innocent person? Who is most at risk to be wrongly convicted? What can be done to remedy these miscarriages of justice when they happen, and what can be done to prevent them from happening at all?

This book answers these questions by exploring numerous causes of wrongful conviction (mistaken eyewitness identification, false confessions, unreliable informants, and flawed forensic science, to name a few) as well as the social characteristics of the offenders (their race, ethnicity, and education level, for example) who appear to be at highest risk of a wrongful conviction. In addition, case studies provide specific examples of how these flaws, mistakes, and biases can work together to convict an innocent person. Finally, several chapters explore possible remedies: ways to prevent wrongful convictions from occurring and ways to bring them to light when they do occur. For example, restrictions on the use of informants, better support for defense counsel services, and stricter enforcement of guidelines for police and prosecutorial conduct may help prevent wrongful convictions, while the widespread use of DNA testing and the development of a network of innocence projects that revisit questionable cases after conviction can help remedy them once they occur. In sum, the book examines the causes and characteristics of wrongful convictions as well as responses to the problem.

This book is unique in several respects. First, it features researchers and practitioners who have written widely cited and influential books and articles on the causes of wrongful convictions, litigated well-known cases of such convictions, and helped implement in state legislatures some of the most promising remedies to prevent them. At the forefront of the field, the contributors are well situated to discuss the current state of knowledge about wrongful conviction. Second, with contributions from lawyers, sociologists, criminologists, and psychologists, this book provides a cross-disciplinary perspective on the conviction of the innocent—a dialogue that is essential to advancing knowledge on this issue. Lawyers must understand the significance and utility of the research findings of sociologists, criminologists, and psychologists, who in turn must understand the problems faced by attorneys who are litigating these cases and learn how academic research can be made more useful in the courtroom. As the first to combine all these perspectives into one volume, the book shows readers how each point of view contributes to a fuller understanding of the issue. Finally, each chapter has been specifically written for this book, ensuring that contributors are presenting the most current information in their particular fields.

By bringing together the most recent research on the problem of wrongful conviction, we hope to provide the academic community, both researchers and students, with a better understanding of the legal and social dynamics that may result in a wrongful conviction and inspire their own research and advocacy efforts. In addition, we hope that this book is a useful resource for those directly involved in improving our system of justice.

Defining Wrongful Conviction

Wrongful convictions may occur in two ways: (1) the defendant is found guilty at trial but, in fact, is innocent; and/or (2) the adjudicatory process is significantly compromised by prejudicial and other potentially reversible errors, regardless of the accused's guilt or innocence. Prejudicial errors may involve, for example, the propensity of juries to convict when cases involve minority and economically disadvantaged defendants or victims who are markedly more socially valued than their offenders. Reversible errors involve any compromise of the constitutional rights of the accused or the rules of criminal procedure. Thus, some wrongful convictions involve factually guilty individuals whose convictions are overturned because of a procedural error or a violation of their rights. Other wrongful convictions may result from these same types of errors but also involve factually innocent people.

This book focuses on the latter category: the wrongful conviction of an innocent person. Although identifying such people may appear to be a straightforward process, determining whether a convicted person is really factually innocent can in practice be difficult. The level of certainty about actual innocence often varies. In some cases, the factual innocence of a convicted person is formally recognized through a state's legal exoneration process, which provides a fairly high degree of certainty that the individual is really innocent. For example, a governor may issue a pardon based on his or her belief in the defendant's innocence, or an appellate court may overturn a conviction and government officials declare the convicted person to be factually innocent. Another form of legal exoneration may occur when a conviction is reversed by an appellate court and the defendant is found not guilty on retrial. Although a not guilty verdict does not exactly equal a finding of innocence (technically, *not guilty* means that the state has not proven guilt beyond a reasonable doubt), it does represent the legal exoneration of the defendant and raises serious doubts about the guilt of the accused.

One can argue, however, for the factual innocence of a convicted person without a formal legal exoneration, which many of our contributors do. It may not be wise to rely solely on the very system that erroneously convicts a person to recognize and rectify its own mistakes. In fact, as many of the chapters demonstrate, criminal justice officials are often reluctant to admit error even in the face of overwhelming evidence of innocence. Thus, the absence of a formal state exoneration does not necessarily preclude a convicted person's factual innocence. In many such cases, independent investigators, scholars, and journalists review the available evidence and even find new evidence that leads them to question a defendant's guilt.

These cases can be resolved in several ways: (1) an appellate court may reverse a conviction because of insufficient evidence but fall short of declaring the defendant's innocence; (2) after an appellate reversal, the prosecutor may drop charges due to insufficient evidence without a statement regarding the defendant's innocence; or (3) after an appellate reversal, a prosecutor may offer a defendant the option to plea to a lesser charge (rather than face retrial) in return for immediate release from incarceration. In these types of cases, the defendant is released from incarceration and cleared of the initial charges against him or her, although the person is not formally declared innocent of those charges. Despite this remaining uncertainty about their factual innocence compared with those who are legally exonerated, these defendants may still be innocent.

Of course, in some cases, independent investigations and scholarly attention may create a reasonable doubt about the defendant's guilt but fail to secure his or her exoneration or release. For example, two chapters in this book reveal substantial evidence about the innocence of several people who have been executed in the United States. Obviously, these defendants were not formally exonerated and have not been since their executions (no such legal exoneration process is available in the United States after an execution); however, the chapters raise serious questions about their guilt and, in fact, argue for their innocence.

Thus, determining the factual innocence of a wrongly convicted person is complex, and the level of certainty about actual innocence may vary according to the type of exoneration afforded to the defendant. This variation in certainty also may be affected by the type of evidence offered to "prove" a defendant's innocence—that is, the type of exculpatory evidence available.

DNA testing is now being used to reexamine numerous innocence claims of convicted persons; and as of October 2000, eighty-two individuals have been legally exonerated in North America using DNA testing since it first became available in the late 1980s (Scheck et al. 2000). DNA analysis adds a degree of scientific certainty to the determination of innocence that is not subject to the level of controversy that surrounds exonerations based on witness recantations, newly found physical evidence, or the confessions of others. Innocence claims based on errors such as prosecutorial or police misconduct or inadequate assistance of defense counsel may involve even higher levels of uncertainty about actual innocence. Although wrongful convictions have been discovered using all of these types of evidence, the individual's factual innocence is more or less likely to be disputed depending on the type of exculpatory evidence offered.

Without irrefutable physical evidence that the accused either could not have committed the crime or the discovery of the actual perpetrator, studies of wrongful convictions tend to be shrouded in uncertainty. Nonetheless, within this arena of shifting probabilities rather than absolute certainty, scientific inquiry is carried out. So, too, are investigations of wrongful convictions.

Structure of the Book

Wrongly Convicted: Perspectives on Failed Justice is organized into four parts. Part 1 considers the causes of wrongful convictions, exploring many of the factors that lead to them: biased police lineups, mistaken eyewitness identification, and faulty forensic science (chapter 1); coerced false confessions (chapter 2); and unreliable informants (chapter 3). As discussed in chapter 4, these flaws occur primarily within two organizational contexts within the criminal justice system: the pressure-filled environment surrounding high-profile, heinous crimes, and the routine environment in which the "usual suspects" are processed on little evidence other than they were previously known to the police. This chapter also demonstrates that the causes of wrongful convictions common to U.S. cases exist in similar cases throughout the common law world.

The chapters in part I make clear that wrongful convictions do not result from a single flaw or mistake; many factors can be at the root of a wrongful conviction. Although each chapter may explore only one or two of these flaws fully, none of the contributors contends that one cause is the singular, or even primary, reason for wrongful convictions. Each chapter merely illuminates one detail of a much larger puzzle. The chapters in part I also make clear that wrongful convictions can result from both intentional abuses and unintentional mistakes that can occur in every stage of the criminal justice process. In fact, failures and mistakes that happen early in the process can influence later stages, compounding the problem or even causing other mistakes. For example, a poorly managed police lineup can lead to a mistaken eyewitness identification, which in turn can be used by police to pressure an innocent suspect into a confession. A prosecutor, relying heavily on the eyewitness and the confession, may choose to ignore or overlook evidence of the suspect's innocence and, believing that he or she has the correct person in custody, may choose to withhold that potentially exculpatory evidence from the defense. A jury, then, will hear only the flawed and incriminating evidence, not the potentially exculpatory evidence, and will most likely return a guilty verdict. Thus, while focusing on the details in each chapter, the reader must keep the larger picture in mind.

Part II explores the social characteristics of the wrongly convicted, emphasizing that flaws and mistakes in the legal processing of a case are not the only factors that can put an innocent person at risk of conviction. Extralegal factors are also at work. Chapter 5 provides an empirical overview of the number of wrongful convictions found on death rows across the country and the social characteristics of these particular individuals (for example, their ethnicity, level of education, and marital status). Chapter 6 offers a more in-depth examination and explanation of the link between the race of the defendant and the increased likelihood of a wrongful conviction in the United States. Because these extralegal factors have not received extensive systematic attention in the research on wrongful convictions, the chapters in part II provide one of the first empirical investigations into the relationship between social characteristics and wrongful convictions (in chapter 5) and demonstrate the significance of these factors to the overall analysis of the causes of such convictions.

Part III introduces readers to a few of the faces of the wrongly convicted, reviewing the cases of persons who have been wrongly convicted, some who were exonerated, and others who were not so lucky.

These case studies detail the social characteristics of the individuals involved, the crime incident, the investigative process, the trial, and the postconviction appeal process. Each case illustrates many of the points made in parts I and II. For example, chapter 7's discussion of Frank Ewing makes a case for his innocence, although he was executed in 1919, and explores the role of mistaken eyewitness identification, a pressured confession, and racial bias (all discussed in earlier chapters) in the production of his alleged wrongful conviction. Chapter 8 presents the cases of eight individuals executed in New York whom scholars believe to have been wrongfully convicted. All of these cases illustrate the factors discussed in previous chapters: perjury by informants, mistakes by eyewitnesses, police tunnel vision, coerced and fabricated confessions, ill-prepared defense attorneys, prosecutorial misconduct, and the targeting of ethnic groups. Finally, chapter 9's discussion of the case of Dale Johnston reveals many of these same failures and mistakes while explaining how the normally operating organizational context that prevails in the criminal justice system allows them to go unremedied.

After devoting much of the book to investigations of the factors that cause wrongful convictions, we believed it was important to conclude with a consideration of remedies and solutions. Part IV explores some visions for change in the twenty-first century, evaluating several strategies for more effectively assessing informants' testimony, methods for ensuring effective assistance of defense counsel, the use of DNA evidence in the processing of a criminal case, and ways to ensure that police and prosecutors reveal exculpatory evidence to the defense. The chapters in this section provide excellent examples of the variety of approaches currently being proposed as responses to the wrongful conviction problem. Some offer specific, concrete remedies to several of the causes of wrongful conviction discussed in part I, while others suggest strategies for reorganizing or reconceptualizing the criminal justice system to reduce such convictions, although these chapters fall short of proposing specific policies or practices.

Given that both the problem and possible remedies are just beginning to receive widespread attention in the criminal justice and academic communities, we argue that a variety of strategies must be examined and avenues pursued in the process of developing solutions. Therefore, part IV brings together a number of different vantage points. For example, in chapter 3, Clifford Zimmerman explains the role of informant use in causing wrongful convictions. In chapter 10, he returns to this subject and provides a practical set of guidelines for police and prosecutorial use of informants that could limit informant misuse and misconduct. Chapter 11 explores the issue of ineffective assistance of counsel, a problem that undergirds many of the flaws and mistakes discussed throughout the book. In many cases, the unintentional mistakes and intentional abuses common in wrongful conviction cases are not found early and remedied because defendants are represented by ill-prepared, underfunded, overworked defense counsel. The chapter explains the impact of ineffective assistance of counsel on the wrongful conviction problem and suggests some strategies for improvement.

Chapter 12 discusses the tremendous impact of DNA technology on the identification and correction of wrongful convictions and argues for the development of a network of innocence projects across the country dedicated to the prevention and redress of wrongful convictions. Since the late 1990s, DNA has provided convincing evidence that sixty-nine factually innocent persons had been placed on death row in the United States (Dwyer et al. 2000). The Innocence Project at the Benjamin N. Cardozo School of Law (headed by chapter 12 authors Barry Scheck and Peter Neufeld) has spearheaded efforts to institutionalize the use of DNA testing and facilitate its admissibility in state and federal courts. Attorneys Scheck and Neufeld have recommended that "DNA testing should be done within seven to fourteen days of a crime to make sure innocent suspects are not incarcerated and to improve the chances of catching the guilty" (Scheck et al. 2000: 255). In chapter 12, they call for the expansion of the innocence project model used at Cardozo to law schools across the country.

Part IV ends with a reconsideration of two issues fundamental to the current wrongful conviction problem and debate: the relative merits of the adversarial system, and the ultimate cost of an erroneous outcome of adversarial justice—the death penalty. Chapter 13 argues that the system of adversarial justice currently in use in the United States calls into question the notion that a trial is a "truth-seeking" enterprise. Given that courts are more concerned with dispute resolution than truth determination, the rules of the trial game are not really aimed at ensuring that the truth of the criminal event is discovered, which can lead to the conviction of innocent people.

Finally, chapter 14 addresses the significance of the wrongful conviction problem to the current death penalty debate. With the discovery of an increasing number of wrongful convictions in our justice system, the possibility, if not probability, that Americans have and will execute an innocent person looms. The chapter discusses public concern about the death penalty and the growing fear that the execution of an innocent person is inevitable, concluding with a call for the end of the death penalty in the United States. As such, the chapter is more of a response to the wrongful conviction problem than a solution: until those inside and outside the criminal justice system find ways to reduce the number of wrongfully convicted people in the system, we should at least be sure that the United States does not participate in the ultimate constitutional violation—the ultimate human rights violation—by executing an innocent person.

Conclusion

We hope that the original work of the innovative researchers and legal advocates who have contributed to this book will draw increased attention to the issue of wrongful conviction. It is disquieting to realize that wrongful convictions are a consequence of our inability to strike a balance between our need for "justice" and our desire to provide due process rights to the criminally accused. As Judge Sarokin stated in the 1985 ruling that released Rubin "Hurricane" Carter after nineteen years of imprisonment, "there is a substantial danger that our society, concerned about the growth of crime, will retreat from the safeguards and rights accorded to the accused by the constitution. The need to combat crime should never be utilized to justify an erosion of our fundamental guarantees. Indeed, the growing volume of criminal cases should make us even more vigilant; the greater the *quantity*—the greater the risk to the *quality* of justice" (*Carter v. Rafferty* 1985: 560). We hope that the social and legal processes that give rise to the way in which we define and administer *quality* justice will be continually scrutinized by us all.

REFERENCES

Associated Press. 2000. "Illinois Puts Executions on Hold," 31 January. Available at http://www.apbnews.com. [Internet]

Chen, Hans H. 2000. "U.S. Prison Population Hits All-Time High," 19 April. Available at http://www.apbnews.com. [Internet]

Connors, Edward, Thomas Lundregan, Neal Miller, and Tom McEwan. 1996. *Convicted by Juries, Exonerated by Science: Case Studies in the Use of DNA Evidence to Establish Innocence after Trial.* Washington, D.C.: National Institute of Justice.

Davies, Frank. 2000. "Group to Review Death Penalty." *San Jose Mercury News,* 12 May. [Internet]

Death Penalty Information Center. 2000. Available at http://www.essential.org/dpic/.

Dieter, Richard C. 1997. *Innocence and the Death Penalty: The Increasing Danger of Executing the Innocent.* Washington, D.C.: Death Penalty Information Center.

Dwyer, Jim, Peter Neufeld, and Barry Scheck. 2000. "When Justice Lets Us Down." *Newsweek*, 14 February. Available at http://www.newsweek.com. [Internet]

McCloskey, Jim. 1999. "The Kerry Cook Story." Centurion Ministries, Princeton, N.J. Unpublished.

Radelet, Michael L., Hugo Adam Bedau, and Constance E. Putnam. 1992. *In Spite of Innocence.* Boston: Northeastern University Press.

Scheck, Barry, Peter Neufeld, and Jim Dwyer. 2000. *Actual Innocence.* New York: Doubleday.

CASES CITED

Carter v. Rafferty, 621 F.Supp. 533 (1985).
Rafferty v. Carter, 484 U.S. 1011, 108 S.Ct. 711 (1988).

PART

I

Causes of Wrongful Convictions

GEORGE CASTELLE

ELIZABETH F. LOFTUS

1 | Misinformation and Wrongful Convictions

A young man fidgets nervously at counsel table. A trembling but determined victim takes the witness stand and identifies the young man as the person who viciously assaulted her. A police officer reinforces the victim's testimony, stating that her previous identification of the young man in the police lineup was the most convincing he had ever seen.

The jury returns a verdict of guilty. The young man's family sobs as he is led away in chains. He turns to his family, in tears, and mouths the words "I didn't do it." The prosecutor announces to the press that "justice has been done." A decade later, DNA testing proves that the young man, now in his thirties, is innocent. He is released from prison, hoping to rebuild his life. Through her lawyer, the victim states that, despite the DNA results, she is still certain that she identified the right person.

This disturbing scenario has repeated itself countless times in courtrooms throughout the country. Current news reports routinely count case after case in which innocent people have spent years, sometimes decades, behind bars before their convictions were set aside.

Given the growing list of innocent people condemned to prison, we find it natural to wonder whether there is something fundamentally wrong with our system of justice. In this chapter we identify some of the flaws in our justice system that allow wrongful convictions to occur, with the hope of illuminating patterns in these cases and identifying some of the legal and psychological factors that combine to put innocent people behind bars. In particular, we examine how mistakes at each stage of the case preparation—the police investigation, the laboratory analysis, and the trial—build on each other to disrupt the criminal justice process and convict an innocent person. By studying the details of wrongful conviction cases and following the trail of misinformation from its origins as mistaken or misinterpreted crime scene evidence to its introduction at trial as "convincing" evidence of guilt, we can gain insight into how wrongful convictions occur.

In this chapter we focus on suggestive interviews and lineups conducted by law enforcement authorities and examine the troubling practice among some of these officials of withholding evidence favorable to the defense. More important, while our study reveals errors in the collection of physical evidence and the testing and reporting of forensic science results, it also considers the poorly understood effect of the cross-contamination of evidence: when one piece of misinformation contaminates other information in a case and ultimately results in the conviction of the innocent. When an innocent person is convicted, that conviction is often attributed to a single mistake—a victim misidentified a suspect in a lineup; a faulty lab report implicated the wrong person; an innocent passerby was the only person observed at the scene; a police officer erroneously believed that a suspect knew something that only the real killer would know. Indeed, much of the current research into wrongful conviction cases focuses on one mistake or one part of the criminal justice process in which a mistake occurred. Nevertheless, while these studies are important because they detail how such mistakes happen, they do not explain how failures in one part of the process can shape the development of the case later on.

A deeper, more careful, analysis reveals that wrongful convictions do not usually occur because one person made one mistake. Rarely is someone innocent for one reason alone; on the contrary, a person who is innocent for one reason should be innocent for many. When an error in identification is made, such as the erroneous identification of a suspect's face in a lineup, other evidence should conflict with this identification. If the wrong face has been identified, the person with the wrong face will also have the wrong fingerprints and will likely be the wrong height, the wrong weight, and the wrong age and have the wrong DNA, the wrong hair, the wrong clothes, the wrong jewelry, the wrong scars, and the wrong tattoos. Moreover, the person with the wrong face will have been somewhere else at the time of the crime.

Undeniably, something else comes into play when an initial piece of evidence is mistaken: that mistake causes other things to happen. When communicated to people who have knowledge of the case, the mistake appears to transform something in their thoughts, their memories, and their approach to potentially every other piece of evidence in the case. What exactly occurs is poorly understood within the judicial system and the law enforcement community and is rarely acknowledged. But understanding exactly what happens is essential to understanding why wrongful convictions occur and what can be done to prevent them.

Although there has been longstanding interest in cases of wrongful conviction (for example, Borchard 1932; Loftus 1979), a more recent report commissioned by the National Institute of Justice (Conners et al. 1996) has heightened interest in the subject. The report describes twenty-eight cases of wrongfully convicted persons who were exonerated by DNA evidence after spending an average of seven years in prison. To this figure Wells et al. (1998) add twelve cases, and Scheck et al. (2000) conclude that sixty-four innocent people imprisoned for serious crimes have been released because DNA analysis has proven their innocence. At least seven of those people were on death row.

An additional series of wrongful convictions resulted from the fraudulent forensic science of state trooper Fred Zain, who was found to have fabricated serology results, falsely reporting blood and semen characteristics in sexual assault and murder cases during a sixteen-year career in crime labs in West Virginia and Texas.[1] Seven convictions have been set aside since the exposure of Zain's fraudulent results, and more are currently under review (Castelle 1999).

In the National Institute of Justice study (Connors et al. 1996), twenty-four out of twenty-eight wrongful convictions occurred at least in part from erroneous eyewitness identification. In fifty-two of the cases of DNA exonerations discussed by Scheck et al. (2000), mistaken eyewitness identification was used to convict the innocent defendant. In each of these cases, the innocent person was innocent for other reasons as well. Similarly, those wrongfully convicted on the basis of Trooper Zain's false serology tests were surely innocent for other reasons also. What happened to those other reasons? Why didn't they serve to overcome or correct the erroneous eyewitness identification or the faulty forensic science?

The William Harris Case

For those seeking to understand how wrongful convictions occur, the case of William Harris is particularly instructive. This disturbing case, which appears in both the National Institute of Justice study and the Fred Zain list of wrongful convictions, highlights the multiple factors that frequently contribute to such convictions: suggestive police interviews and lineups, evidence of innocence withheld by the police, and erroneous or misinterpreted forensic science. More important, the case illustrates the cross-contamination of seemingly independent pieces of evidence as mistakes build on each other to produce a wrongful conviction.

William Harris was a talented young athlete with college scholarships and a bright future ahead of him. But his promising future began to collapse in December 1984, when a young woman was sexually assaulted outside her house in William's hometown of Rand, West Virginia. The sexual assault occurred from behind, in the dark. The victim obtained a brief view of the assailant's face during the assault and again as the assailant fled the scene, when the side of his face was briefly illuminated by light from nearby windows.[2] The victim was examined at the hospital, and the sexual fluids from the assault were collected and sent for analysis to the serology division of the West Virginia State Police Crime Laboratory, which was headed by state trooper Fred Zain.

At trial, William Harris was convicted on the basis of two key pieces of evidence. First, the jury heard the fraudulent scientific testimony of Fred Zain, who falsely claimed to have identified genetic markers in the semen consistent with only a small percentage of the population, including William Harris.[3] Second, the jury heard the victim identify William as her assailant, stating that there was no doubt in her mind that he was the person who had assaulted her.[4] The deputy sheriff who conducted the lineup emphatically supported her testimony. In his own trial testimony, he described the victim's reaction as she selected William from among those standing in the jailhouse lineup:

> A: [deputy sheriff] . . . she glanced across the people standing there; and immediately her vision became focused on a particular person; she said, "That's him." She began to cry; and when asked which person it was, she said it was No. 3 [William Harris]. And

when asked if she was absolutely certain about that, she said "There was no question, that was absolutely him."

Q: [assistant prosecutor]: Okay. You said she showed certainty, in fact expressed her certainty to you?

A: It was a very convincing identification. It was very clear. She had no doubt in her mind. It was probably the, the most dramatic sort of identification I had ever seen. (*State of West Virginia v. William O'Dell Harris, Jr.* 1987: 379)

On the basis of this testimony, William was convicted of sexual assault and sentenced to a term of ten to twenty years in the West Virginia Penitentiary.

William's ill-fortune began to change in 1993, when the West Virginia Supreme Court of Appeals ordered an investigation into the serology division of the State Police Crime Laboratory. In early 1993, a prosecutor disclosed an internal audit of the lab in a petition to the West Virginia Supreme Court of Appeals, revealing a history of problems with Zain's work. The court responded by ordering a full investigation, afterwards concluding that Zain had faked data in virtually every case for which there was sufficient evidence to review.[5] On the basis of this finding, lawyers for William Harris were able to obtain DNA testing of the remaining evidence in his case—testing that did not exist at the time of his 1987 trial. The test showed conclusively that William could not have been the assailant (Messina 1995a, 1995b).

The exoneration of William Harris by DNA testing stands in marked contrast to the eyewitness testimony—the "most convincing" identification that the investigating officer had ever seen. How can such unequivocal eyewitness testimony be so unequivocally wrong? We can shed light on this mystery by examining the original police records in the case, which were withheld for ten years and ultimately disclosed during the civil litigation that followed William's release. Controverting the trial testimony of the victim and the investigating officer, the concealed police report contains the victim's original observations: "Suspect [William Harris] eliminated with photo lineup on March 4, 1985. Victim said she knew him and it wasn't him."[6]

This disturbing disclosure of the victim's original observations and their contradiction during the trial testimony has many implications for our study. Among other points, it allows us to observe the effect of misinformation on witnesses' memories: the transformation of a victim's testimony from the absolute elimination of a suspect to an equally absolute (and absolutely false) identification of the suspect in a police lineup and at trial. We can reconstruct much of the transformation by reviewing the complete police file (which was withheld from William's defense attorneys), the trial testimony, and the deposition testimony of the police officers in the civil litigation that followed William's release.

As reconstructed from courthouse records, the transformation of the victim's identification of her assailant occurred in nine stages. First, on 16 December 1984, the evening of the assault, the victim described her assailant as approximately five feet, seven inches tall and in his early twenties.[7] (William was more than six feet tall and seventeen years old.[8])

Second, the victim's description of her assailant was tape-recorded several days later. At this time, she told police that the assailant was wearing a jogging suit and had a short Afro haircut.[9] (William did not own a jogging suit at the time and has never worn his hair in an Afro.[10])

Third, in March 1985, the police again interviewed the victim, this time providing her with a series of photographs, including one of William. As previously discussed, the police report states: "Suspect [William Harris] eliminated with photo lineup on March 4, 1985. Victim said she knew him and it wasn't him."[11]

Fourth, in late March 1985, when William won the heavyweight division of the state high school wrestling championship, photographs of him were prominently featured in television and newspaper coverage of the championship. The victim appears to have casually glanced at those photographs an unknown number of times.[12]

Fifth, in June 1985, the police again approached the victim with photographs, this time displaying William's high school yearbook with the names under the photographs blocked from the victim's view. According to trial testimony, upon viewing William's yearbook photograph, the victim—for the first time—recognized the person in the photograph as her assailant.[13]

Sixth, on 25 July 1985, police arrested William and placed him in a five-person jailhouse lineup. In a recorded interview with the victim after the conclusion of the lineup, the victim identified "number 3" (William Harris) as her assailant.[14]

Seventh, on the basis of the victim's statement, the police obtained a court order allowing them to draw William's blood for comparison with the semen left by the assailant. On 30 October 1985, the serology division of the West Virginia State Police Crime Lab, headed by the later discredited state trooper Fred Zain, reported that serological examination of the sexual assault fluids contained genetic markers consistent with the known blood of William Harris.[15] The results of this "match" were communicated to the investigating officers and, in turn, communicated to the victim.

Eighth, in pretrial proceedings nearly two years later, the victim described her selection of William Harris from the police lineup:

Q: What were you instructed to do [at the lineup]?

A: Just to, you know, just to look at them very carefully; and they brought them—then they brought them up closer. First they were back, and then they brought them up close to me. And to look them over. And he had one, each one of them to step up for me to get a closer look. He did all of them that way. And then they all stood back in the line, and then I chose. (*State of West Virginia v. William O'Dell Harris, Jr.* 1987: 88)

Finally, the ninth step occurred at trial, where the thoughtful lineup process that the victim described in the eighth step seemed to disappear from memory. Instead, the deputy sheriff who had conducted the lineup testified to a dramatic, immediate recognition: "She glanced across the people standing there; and immediately her vision became focused on a particular person; and she said, 'That's him. . . . There was no question, that was absolutely him. . . . ' It was probably the, the most dramatic sort of identification I had ever seen" (*State of West Virginia v. Williams O'Dell Harris, Jr.* 1987: 379).

The fact that the victim had initially viewed William's photograph and eliminated him as the suspect was never revealed to the jury because the police had not disclosed that information. In fact, the prosecutor repeatedly asserted that the victim had "never wavered."[16]

Causes of Wrongful Convictions

Four primary components led to the wrongful conviction of William Harris, each representing a recurring theme that appears in numerous cases of wrongful convictions. First, the victim appears to have been repeatedly exposed to suggestive interviewing techniques that subjected her memory of the assailant to the distorting effects of unconscious transference, a photo-biased lineup, and false reinforcement. Second, whether intentionally or not, the police or the prosecutors appear to have withheld from the defense, and from the jury, crucial information that was favorable to the defense and necessary to ensure fairness at trial. Third, erroneous or exaggerated forensic science was communicated to the jury in a manner that gave a false aura of scientific expertise to the prosecution's case. Finally, the false scientific testimony and the erroneous eyewitness identification appear to have affected one another, resulting in cross-contamination and a false reinforcement that enhanced the errors and blinded police, prosecutors, judges, and jurors to the true weaknesses in the prosecution's case. Let us briefly discuss each of these factors in more depth.

Suggestive Police Interviews

It is not clear why the investigating officers in the William Harris case returned to William as a suspect after the victim's unequivocal assertion that "she knew him and it wasn't him." The victim knew she had been assaulted by a young, athletic, black male. The officers' pursuit of William may simply have been linked to the population makeup of Rand, West Virginia, a small rural community in which few candidates met even this broad, vague description.

What is clear, however, is that the victim's repetitious exposure to William Harris's name and photograph transformed her memory from its original state to something very different by the time of trial. *Unconscious transference* is the term applied to the phenomenon in which a person seen in one situation is confused with or recalled as a person seen in another situation (Loftus 1979; Loftus and Doyle 1997). The victim's repeated exposure to photographs of William may have ultimately led to the substitution of those photographs for her hazy memory of the assailant's face, which she acquired in brief views, in the dark, on the night of the crime.

Additionally, the victim originally stated that she knew William, subsequently reviewing his photograph and eliminating him as her assailant. Months later, she selected his photograph from his yearbook, reversing herself and now identifying him as her assailant. The effect on the jailhouse lineup should be readily apparent: only one person in the lineup was familiar—the person in the previously seen photograph. Such a photo-biased lineup can produce a form of unconscious transference, further increasing the likelihood of an erroneous identification (Loftus 1979).

The victim's confidence in her new identification of William was probably boosted when she learned about the erroneous forensic science "matching" William to the sexual assault fluids. To appreciate how the victim might have completed the transition from "not him" to "absolutely sure it was him," we need to understand a concept that psychologists call the *malleability of confidence,* a phenomenon studied extensively by researchers at Iowa State University (see Wells and Bradfield 1998, 1999). They have shown that witnesses who identify a suspect from a police lineup or a group of photos are far more confident of their choice if given positive feedback, even in casual conversation.

In the first Iowa State study (Wells and Bradfield 1998), more than 350 subjects watched a grainy surveillance-camera videotape of a person who later shot and killed a store security guard at a Target store. Subjects were told that the person they saw had shot a security guard and were shown either a lineup or photographs and asked to identify the gunman. In fact, the gunman was in neither the lineup nor the photos. All subjects chose someone and, of course, in doing so made a false identification. Later some subjects were told, "Good, you identified the actual suspect." These subjects were subsequently far more confident about their choices than were those who heard nothing about whether or not they had identified the right man. Even more disturbing, in addition to being more confident, the first group of subjects also remembered having a better view of the suspect, having paid greater attention to the videotape, having had an easier time making the identification, needing less time to make the identification, and being better able to make out details of the suspect's face than did those who received no feedback. For the most part, subject eyewitnesses were completely unaware that feedback manipulation had influenced their certainty.

In a subsequent study, Wells and Bradfield (1999) again showed that giving eyewitnesses confirming feedback after they had made an identification inflated their confidence and affected other testimony-relevant judgments, such as how good their view was or how much attention they had paid during the event itself. Privately thinking about the identification reduced the confidence-inflating effects of the feedback but only if the private thinking occurred before the feedback, not after.

These findings have important implications for the criminal justice process. One immediate lesson is that giving feedback of any kind (for example, "you identified the suspect" or "you identified the person whose DNA was found at the scene") can inflate confidence artificially and must be avoided to keep the witness from having an unjustified influence on the trier of fact (that is, the judge or the jury). A way to minimize post-identification feedback is to conduct an identification test as one would conduct a good scientific experiment: doing the test "blind." If the agent conducting the lineup does not know which person in the lineup is the suspect, the agent cannot communicate any information about the status of the identified person.

These findings also call into question the criteria used by the courts in determining the likely accuracy of an identification. In *Neil v. Biggers* (1972), the U.S. Supreme Court set forth five criteria: (1) the eyewitness's opportunity to view the suspect, (2) the attention paid by the eyewitness, (3) the accuracy of the eyewitness's pre-lineup description of the suspect, (4) the certainty of the witness, and (5) the amount of time between the event and the attempt to identify the suspect. Most of these criteria, however, rely on the memory of the witness who is being scrutinized or called into question in the case. If post-identification feedback has altered confidence as well as the memory of the viewing opportunity and the attention paid, use of these criteria becomes almost meaningless.

Fortunately, the U.S. Department of Justice (1999) has developed national guidelines that, if followed, will reduce the likelihood of wrongful convictions. Among other things, the guidelines explicitly caution investigators to avoid communicating information to eyewitnesses that might contaminate their subsequent testimony.

Withholding Evidence Favorable to the Defense

A deeply disturbing aspect of the William Harris case and other cases involving wrongful convictions is the concealment of evidence favorable to the defense. The U.S. Supreme Court prohibits police and prosecutors from pursuing a prosecution while withholding evidence that supports a claim of innocence (*Brady v. Maryland* 1963). The requirement to disclose evidence favorable to the defense includes matters affecting the reliability or credibility of key prosecution witnesses (*Giglio v. United States* 1972). Additionally, the prosecutor has a duty to learn about evidence favorable to the defense that may be in police possession. The prosecutor is required to have procedures and regulations in place to ensure communication of all such information from the police to the prosecution so that the prosecution, in turn, can give the required information to the defense (*Giglio v. United States* 1972; *Kyles v. Whitley* 1995). The requirements regarding the disclosure of evidence favorable to the defense go to the heart of a fair trial. In setting forth those requirements (*Brady v. Maryland* 1963: 87), the Supreme Court stated: "Society wins not only when the guilty are convicted but when trials are fair." A trial is not fair when the prosecution has exclusive possession of information favorable to the defense but withholds it, a practice often called a "*Brady* violation." Scrupulous adherence to the requirements of *Brady v. Maryland* (1963) is essential to avoiding wrongful convictions (Connors et al. 1996: 15, 18; Scheck et al. 2000).

A review of the William Harris case, as well as many other wrongful convictions, reveals disturbing examples of violations of the duty to disclose information favorable to the defense. In the civil litigation that followed William's release, both police and prosecutors insisted that the prosecutors were not told that the victim had previously seen William's photograph and eliminated him as the suspect.[17] If, in fact, this claim is true, it is clear that the prosecution did not have effective mechanisms in place to ensure the communication of information favorable to the defense. Without such mechanisms, a "don't ask, don't tell" relationship evolves between police and prosecutors. In the William Harris case, the failure to follow the requirements set out in *Brady v. Maryland* (1963) allowed the prosecutor to claim dramatically to the jury that the victim "never wavered" in her identification of William, while the police kept to themselves the vital information that the victim had not only wavered but completely reversed herself.[18]

Similarly, vital information that would have cast doubt on the forensic science testimony was also concealed from the defense. During the investigation of the West Virginia State Police Crime Laboratory, Fred Zain's assistants testified that they observed Zain faking data in nearly one hundred instances and had reported the fraud to his supervisors.[19] Despite their reports, however, the fraud remained concealed for nearly ten more years while Zain continued to testify in rape and murder trials.

The failure to convey information affecting the reliability of key prosecution witnesses strikes at the heart of *Brady* violations and strips the judicial process of one of the principal safeguards against wrongful convictions. Such convictions will be avoided in the future only if police and prosecutors renew their commitment to identify and disclose required information and if judges and disciplinary authorities over-come their traditional reluctance and address *Brady* violations more vigorously.

Erroneous Forensic Science

The recent history of wrongful convictions has been accompanied by a parallel history of erroneous and sometimes fraudu-lent forensic science (Castelle 1999). Unfortunately, the fraud commit-ted by Fred Zain is not unique. Between 1992 and 1995, five state troopers pled guilty and were sentenced to prison for repeatedly plant-ing fingerprints in criminal cases in New York State (Goldin 1995; Perez-Pena 1997). In 1997, a New Jersey medical examiner was con-victed of witness tampering while on trial for faking an autopsy re-port (Hanley 1997). In 1992, a Texas pathologist entered a no-contest plea to faking autopsies in murder cases (Fricker 1993). A North Caro-lina footprint expert faked results in cases across the United States and Canada throughout a ten-year courtroom career (Hanson 1993, 1996). In the inspector general's 1996 investigation of the FBI Crime Laboratory, one FBI agent reported that "there was an unidentified [FBI] laboratory division technician or examiner who would determine if suspects were Afro-Americans. If so, he would manipulate tests to prove guilt" (U. S. Department of Justice 1996).

In addition to these disturbing examples of outright crime lab fraud, inadvertent error, sloppiness, exaggeration, and bias also contaminate the process. Lab samples have been inadvertently mislabeled when collected at the crime scene and mislabeled or accidentally switched upon receipt at the lab. Additionally, lab results have been all too fre-quently misread or misinterpreted, mistyped, mistranscribed, and misreported (Castelle 1999).

In the 1990s, the Supreme Court adopted procedural safeguards to protect juries from the introduction into evidence of unreliable fo-rensic science. The Court now requires a reliability assessment before the introduction of expert testimony, if challenged (see *Daubert v. Merrell Dow Pharmaceuticals, Inc.* 1993; *Kumho Tire Co. v. Carmichael* 1999). Defense lawyers can reduce the likelihood of erroneous foren-sic science results by conscientiously insisting on a thorough reliability assessment in disputed cases. They can also reduce the likelihood of errors by obtaining the raw data from the prosecution forensic scien-tists and submitting it for independent review, obtaining independent retesting of questionable lab results, and subjecting the trial testimony of prosecution experts to more rigorous scrutiny.

Cross-contamination of Evidence

Courts have traditionally tended to view categories of evidence as separate and discrete units. In pretrial proceedings as well as at trial, they typically sift through the evidence in a case, determining which items will be presented to the jury and which will not. Unreliable, prejudicial, and illegally seized evidence ordinarily cannot be presented to the jury. The results of lie detector tests, for example, are generally held to be inadmissible, as are confessions obtained involuntarily and physical evidence illegally seized.

On appeal, higher courts traditionally review the decisions of trial judges and will occasionally reverse a conviction, ordering a retrial or review of the case with a particular piece of evidence removed from consideration. In the Fred Zain cases, for example, after the fraud was exposed, the trial judges were required to review convictions that had been based at least in part on Zain's testimony by removing his testimony from consideration and weighing the sufficiency of what remained.[20]

The problem with this process is that evidence in a criminal case does not exist in discrete and immutable units, with each piece isolated from the other. Instead, the knowledge that a suspect passed or failed a lie detector test, supposedly confessed, or knew something that "only the real killer could have known" can permeate every aspect of a case, even if excluded from trial.

The effects of post-event information in altering memories have been thoroughly documented in numerous laboratory experiments (Loftus 1979). Nevertheless, the resulting impact of one piece of evidence on another—the cross-contamination of evidence—has rarely been discussed. Cross-contamination can take several forms. In the forensic sciences, for example, certain types of testing can produce ambiguous results that may be interpreted using a high degree of subjective judgment. Consider a forensic scientist faced with ambiguous test results who has been informed that the suspect was identified by the victim. Because he or she may be affected by that knowledge, even unwittingly, the scientist may read into those results a confirmation of guilt that might not otherwise be apparent (Thompson 1997).

The less neutral the scientist or the more the scientist feels a part of the prosecution team, the more likely that nonscientific evidence will bias the supposedly neutral scientific results. The most extreme examples, of course, are the Zain cases, in which Zain, as a state trooper and a forensic scientist, appears to have determined first who was the principal police suspect and then simply produced whatever combination of real and fictional scientific data served to confirm guilt.

If evidence from lay witnesses is capable of affecting scientific results, the reverse is even more true: scientific evidence may have an enormous influence on the testimony of lay witnesses. The William Harris case provides a valuable example. Consider the transformation of the victim's belief that William was not the assailant to her unequivocal assertion of the exact opposite, in which her knowledge of Zain's fraudulent results may have played a vital contaminating role. Suppose, for example, that the victim and the investigating officer had instead been told that scientific testing had eliminated William as a suspect. It seems unlikely that in such a case the officer would have overlooked or forgotten the victim's earlier statements and described her identification of William as the "most dramatic," the "most convincing" that he had ever seen. The victim's knowledge that scientific testing had confirmed her identification of William surely bolstered her confidence that she was right.

After Zain's fraud was exposed, the judge in the William Harris case was required to remove from consideration Zain's evidence and weigh the sufficiency of what remained. What remained (while the victim's original statements were still concealed) was the dramatic trial testimony of the victim and the investigating officer identifying William as the assailant. On the basis of this analysis, the prosecution opposed DNA testing for William and urged that he remain in prison based on the "unshakable" independent evidence of guilt.[21] Unfortunately, it was not independent evidence at all but apparently the product of suggestion and false reinforcement, contaminated by the misinformation provided by Fred Zain.

The same influences are likely to affect investigating officers and eyewitnesses in other contexts. The knowledge that a suspect has failed a lie detector test, confessed, or knows something "that only the real killer could know"—whether accurate or not—can color the perceptions of other pieces of evidence. Every memory of the suspect's actions, words, or demeanor can be reinterpreted in light of the contaminating effect of the "knowledge" of guilt. As in the case of William Harris, independent evidence of innocence—that the assailant was initially described as being a different height, a different age, and wearing different clothing—tends to fade in significance and even disappear from witnesses' memories.

William Harris's case is probably not unique. In many cases of wrongful convictions, independent evidence of guilt introduced at trial turns out to be erroneous. In reality, this independent evidence may not be independent at all but the product of the cross-contaminating effect of misinformation, as in the case of William Harris. Consequently, an understanding of the potential for cross-contamination of evidence and the implementation of safeguards against it are essential steps in reducing the likelihood of wrongful convictions in the future.

Conclusion

The wrongful conviction of William Harris and others like him could have been avoided. The suggestive interrogations, the photo-biased lineup, the erroneous forensic science, the withholding of exculpatory evidence (that is, evidence of William's innocence), and the cross-contaminating effect of the misinformation on the witnesses in the case all contributed to William's conviction, despite the many overlooked or ignored indications of innocence. What occurred in his case is not unique: many of the factors that contributed to his wrongful conviction can be observed repeatedly in an examination of the growing number of wrongfully convicted persons.

Exercising greater caution at numerous stages in the legal process may help reduce wrongful results. Caution could be increased by (1) adherence to the recently adopted guidelines for avoiding suggestive eyewitness interviews and identification procedures, (2) more scrupulous adherence to rules regarding disclosure of evidence favorable to the defense, (3) more probing reliability assessments of forensic science results, and (4) adoption of steps to minimize the cross-contamination of evidence by carefully recording and disclosing witnesses' initial observations before exposing witnesses to post-event information.

It is important to note, however, that many of the recent wrongful convictions would not have been identified and overturned without the development of DNA testing and its availability in post-conviction proceedings. Instead, William Harris and others like him would still be in prison today, convicted on the basis of seemingly overwhelming evidence of guilt. In cases without evidence to submit to DNA testing or those in which judges in post-conviction proceedings will not permit it, innocent people remain in prison today, some possibly facing sentences of death.

In cases without evidence to submit to DNA testing, the same factors that produced wrongful convictions in the past are producing more wrongful convictions today. To reduce the growing number of innocent people in prison, responsible law enforcement officers, prosecutors, defense lawyers, and judges must carefully study the recent wave of wrongful convictions, learn from the experience, and resolve to take the necessary steps to assure that they will never occur again.

NOTES

1. See *Investigation into the West Virginia State Police Crime Laboratory, Serology Division* (1993). The West Virginia Supreme Court of Appeals summarized what it described as Zain's "long history of falsifying evidence" in criminal prosecutions:

    The acts of misconduct on the part of Zain included 1) overstating the strength of the results; 2) overstating the frequency of genetic matches on individual pieces of evidence; 3) misreporting the frequency of genetic matches on multiple pieces of evidence; 4) reporting that multiple items had been tested, when only a single item had been tested; 5) reporting inconclusive results as conclusive; 6) repeatedly altering laboratory results; 7) grouping results to create the erroneous impression that genetic markers had been obtained from all samples tested; 8) failing to report conflicting results; 9) failing to conduct or to report conducting additional testing to resolve conflicting results; 10) implying a match with a suspect when testing supported only a match with the victim; 11) reporting scientifically impossible or improbable results. (*Investigation into the West Virginia State Police Crime Laboratory, Serology Division* 1993: 503)

2. See the police interview of the victim, 18 December 1984; the transcript of the juvenile transfer hearing, 10 January 1986; and the trial transcript (*State of West Virginia v. William O'Dell Harris, Jr.* 1987).

3. See the trial transcript (*State of West Virginia v. William O'Dell Harris, Jr.* 1987: 268–315).

4. See the trial transcript (ibid.: 453).

5. See *Investigation into the West Virginia State Police Crime Laboratory, Serology Division* (1993).

6. See the Kanawha County Sheriff's Department, Law Enforcement Division, 29 April 1985, report of investigation (*State of West Virginia v. William O'Dell Harris, Jr.* 1987). At trial, the prosecution acknowledged that the victim initially stated that she knew William Harris and that "it wasn't him." The prosecution dismissed this statement, however, explaining that the victim was referring to William's father, William O'Dell Harris, Sr. (ibid.: 198–99). At no time did the prosecution or the police acknowledge that the victim had viewed the photograph of William, Jr. (the defendant) and eliminated him as the assailant. In the subsequent civil litigation, the po-

lice testified that they did not tell the prosecutors that the photographic elimination had occurred (*William O. Harris, Jr., v. Fred S. Zain, et al.* 1995: 62–66).

7. See the trial transcript (*State of West Virginia v. William O'Dell Harris, Jr.* 1987: 215).
8. See the trial transcript (ibid.: 158).
9. This is the victim's statement to the Kanawha County sheriff on 18 December 1984 (ibid.: 13).
10. See the trial transcript (ibid.: 550, 565, 590, 608, 621, and 635).
11. See the Kanawha County Sheriff's Department, Law Enforcement Division, 29 April 1985, report of investigation (ibid.).
12. See the transcript of the suppression hearing on 15 July 1987 (ibid.: 35).
13. See the trial transcript (ibid.: 360–65).
14. This is the victim's statement to a Kanawha County deputy sheriff on 25 July 1985 (ibid.).
15. See the forensic report, West Virginia State Police Crime Laboratory, S-85–378, 30 October 1985 (ibid.).
16. See the trial transcript (ibid.: 794, 797, and 800).
17. See the deposition of deputy sheriff John W. Johnson on 8 April 1996 (*William O. Harris, Jr., v. Fred S. Zain, et al.* 1995: 62–66).
18. See the trial transcript (*State of West Virginia v. William O'Dell Harris, Jr.* 1987: 794, 797, and 800).
19. See the deposition of state trooper Sabrina Gayle Midkiff and the deposition of former state trooper Lynn Inman (Moreland) (*Investigation into the West Virginia State Police Crime Laboratory, Serology Division* 1993: 11–19, 22, and 39–44). In her 1993 deposition, Trooper Midkiff testified:

> Q: [George Castelle] How many did you see that were clear cut where [Fred Zain] appeared to be making up results that didn't exist?
>
> A: I couldn't give you a number. It's a large number though.
>
> Q: I won't put words in your mouth, but to give us a better understanding, by "large," would that be 10 or 20 or 100 or 1000?
>
> A: Probably, considering over the period of time, it may be close to 100. It became routine, and it got to the point where I didn't pay any attention.

Both Trooper Midkiff and Trooper Inman testified in the 1993 investigation that they reported the fraud to Zain's state police supervisors and showed them examples of the fraud, yet the supervisors continued to praise Zain and recommend him for promotions. Trooper Inman stated:

> A: Our complaint was that [Zain] was calling things that weren't there. Then I really felt it was kind of up to the supervisors to take a look at that.
>
> Q: Did you discuss it with the supervisors?
>
> A: Yes sir, we did. . . .
>
> Q: What did they do?
>
> A: I don't know; nothing was changed.

A review of Zain's personnel file during the period of time in question confirms Troopers Midkiff and Inman's disappointment in Zain's supervisors. His evaluations during and after the time of the complaints read as follows: "Sergeant Zain will go beyond what is normally required to assist field investigators and to keep the backlog down to a minimum in this section. Sergeant Zain is continually attempting to improve advanced

Serology techniques in this section" (West Virginia State Police personnel file of state trooper Fred S. Zain, semi-annual evaluation report, 1 January– 30 June 1985, investigative file [*Investigation into the West Virginia State Police Crime Laboratory, Serology Division* 1993]); "Continues to demonstrate a high level of job interest. Level of productivity is excellent in the Serology section" (semi-annual evaluation report, 1 January–30 June 1986); "An efficient run section. Sgt. Zain continues to demonstrate a high level of job interest in the field of serology. He goes the extra step when trying to assist the investigator and prosecutor" (semi-annual evaluation report, 1 July–31 December 1987); "Recommended for promotion" (semi-annual evaluation report, 1 January–30 June 1988).

20. See *Investigation into the West Virginia State Police Crime Laboratory, Serology Division* (1993: 505–6).

21. See the respondent's memorandum in opposition to petition for *Writ of Habeas Corpus Ad Subjiciendum* (*State of West Virginia ex rel. William O. Harris, Jr., v. Trent* 1993: 8).

REFERENCES

Borchard, Edwin. 1932. *Convicting the Innocent.* New Haven: Yale University Press.

Castelle, George. 1999. "Lab Fraud: Lessons Learned from the 'Fred Zain' Affair." *Champion* 23 (May): 12–16, 52–57.

Conners, Edward, Thomas Lundregan, Neal Miller, and Tom McEwan. 1996. *Convicted by Juries, Exonerated by Science: Case Studies in the Use of DNA Evidence to Establish Innocence after Trial.* Washington, D.C.: National Institute of Justice.

Fricker, Richard L. 1993. "Pathologist's Plea Adds to Turmoil." *American Bar Association Journal* (March): 24.

Goldin, Davidson. 1995. "5th State Trooper Pleads Guilty in Scandal." *New York Times,* 8 April, p. A29.

Hanley, Robert. 1997. "Jury Convicts an Ex-Coroner of Tampering with a Witness." *New York Times,* 29 October, p. B8.

Hanson, Mark. 1993. "Believe It or Not." *American Bar Association Journal* (June): 64.

———. 1996. "Out of the Blue." *American Bar Association Journal* (February): 50.

Loftus, Elizabeth F. 1979. *Eyewitness Testimony.* Cambridge: Harvard University Press.

Loftus, Elizabeth F., and James M. Doyle. 1997. *Eyewitness Testimony: Civil and Criminal.* 3d ed. Charlottesville, Va.: Lexis Law Publishing.

Messina, Lawrence. 1995a. "Harvard Lab Tests Show Ex-Wrestling Star Couldn't Be Rapist." *Charleston Gazette,* 3 May, p. A6.

———. 1995b. "Harris Won't Forget Wrongful Rape Conviction." *Charleston Gazette,* 2 August, pp. A1, A11.

Perez-Pena, Richard. 1997. "Report Faults Supervision of State Police: Free Rein Said to Lead to Evidence Tampering." *New York Times,* 4 February, pp. B1, B4.

Scheck, Barry, Peter Neufeld, and Jim Dwyer. 2000. *Actual Innocence.* New York: Doubleday.

Thompson, William C. 1997. "A sociological perspective on the science of forensic testing." *University of California Davis Law Review* 30: 1113–36.

U. S. Department of Justice, Office of the Inspector General. 1996. Investigation of FBI laboratory, memorandum of investigation, and interview of FBI agent Greg Parsons, 23 January.

———, Office of Justice Programs. 1999. *Eyewitness Evidence: A Guide for Law Enforcement.* Washington, D.C.: National Institute of Justice.

Wells, Gary L., and Amy L. Bradfield. 1998. "'Good, You Identified the Suspect': Feedback to Eyewitnesses Distorts Their Reports of the Witnessing Experience." *Journal of Applied Psychology* 83: 360–76.

———. 1999. "Distortions in Eyewitnesses' Recollections: Can the Postidentification-Feedback Effect Be Moderated?" *Psychological Science* 10: 38–144.

Wells, Gary L., Mark Small, Steven Penrod, Roy S. Malpass, Solomon Fulero, and C. Elizabeth Brimacombe. 1998. "Eyewitness Identification Procedures: Recommendations for Lineups and Photospreads." *Law and Human Behavior* 22: 603–47.

CASES CITED

Brady v. Maryland, 373 U.S. 83 (1963).

Daubert v. Merrell Dow Pharmaceuticals, Inc., 509 U.S. 579 (1993).

Giglio v. United States, 405 U.S. 150 (1972).

Investigation into the West Virginia State Police Crime Laboratory, Serology Division, 190 W.Va. 321, 438 S.E.2d 501 (1993).

Kumho Tire Co. v. Carmichael, 119 S.Ct. 1167 (1999).

Kyles v. Whitley, 514 U.S. 419 (1995).

Neil v. Biggers, 409 U.S. 188 (1972).

State of West Virginia v. William O'Dell Harris, Jr., No. 86–F-442 (Circuit Court, Kanawha County, W. Va., 1987).

State of West Virginia ex rel. William O. Harris, Jr., v. Trent, No. 93–W-43 (Circuit Court of Kanawha County, W.Va., 1993).

William O. Harris, Jr., v. Fred S. Zain, et al., Civil Action No. 2:95–1121 (U.S. District Court, Southern District of W.Va., 1995).

RICHARD A. LEO

2 False Confessions
Causes, Consequences, and Solutions

Despite popular perceptions, innocent individuals sometimes confess to crimes they have not committed. For example, of sixty-two wrongly convicted individuals who have been exonerated by DNA evidence in the United States, Scheck et al. (2000) note that fifteen originally confessed to the crime. A confession is one of the most powerful pieces of evidence that can be presented in court: juries almost always believe a defendant who confesses to a crime, in spite of any other evidence to the contrary (Kassin and Sukel 1997; Leo and Ofshe 1998). Why, they ask, would a person admit to committing a crime if he or she had not? It is thus essential to understand how false confessions are produced and how they influence the police investigation, the prosecution's presentation of the case, and the jurors' and judges' decisions. A false confession can bias every part of the criminal justice process that follows, often resulting in the wrongful conviction of an innocent person (Leo and Ofshe 1998).

This chapter reviews the existing psychological, criminological, and sociolegal literature on police interrogation and false confession to answer three questions. First, how can police interrogators' techniques, methods, and strategies cause innocent suspects to make false confessions? Second, what is the impact of demonstrably unreliable confession evidence on the perceptions, decision making, and actions of judges and juries? Third, what policy reforms are most likely to reduce police-induced false confessions and thus minimize the number of unjust deprivations of liberty and wrongful convictions?

The Causes of Police-Induced False Confession

From the Third Degree to the Age of Psychological Interrogation

If we examine earlier eras of American history, we can see how and why police interrogators sometimes elicited false confessions from criminal suspects. Through at least the early 1930s, police regularly relied on physical coercion and psychological duress to extract confessions (Hopkins 1931). In the past sixty years, however, more subtle and sophisticated psychological interrogation methods have replaced those third-degree tactics (Leo 1992). As a result, it is no longer obvious how American police elicit confessions from the innocent or why the innocent falsely confess to crimes that carry lengthy prison sentences, life imprisonment, or execution (Gudjonsson 1992; Wrightsman and Kassin 1993). With the decline of the third degree, the phenomenon of police-induced false confession has become counter-intuitive (White 1997).

The Myth of Psychological Interrogation

Most people do not appear to know that police-induced false confessions even exist (Ainsworth 1995; Johnson 1997; Kassin and Neumann 1997). Like many criminal justice officials (especially police and prosecutors), most people believe in what I call the *myth of psychological interrogation*: that an innocent person will not falsely confess to police unless he or she is physically tortured or mentally ill (Ainsworth 1995; Johnson 1997; White 1997). This myth is, of course, completely false. The social science research literature has amply documented that contemporary methods of psychological interrogation can, and sometimes do, cause cognitively and intellectually normal individuals to give false confessions to serious crimes of which they are entirely innocent (Gudjonsson 1992; Kassin 1997; Leo and Ofshe 1998). The central issue, then, is no longer whether police-induced false confessions exist but why they occur and what can be done to prevent them.

The Social Psychology of Police Interrogation

Modern interrogation techniques and strategies are designed to break the resistance of rational people who know they are guilty, manipulate them to stop denying their culpability, and persuade them to confess (Inbau et al. 1986; Ofshe and Leo 1997a, 1997b). Police interrogators elicit the decision to confess by influencing the suspect's perception of (1) the nature and gravity of his immediate situation, (2) the suspect's available choices or alternatives given that situation, and (3) the consequences of each of these choices (Ofshe and Leo 1997a, 1997b). By continually manipulating the suspect's perception of the situation and his available alternatives, the interrogator labors to persuade the suspect that he has few options except confession and that the act of admitting culpability is the most optimal, and thus the most sensible, course of action.

Step 1: Shifting the Suspect from Confident to Hopeless. American police interrogation is essentially a two-step process (Ofshe and Leo 1997a, 1997b). The goal of the first step is to break the suspect's resistance by causing her to perceive the situation as hopeless. The interrogator leads the suspect to believe that she has been caught; that guilt can be objectively demonstrated to the satisfaction of any reasonable person; that this fact is indisputable and cannot be changed; that there is no way out of this predicament; and that, as a result, the suspect is trapped and her fate determined.

Presuming that the suspect is guilty, the interrogator is likely to rely on several well-known interrogation techniques and strategies to successfully communicate the message that the suspect is caught and persuade him that the situation is hopeless. The interrogator is likely to (repeatedly) accuse the suspect of having committed the crime and express unwavering confidence in these repeated assertions of guilt, ignoring or rolling past any of the suspect's objections. This may cause the unknowing suspect to believe that he bears the burden of proving innocence, yet the interrogator may seek to prevent the suspect from issuing denials or asserting innocence. If the suspect offers an alibi, the interrogator may attack it as inconsistent, implausible, contradicted by all the case evidence, or simply impossible—even if none of these characterizations is true.

The most important and effective technique that police use to convince the suspect that her situation is hopeless is to confront her with objective and irrefutable evidence of guilt, whether or not any actually exists. American law permits interrogators to pretend they have evidence when they do not, and police often confront suspects with fabricated evidence, such as nonexistent eyewitnesses, false fingerprints, make-believe videotapes, fake polygraph results, and so on (Leo 1992, 1996a, 1996b). Because they are legally permitted to lie about the evidence during interrogation, police may also exaggerate the nature, type, amount, or strength of evidence they already have. The purpose of this technique is to convince the suspect that the case against her is so objectively irrefutable that guilt will be established beyond any possible doubt and that conviction and imprisonment are inevitable. Thus, the suspect believes that she has no choice but to confess to the crime.

Step 2: Offering the Suspect Inducements to Confess. In the second phase of interrogation, the detective seeks to influence the suspect to perceive that the only way to improve this otherwise hopeless situation is by admitting to the offense (Ofshe and Leo 1997a, 1997b). The interrogator's general strategy is to persuade the suspect that the benefits of admitting guilt clearly outweigh the costs of continuing to assert innocence. To accomplish this goal, the interrogator presents the suspect with inducements that communicate that he will receive some personal, moral, communal, procedural, material, legal, or other benefit if he confesses to the offense. These inducements can be arrayed along a continuum ranging from legally permissible benefits (low-end inducements) to explicitly coercive threats and promises (high-end inducements). Given the suspect's perception of the immediate situation and his limited choices, these inducements convey that it is in his self-interest to confess. For analytic purposes, researchers have classified these inducements into three categories: low end, systemic, and high end (Ofshe and Leo 1997a, 1997b).

Low-end inducements refer to self-image, interpersonal, or moral appeals that suggest the suspect will feel better or improve her social standing if she confesses. They are intended to manipulate the guilty suspect who is either (1) experiencing a troubled conscience, remorse, or low self-esteem because of her offense or (2) vulnerable to moral suasion. The interrogator tells the suspect that if she denies any culpability, she will continue to experience guilt and anxiety. Once she accepts responsibility for her actions by confessing, however, she will be relieved of this tormenting distress. She also will be viewed as a better person—by her own conscience; her family, friends, peers, or employer; and the victim, the victim's family, or the community more generally. Classic low-end inducements include imploring the suspect to confess because "you will get it off your chest," "the truth will set you free," "honesty is the best policy," "it's the honorable thing to do," "it will cleanse your soul," "you will be tormented by your conscience if you don't," or "the victim, your family, or God will only forgive you if you confess."

Systemic inducements focus the suspect's attention on the discretionary ability of criminal justice officials to positively influence his case as well as the systemic benefits for confessing and the costs for continuing to deny guilt (Ofshe and Leo 1997a, 1997b). The interrogator's goal in relying on systemic inducements is to lead the suspect to reason that his case is likely to be processed more favorably by all actors in the criminal justice system if he accepts responsibility, demonstrates remorse, cooperates with authorities, and admits guilt. They also remind him that he will be treated less favorably if he continues to deny any involvement in the offense. The interrogator seeks to motivate the suspect to admit responsibility by placing his actions in the best possible light from the perspective of the criminal justice system. For example, an interrogator may tell a suspect that he is the suspect's ally and will try to help him out, both in his discussions with the prosecutor as well as in his role as a professional witness at trial; however, the interrogator claims that he can only do so if the suspect first admits guilt. Or the interrogator may ask the suspect how he expects the prosecutor to react if the suspect does not cooperate with authorities. Or the interrogator may ask the suspect how a judge and jury are going to view him if he does not demonstrate remorse and admit his guilt to authorities.

High-end inducements communicate the message that the suspect will receive less punishment; a lower prison sentence; or some form of investigative, prosecutorial, judicial, or juror leniency or clemency if she complies with the interrogator's demand that she confess and that the suspect will receive a higher charge or longer prison sentence if she does not comply with the interrogator's demand (Ofshe and Leo 1997a, 1997b). These inducements may be either implicit or explicit: the important question is whether the interrogation technique communicates the message, or is understood to communicate the message, that the suspect will receive a lower criminal charge or lesser punishment if she confesses (minimization) as opposed to a higher criminal charge or a greater amount of punishment if she does not (maximization) (see Kassin and McNall 1991). For example, interrogators sometimes try to persuade suspects that their behavior was merely an accident, a reasonable response to the victim's provocation, or a heroic act of self-defense. By portraying the suspect's behavior as an accident or reasonable response to provocation, the interrogator communicates the message that the suspect did not intend to harm the victim, that the act was not a crime or was a significantly lower level of crime, and that the suspect will therefore receive little or no punishment if she agrees to this minimized version of what the interrogator is suggesting might have happened. By portraying the suspect's behavior as self-defense, the interrogator communicates that no crime at all even occurred and that the suspect will receive no punishment at all (since self-defense is not a crime but a legally justified response to physical aggression) if she agrees to this version of what the interrogator is suggesting (Ofshe and Leo 1997a, 1997b).

Effective psychological interrogation is a gradual yet cumulative process. As they progress through the two steps of interrogation, detectives work to structure the suspect's perceptions about the nature of his immediate situation, the limited choices available to him, and what follows from these choices. Through techniques that rely on deception, manipulation, and sometimes coercion, an interrogator seeks to transform the psychological context within which the suspect comes to perceive his situation and make the decision about whether to confess. At the beginning of the interrogation (when the suspect's subjective confidence of leaving the interrogation without incriminating himself is high), the suspect may never have agreed to make an admission. At that point, the suspect would have had nothing to gain and everything to lose by making an admission and thus may not have even thought it possible that he would be made to confess. Once the suspect has been convinced that he will almost certainly be arrested, convicted, and punished, however, his evaluation of the immediate situation and his decision-making calculus are likely to change. Once the suspect has been persuaded that he is caught and that his situation is hopeless, the act of confessing may appear (given how he now views his circumstances and limited alternatives) to be in his rational self-interest (Ofshe and Leo 1997a, 1997b).

The Different Types of Police-Induced False Confession

Kassin and Wrightsman (1985) identified three conceptually distinct types of false confession: voluntary, coerced-compliant, and coerced-internalized. This typology or classification scheme has offered a useful conceptual framework for scholars of interrogation and confession (Gudjonsson 1992), although it has been criticized by others (Davison and Forsaw 1993; McCann 1998; Ofshe and Leo 1997b). Synthesizing the existing research literature, Ofshe and Leo (1997b) have extended and modified Kassin and Wrightsman's initial typology to include five distinct types of false confession: voluntary, stress-compliant, coerced-compliant, coerced-persuaded, and non-coerced–persuaded.

A *voluntary false confession* is offered either without police interrogation or in response to minimal police pressure. As Kassin and Wrightsman (1985) state, individuals volunteer false confessions without police questioning for a variety of reasons: a morbid desire for notoriety, the need to expiate guilt about imagined as well as real acts (Gudjonsson 1992), the need to receive attention or fame, the desire to protect or assist the real offender, an inability to distinguish between fantasy and reality, or a pathological need for acceptance or self-punishment (Kassin 1997). High-profile crimes such as the Lindbergh kidnapping in the 1930s, the Black Dahlia murder in the 1940s, and the JonBenet Ramsey and Nicole Brown Simpson murders in the 1990s may attract hundreds of voluntary false confessions (Kassin 1997).

A *stress-compliant false confession* occurs when the stresses and pressures of custodial questioning overwhelm the suspect and she comes to believe that the only way to terminate the punishing experience of interrogation is by confessing (Ofshe and Leo 1997b). Three primary sources of stress are present during interrogation: the interrogation environment, the interrogator's interpersonal style, and the interrogator's techniques and strategies. Detectives intentionally structure the environment to create tension and induce distress by making the suspect feel both powerless and anxious: they typically place the suspect in a cramped and unfamiliar setting; isolate her from personal contact or social support;, and do not permit her to exercise any control over the pace, length, or intensity of interrogation. Interrogators' interpersonal styles may also be a source of distress: as they exert pressure on the suspect to confess, they may, by turns, be confrontational, insistent, demanding, overbearing, deceptive, hostile, and manipulative. An interrogator's techniques and strategies are also designed to induce distress and anxiety systematically by attacking the suspect's self-confidence, not permitting her to assert her innocence or deny her guilt, causing her to feel powerless and trapped, and exerting pressure on her to comply with the interrogator's demand that she confess. Even though she privately knows that she is innocent, the stress-compliant false confessor complies with the interrogator's demand that she confess because the prospect of continued interrogation is subjectively intolerable.

According to Kassin (1997: 225), "coerced compliant false confessions occur when a suspect confesses in order to escape or avoid an aversive interrogation or to gain a promised reward." A *coerced-compliant false confession* is therefore similar to a stress-compliant false confession insofar as the individual knowingly confesses falsely to escape an aversive interrogation. As Ofshe and Leo (1997b) point out, however, two major differences exist between coerced- and stress-compliant false confessions. First, coerced-compliant false confessions are caused by coercive techniques such as threats and promises. Second, the suspect may consciously decide to terminate the interrogation to escape the aversive questioning or gain a promised reward (Ofshe and Leo 1997b). Social scientists, appellate courts, and others have documented numerous cases of coerced-compliant false confessions in American history, both in the era of the third degree (see, for example, Hopkins 1931) as well as in the age of psychological interrogation (see, for example, Leo and Ofshe 1998).

A *coerced-persuaded false confession* occurs when the interrogator's use of coercive influence techniques causes a suspect to temporarily doubt the reliability of his memory; believe that he probably did, or logically must have, committed the crime under question; and confess to it, despite having no memory or knowledge of participating in or committing the offense (Ofshe and Leo 1997b). A coerced-persuaded false confession typically unfolds in three steps. First, the interrogator successfully attacks the suspect's confidence in the reliability of his memory, causing the suspect to doubt his actual knowledge, recollections, or framing of his situation. Second, the interrogator offers the suspect an acceptable amnesia-based explanation for his apparent lack of memory of having committed the crime (such as post-traumatic stress disorder, dry or alcoholic blackout, repressed memory, and so on). Third, after the suspect comes to believe that he must have committed the crime despite his absence of memory, the interrogator and the suspect jointly construct a confession to explain how and why it occurred (Ofshe and Leo 1997b). Since the suspect did not commit or participate in the crime, his confession comes from information that the interrogator has fed to him or that he has obtained from other sources (such as the media or community gossip), inferences from the interrogator's questions and suggestions about how the crime occurred, and good faith guesses (that is, confabulations) about how the crime could or should have occurred. Because coerced-persuaded false confessors lack any knowledge or memory of having committed the crime, they confess in hypothetical, tentative, and speculative language ("I could have," "I would have," "I probably did," "I must have," and so on), reflecting their uncertainty and lack of knowledge (Ofshe and Leo 1997a, 1997b).

As Ofshe and Leo (1997b) point out, a *non-coerced–persuaded false confession* follows the same structure, sequence, and logic as a coerced-persuaded one. The major difference is that a non-coerced–persuaded false confession is not elicited in response to coercive interrogation techniques. Accordingly, "a non-coerced persuaded confession is elicited in response to the influence tactics and techniques of modern, psychologically sophisticated accusatorial interrogation, and given by a suspect who has temporarily come to believe that it is more likely than not that he committed the offense despite no memory of having done so" (Ofshe and Leo 1997b: 215). As with coerced-persuaded false confessions, non-coerced–persuaded false confessions are delivered in the grammar of confabulation. Once the persuaded false confessor is removed from the influences and pressures of the interrogation environment, the person—whether coerced or not—comes to realize that she could not have possibly committed the crime and typically recants her confession (Ofshe and Leo 1997b).

The Consequences of Police-Induced False Confession

Police-induced false confession has always been one of the primary causes of miscarriages of justice in the United States (Bedau and Radelet 1987; Borchard 1932; Leo and Ofshe 1998). While it is not presently possible to provide a valid quantitative estimate of the incidence or prevalence of police-induced false confession (Gudjonsson 1992; Kassin 1997; White 1997), the social science research literature has established that such confessions occur with troubling regularity and are highly likely to lead to unjust deprivations of liberty and the wrongful conviction of the innocent (Gudjonsson 1992; Leo and Ofshe 1998; Wrightsman and Kassin 1993). Psychologists, criminologists, and others have documented so many examples of police-induced false confession that there is no longer any dispute about their occurrence. Nevertheless, because most are likely to go unnoticed by researchers, unacknowledged by police and prosecutors, and un-reported by the media, they are not easily discovered and are rarely publicized. As a result, the documented cases likely represent only the tip of a much larger false confession (and wrongful conviction) iceberg.

Historically regarded as a form of self-conviction, false confessions are very likely to lead to miscarriages of justice because of their ex-treme biasing effect on the perceptions and decision making of crimi-nal justice officials and lay jurors (Kassin and Sukel 1997; Leo and Ofshe 1998; Wrightsman and Kassin 1993). Except for the rare instance in which a perpetrator is caught in flagrante (more common in cin-ema than in real life), a confession is regarded as the most powerful, persuasive, and damning evidence of guilt that the state can bring against an accused (Kassin and Wrightsman 1985; Leo 1996a; Leo and Ofshe 1998). A false confession is therefore the most powerful, per-suasive, and damning *false* evidence of guilt that the state can bring against an accused—more prejudicial than any other potential source of evidence.

A suspect's confession sets in motion a virtually irrefutable pre-sumption of guilt among criminal justice officials and lay jurors (Johnson 1997). As a result, a suspect who confesses will be treated more harshly at every stage of the criminal process (Leo 1996a; Ofshe and Leo 1997b). Consider police and prosecutors. Once police obtain a confession (and their preconceived bias is confirmed), they invari-ably shut down their investigation, clear the case as solved, and—even if the suspect's guilt is far from certain—make no effort to pursue other possible leads (Leo and Ofshe 1998). Because they are reluctant to admit their mistakes and are committed to the belief that innocent people do not falsely confess, police almost never consider the possibility that they may have mistakenly elicited or coerced a false confession from an entirely innocent suspect, and district attorneys almost never con-sider the possibility that they may be prosecuting an innocent defen-dant based on a police-induced false confession (Johnson 1997; Ofshe and Leo 1997b). If the defendant retracts his confession, police and prosecutors dismiss the recantation with sneering derision. Prosecutors tend to make the confession the dramatic centerpiece of their case; charge the defendant with the highest possible offense, set of offenses, or number of counts that the law allows; and are less likely to either initiate or accept a plea bargain to a reduced charge (Leo and Ofshe 1998). Because they are so committed to a belief in a suspect's guilt once a confession is obtained, police and prosecutors often selectively ignore virtually any evidence that fails to fit their presumption of guilt—for example, when none of the physical evidence (blood, saliva, semen, DNA, and so on) left by the perpetrator of the offense at the crime scene matches the confessor. They rationalize even the most innocent case discrepancies as evidence of the suspect's guilt that "corroborates" his confession (Leo and Ofshe 1998).

Police and prosecutors are not uniquely affected by the extreme biasing power of confession evidence: *all* criminal justice officials presume the guilt of any defendant who has confessed and treat her more harshly as a result (Johnson 1997; Leo 1996a). Suspects who confess will experience greater difficulty making bail (especially in serious cases), a disadvantage that significantly reduces a criminal defendant's likelihood of acquittal (Walker 1994). Defense attorneys are more likely to pressure their clients to waive their constitutional right to a trial and accept a guilty plea to a lesser charge because they realize that the defendant's confession, even if coerced or unreliable, virtually ensures her conviction (Johnson 1997).

So, too, are triers of fact biased in favor of conviction by the mere fact of an admission. Judges are conditioned to disbelieve claims of innocence and almost never suppress confessions, even highly questionable ones (Givelber 1997). If the defendant's case goes to trial, the jury will treat the confession as more probative of the accused's guilt than any other type of evidence (Kassin and Neumann 1997; Leo and Ofshe 1998; Miller and Boster 1977)—especially if the confession receives negative pretrial publicity (Pratkanis and Aronson 1991), as in virtually all high-profile cases. Juries are often so unwilling to believe that anyone would confess to a crime that he did not commit that they are likely to convict on the basis of the confession alone, even if no significant or credible evidence confirms the confession and considerable evidence disconfirms it (Kassin and Sukel 1997; Leo and Ofshe 1998; White 1997).

Once convicted, a false confessor will be sentenced more harshly. Trial judges are conditioned to punish defendants for claiming innocence (the logical extension of not accepting the trial tariff offered in plea bargaining negotiations) and for failing to apologize for their wrongdoings (Givelber 1997). It is the rare innocent defendant who expresses remorse at his post-conviction sentencing hearing, even when doing so would significantly reduce his sentence. Once incarcerated, no criminal justice official will take seriously the defendant's insistent claim that he confessed falsely and was wrongfully convicted. As Gudjonsson (1992) points out, the judiciary performs extremely poorly at discovering, admitting to, or doing something about its errors. Moreover, mistakes in the administration of criminal justice become more difficult to correct the farther a case progresses in the system (Givelber 1997; Huff et al. 1996). Thus, this one biased piece of evidence contaminates the perception and treatment of a case as it makes its way through the entire criminal justice process.

Policy Solutions

There is no worse error in American criminal justice than the wrongful prosecution, conviction, and incarceration of an innocent person, especially in capital cases—where the risk that a police-induced false confession will lead to a miscarriage of justice may be four times higher than in noncapital cases (Gross 1996). It is important to emphasize, however, that every wrongful prosecution and conviction represents a *systemic,* not an individual, failure. No one is accusing police of intentionally coercing false confessions, district attorneys of intentionally charging and prosecuting innocent defendants, or juries of intentionally convicting innocent men and women. When police-induced false confessions lead to miscarriages of justice, the procedural safeguards and multiple points of official discretion built into the system to prevent these outcomes have failed. The series of perceptions, decisions, and actions that ultimately lead to unjust deprivations of liberty and miscarriages of justice are typically based on ignorance, bias, and negligence—not malice. Yet because these errors are preventable, it is imperative that all reasonable steps be taken to prevent them. In the remainder of this chapter, I advance three policy recommendations that can reduce the number of police-induced false confessions and their likelihood of leading to unjust deprivations of liberty and miscarriages of justice: improved police training, mandatory video recordings of interrogations, and the provision of expert witness testimony.

Improved Police Training

American police are poorly trained to understand the psychology of interrogation, suspect decision making, and confession; evaluate the likely unreliability of confession statements; and recognize and prevent false confessions. Because they are not properly trained, most interrogators do not realize how their commonly taught and practiced methods of psychological interrogation can set up an innocent person to make a false confession. To reduce the number of false confessions, police interrogation training needs to be significantly improved in at least two ways.

First, detectives need to receive better training about the existence, variety, causes, and psychology of police-induced false confessions. Contrary to current practice, interrogation trainers (and training manuals) must stop perpetuating the myth of psychological interrogation: interrogators need to be taught that their psychological interrogation techniques can and do cause innocent suspects to falsely confess. More important, interrogators need to be taught *why* their commonly taught and practiced interrogation methods (such as maximization and minimization strategies) may lead both guilty and innocent people to confess. If interrogators learn the logic, principles, and effects of their psychological interrogation methods, they will be not only more knowledgeable about the causes of false confessions but also more effective at eliciting truthful ones. In addition, detectives need to be taught about the different types of false confessions, their distinguishing characteristics, and how to prevent them.

Second, interrogators need to receive better training about the indicia of reliable and unreliable statements and how to properly distinguish between them. It has long been a generally accepted principle in law enforcement (as well as among social scientists and legal scholars) that valid confessions are supported by logic and evidence whereas false ones are not (see, for example, Ayling 1984; Langbein 1978; Spence 1982). In practice, however, detectives virtually always treat a suspect's "I did it" statement as if it is automatically self-validating—even if logic or evidence fails to support it—merely because it validates their own presumption of the suspect's guilt. As Ofshe and Leo (1997b) point out, a suspect's "I did it" statement may turn out to be either evidence of innocence or evidence of guilt; initially it should be treated as a neutral hypothesis to be objectively tested against the case facts. Detectives need to learn that the proper way to assess the likely reliability of a suspect's confession is to analyze the fit of the suspect's post-admission narrative against the underlying crime facts to determine whether it reveals guilty knowledge and is corroborated by existing evidence (Ofshe and Leo 1997b). Assuming no contamination, a guilty suspect's post-admission narrative will reveal knowledge that is known only to the true perpetrator or the police, lead to new or derivative evidence, explain seeming anomalies or otherwise inexplicable crime facts, and be corroborated by existing physical and medical evidence (Leo and Ofshe 1998). An innocent suspect's post-admission narrative will reveal the opposite. Police interrogators need to be trained to recognize their own confirmation biases, initially treat admission statements as neutral hypotheses to be tested against objective case facts, and systematically analyze the probative value of a suspect's post-admission narrative (Ofshe and Leo 1997a).

Mandatory Video Recording

In Alaska (since 1985) and Minnesota (since 1994), police have been required to electronically record all police interrogations in entirety (see *Stephan v. State* 1985; *State v. Scales* 1994). Elsewhere, many American police departments voluntarily record interrogations (Geller 1992). Unlike some potential reforms, the recording of police interrogations is not an adversarial policy suggestion; it favors neither the defense nor the prosecution but only the pursuit of accurate and reliable fact finding. For at least three obvious reasons, American police everywhere should be legally required to electronically record their entire interrogations, not merely the recap or the statement that follows the interrogation.

First, videotaping police interrogations creates an objective, comprehensive, and reviewable record of the interrogation. With videotaping, it is no longer necessary to rely on subjective credibility judgments to resolve any "swearing contests" between the police and the defendant about what occurred during the interrogation. Unlike the testimony of two disputants, the videotape does not suffer from the fallibility and biases of human memory and judgment but preserves a record of the interrogation that is complete and factually accurate. A videotape will capture any police abuses or improprieties as well as protect detectives from false accusations. By preserving the record, videotaping removes the secrecy of interrogation and makes it accessible to criminal justice officials and triers of fact, thus rendering the fact-finding process more accurate and reliable (Johnson 1997; Kamisar 1980; Westling and Waye 1998).

Second, videotaping leads to a higher level of scrutiny (by police officials as well as others) that will deter police misconduct during interrogation, improve the quality of interrogation practices, and thus increase the ability of police to separate the innocent from the guilty. Interrogators are less likely to resort to improper interrogation practices when the camera is rolling and thus are less likely to coerce an innocent suspect into falsely confessing.

Third, a videotaping requirement will create the opportunity for various criminal justice officials to monitor more closely both the quality of police interrogation and the reliability of confession statements. Detectives, police managers, prosecutors, and judges will be able to detect false confessions more easily and thus may be able to prevent their admission into evidence against innocent defendants. Although some unreliable confessions will still inevitably be admitted into evidence at trial, a videotaping requirement will give jurors more knowledge to evaluate the quality of the interrogation and the reliability of the defendant's confession and make a more informed decision about what weight to place on confession evidence during their deliberations.

Expert Witness Testimony

The use of social science expert witness testimony in cases involving a disputed interrogation or confession has become increasingly common (see, for example, *United States v. Hall* 1996, 1997). Expert witness testimony in disputed confession cases is necessary because the traditional procedures of the adversarial system (such as opening and closing arguments, cross-examination of witnesses, cautionary instructions to juries, and so on) are not sufficient to safeguard innocent individuals against the likelihood of wrongful conviction based on unreliable confession evidence (Leo and Ofshe 1998). The purpose of expert witness testimony is to educate triers of fact about the general findings from the scientific research on interrogation and confession so that they can more adequately understand the psychological principles, practices, and processes of modern interrogation and thereby more accurately discriminate between reliable and unreliable confessions.

Expert witness testimony may reduce the number of police-induced false confessions that lead to wrongful convictions in three ways: by its direct effect on the decision making of the judge at pretrial suppression hearings (at which time the judge decides which evidence to allow at trial and which to exclude), its direct effect on the decision making of jurors at trial, and its indirect effect on the behavior of police and prosecutors. The purpose of expert witness testimony at pretrial suppression hearings is to assist the judge in analyzing whether the interrogation was coercive and thus whether the defendant's confession statement should be admissible at trial. Interrogation experts may usefully testify at pretrial suppression hearings about the nature and content of contemporary interrogation training and practices, the scientific research literature on interrogation and confession, and whether and why certain interrogation methods are regarded as coercive and therefore likely to overcome an individual's will. With the use of social science expert witness testimony, judges are more likely to suppress (that is, exclude from evidence) coerced confessions, some percentage of which are likely to be false. As a result, the use of expert witness testimony at pretrial suppression hearings will result in the admission of fewer police-induced false confessions into evidence at trial, which in turn will result in fewer wrongful convictions.

If a factually disputed confession is introduced at trial, the jury will want to know how an innocent person could possibly have been made to confess falsely—especially to a heinous crime. Although the question is obvious, the answer is not. The purpose of social science expert witness testimony at trial is to provide a general overview of the research on interrogation and confession to assist the jury in making a fully informed decision about what weight to place on the defendant's confession in its deliberations. More specifically, social science expert witnesses can aid the jury by (1) discussing the scientific research literature documenting the phenomenon of police-induced false confessions (thereby refuting the myth of psychological interrogation), (2) explaining how and why particular interrogation methods and strategies can cause the innocent to confess, (3) identifying the conditions that increase the risk of false confession, and (4) explaining the generally accepted principles of post-admission narrative analysis. By educating the jury about the existence, psychology, causes, and indicia of police-induced false confession, social science expert witness testimony at trial should reduce the number of confession-based wrongful convictions.

Finally, the use of expert witness testimony in pretrial suppression hearings and at jury trials should exert an educative and corrective effect on the future behavior of police and prosecutors. When interrogation experts testify, police and prosecutors take notice—especially in high-profile cases that rest entirely on disputed confession evidence. Police do not like to have their poor training, technical flaws, or courtroom lies exposed; to be criticized for using inappropriate or coercive methods; or to be shown to have elicited demonstrably false confessions. Prosecutors do not like to be criticized for indicting defendants based solely on coerced or false confessions, to be forced to dismiss charges after a judge suppresses the defendant's confession, or to have defendants acquitted. By exposing flaws in a detective's interrogation methods or in the prosecution's case against a defendant, social science expert witness testimony in disputed confession cases may deter police misbehavior in the long run and improve police and prosecutorial screening practices. It should lead to a decline in the use of psychologically coercive interrogation methods, the number of false confessions that police elicit and prosecutors introduce into evidence at trial, and thus the number of innocent men and women who are wrongfully convicted every year due to false confessions.

REFERENCES

Ainsworth, Peter B. 1995. *Psychology and Policing in a Changing World*. New York: Wiley.

Ayling, Corey. 1984. "Corroborating Confessions: An Empirical Analysis of Legal Safeguards against False Confessions." *Wisconsin Law Review*: 1121–1204.

Bedau, Hugo Adam, and Michael L. Radelet. 1987. "Miscarriages of Justice in Potentially Capital Cases." *Stanford Law Review* 40: 21–179.

Borchard, Edwin. 1932. *Convicting the Innocent*. New Haven: Yale University Press.

Davison, S. E., and D. M. Forshaw. 1993. "Retracted Confessions: Through Opiate Withdrawal to a New Conceptual Framework." *Medicine, Science and the Law* 33: 285–90.

Geller, William. 1992. "Police Videotaping of Suspect Interrogations and Confessions." Report to the National Institute of Justice. Manuscript.

Givelber, Daniel. 1997. "Meaningless Acquittals, Meaningful Convictions: Do We Reliably Acquit the Innocent?" *Rutgers Law Review* 49: 1317–96.

Gross, Samuel R. 1996. "The Risks of Death: Why Erroneous Convictions Are Common in Capital Cases." *Buffalo Law Review* 44: 469–500.

Gudjonsson, Gisli H. 1992. *The Psychology of Interrogations, Confessions and Testimony*. New York: Wiley.

Hopkins, Ernest Jerome. 1931. *Our Lawless Police: A Study of the Unlawful Enforcement of the Law*. New York: Viking.

Huff, C. Ronald, Arye Rattner, and Edward Sagarin. 1996. *Convicted but Innocent: Wrongful Conviction and Public Policy*. Thousand Oaks, Calif.: Sage.

Inbau, Fred E., John E. Reid, and Joseph P. Buckley. 1986. *Criminal Interrogation and Confessions*. 3d ed. Baltimore: William and Wilkins.

Johnson, Gail. 1997. "False Confessions and Fundamental Fairness: The Need for Electronic Recording of Custodial Interrogations." *Boston University Public Interest Law Journal* 6: 719–51.

Kamisar, Yale. 1980. *Police Interrogation and Confessions: Essays in Law and Policy.* Ann Arbor: University of Michigan Press.

Kassin, Saul M. 1997. "The Psychology of Confession Evidence." *American Psychologist* 52: 221–33.

Kassin, Saul M., and Karlyn McNall. 1991. "Police Interrogations and Confessions: Communicating Promises and Threats by Pragmatic Implication." *Law and Human Behavior* 15: 233–51.

Kassin, Saul M., and Katherine Neumann. 1997. "On the Power of Confession Evidence: An Experimental Test of the Fundamental Difference Hypothesis." *Law and Human Behavior* 21: 469–83.

Kassin, Saul M., and Holly Sukel. 1997. "Coerced Confessions and the Jury: An Experimental Test of the 'Harmless Error' Rule." *Law and Human Behavior* 21: 27–46.

Kassin, Saul M., and Lawrence Wrightsman. 1985. "Confession Evidence." In *The Psychology of Evidence and Trial Procedure*, edited by Saul Kassin and Lawrence Wrightsman, 67–94. Beverly Hills, Calif.: Sage.

Langbein, John. 1978. "Torture and Plea Bargaining." *University of Chicago Law Review* 46: 1–21.

Leo, Richard A. 1992. "From Coercion to Deception: The Changing Nature of Police Interrogation in America." *Crime, Law and Social Change* 18: 35–59.

———. 1996a. "Inside the Interrogation Room." *Journal of Criminal Law and Criminology* 86: 266–303.

———. 1996b. "*Miranda*'s Revenge: Police Interrogation As a Confidence Game." *Law and Society Review* 30: 259–88.

Leo, Richard A., and Richard J. Ofshe. 1998. "The Consequences of False Confessions: Deprivations of Liberty and Miscarriages of Justice in the Age of Psychological Interrogation." *Journal of Criminology and Criminal Law* 88: 429–96.

McCann, Joseph. 1998. "A Conceptual Framework for Identifying Various Types of Confessions." *Behavioral Sciences and the Law* 16: 441–53.

Miller, Gerald R., and F. Joseph Boster. 1977. "Three Images of the Trial: Their Implications for Psychological Research." In *Psychology in the Legal Process*, edited by Bruce Sales, 19–38. New York: Pocket Books.

Ofshe, Richard J., and Richard A. Leo. 1997a. "The Decision to Confess Falsely: Rational Choice and Irrational Action." *Denver University Law Review* 74: 979–1122.

———. 1997b. "The Social Psychology of Police Interrogation: The Theory and Classification of True and False Confessions." *Studies in Law, Politics and Society* 16: 189–251.

Pratkanis, Anthony, and Elliot Aronson. 1991. *Age of Propaganda: The Everyday Use and Abuse of Persuasion.* New York: Freeman.

Scheck, Barry, Peter Neufeld, and Jim Dwyer. 2000. *Actual Innocence.* New York: Doubleday.

Spence, Donald P. 1982. *Narrative Truth and Historical Truth: Meaning and Interpretation in Psychoanalysis.* New York: Norton.

Walker, Samuel. 1994. *Sense and Nonsense about Crime and Drugs: A Policy Guide.* Belmont, Calif.: Wadsworth.

Westling, Wayne, and Vicki Waye. 1998. "Videotaping Police Interrogations: Lessons from Australia." *American Journal of Criminal Law* 25: 493–543.

White, Welsh. 1997. "False Confessions and the Constitution: Safeguards to

Prevent the Admission of Untrustworthy Confessions." *Harvard Civil Rights and Civil Liberties Law Review* 32: 105–57.

Wrightsman, Lawrence, and Saul Kassin. 1993. *Confessions in the Courtroom.* Newbury Park, Calif.: Sage.

CASES CITED

State v. Scales, 518 N.W.2d 587 (1994).
Stephan v. State, 711 P.2d 1156 (1985).
United States v. Hall, 93 F.3d 1337 (1996).
United States v. Hall, 974 F.Supp. 1198 (1997).

CLIFFORD S. ZIMMERMAN

3 | From the Jailhouse to the Courthouse
The Role of Informants in Wrongful Convictions

Sycophants, approvers, finks, confidential sources, stoolies, informers, grasses, confidential informants, supergrasses, informants, narcs, undercover informants, snitches, assets, moles, jailhouse informants, or rats: no matter the name, these sources of information enjoy great expectations for reward, a high level of freedom within the criminal justice system, and a vast array of legal protections. Yet these motivations also provide the systemic motivations that lead to the misuse of informants within the criminal justice system.

A former federal prosecutor who instructs prosecutors on the use of informants describes them as willing to do anything: "lying, committing perjury, manufacturing evidence, soliciting others to corroborate their lies with more lies, and double-crossing anyone with whom they come into contact, including—and especially—prosecutors" (Trott 1996: 1383). Nevertheless, law enforcement officials and prosecutors routinely use such people as sources of information and witnesses at trial, choosing to overlook the mounting evidence questioning their reliability. In fact, the use of informants—in particular, jailhouse snitches—has been identified as a powerful factor biasing the criminal justice process and leading to convictions of innocent people.

Of the thirteen Illinois death row inmates found to be wrongfully convicted and released from custody (since the state's reinstatement

55

of capital punishment in 1977), five, or nearly 40 percent, were prosecuted using the testimony of jailhouse informants (Armstrong and Mills 2000). Scheck et al. (2000) reveal that informants have played an important role in numerous wrongful conviction cases: out of sixty-two cases in which DNA has exonerated the innocent defendant, fifteen (24 percent) relied, at least in part, on informants to secure the original conviction. In the now famous Los Angeles County jailhouse informant crisis in 1989, informants who admittedly committed perjury and falsified confessions were linked to 225 murder and other felony convictions (Reinhold 1989; Trott 1996). Like other factors that lead to miscarriages of justice (such as mistaken eyewitness testimony, biased police lineups, and false confessions), informant misuse and misconduct can influence every stage in the adjudication of a case, from the evidence gathered by police to the way in which the prosecution builds the case.

This chapter examines how informant conduct and handling lead to wrongful convictions. First, it presents a brief history of informants and examines the root causes of problems related to them. Then it discusses the link between informants and wrongful convictions by illustrating both police and prosecutorial mishandling of informants as well as jailhouse informant activity.

The Problems with Informants

Informants consist of all persons who provide information to law enforcement officials in exchange for some consideration, such as money or property, or for leniency in charging, sentencing, or release from custody.[1] Criminal justice officials who deal with informants are known as *handlers* and include police, prosecutors, and jail officers. The use of informants to provide information in return for a reward stems from ancient Greece and Rome and has since been firmly institutionalized. Although abuses continually raise questions about the reliability of informants in providing truthful and accurate information, the justice system's reliance on them has proven to be intractable.

The institutionalized nature of informant use facilitates problems and misconduct in four primary ways: (1) officially rewarding informants despite the inaccuracy of their information or their motivation for providing it; (2) promoting law enforcement's use of informants; (3) providing judicial protection for informant confidentiality and security; and (4) maintaining a systemic environment that tends to value speed over accuracy, as when the public pressures criminal justice officials to arrest and convict as quickly as possible. To fully understand the entrenchment of this practice, however, we must review the history of informant use.

A Brief History

In ancient Greece, informers were termed *sycophants*—by definition, persons who put forth false accusations.[2] "The prevalence of malicious and arbitrary prosecution by individual sycophants in a system where the law was the expression of the will of the people led to a permanent situation . . . where the power to impose confiscation of property, dishonour, removal of citizen rights, exile and death was absolute" (Burckhardt 1998: xxxvi).[3] Between the sycophants, the orators, and the threat of public prosecution, an atmosphere of "permanent terrorism" existed (Burckhardt 1998: 73). In ancient Rome, informers received money in exchange for accusations; and slave informers were given their freedom, influencing many to accuse their masters in an attempt to gain release from servitude (Nippel 1995).

Analysis of subsequent informant conduct in the common law system reveals reliance on and systemic incorporation of informants and informant rewards as far back as 1275 (Zimmerman 1994). These early informants, called *approvers,* were confessed felons who, in exchange for freedom and free passage out of the country, gave evidence against others. The system was fraught with problems, particularly because the punishment for the original felony charge, as well as for the false accusation of another, were the same—death.[4] A felon's most likely method of escaping death was to provide information (true or false) about someone else's alleged criminal activity. Thus, from the inception, informants had no incentive to tell the truth and, in fact, a great incentive to blackmail innocent people (Zimmerman 1994).

The approver system led directly to Great Britain's common informer system.[5] Like approvers, common informers were viewed as an evil necessary for the control of crime, particularly in the absence of organized police forces. "Common informers, like approvers, abused their positions, and the government was similarly frustrated in its attempts to control their activity. On a near cyclical basis, statutes were created granting informers benefits, and then later limited by penalizing informer misconduct" (Zimmerman 1994: 158). During this time, informers functioned effectively both within the legal system (through statutory rewards) and outside it (through extortion). For example, informers circumvented Parliament's limitations by entering into formalized agreements with sheriffs (the term for jailers) called *compounding,* wherein the informer exchanged information for money, property, or even marriage of an heir. Widely criticized, the process was abandoned, only to be replaced by another, equally ill-advised one (Zimmerman 1994: 160).

This cycle of acceptance, use, incorporation, disgust, and abandonment continued throughout subsequent centuries. It was brought to the colonies, was part of the newly formed United States, and continues here to this day. Recent episodes of the cycle include informant misconduct and mishandling with the Ku Klux Klan in the 1960s, misuse and mishandling of informants to infiltrate legitimate civil rights organizations and provoke illegal activity in the 1970s, a bevy of jailhouse informant misconduct and mishandling cases in the Los Angeles County Jail in the 1980s, and the highly questionable informant misconduct and mishandling related to the World Trade Center bombings in the 1990s.[6] Thus, the use of informants is firmly rooted in our justice system, despite intermittent attention to the problems it can cause.

Informant Status and Motivations

From the beginning, approvers and common informers were persons who were already involved with the criminal justice system, having been accused of a felony. Currently, the vast majority of people who become informants do so when suspected, accused, or convicted of a crime and offered some degree of leniency in exchange for information and future service. Informants are motivated by a number of factors. Some expect tangible rewards, such as money or property; others look for intangible rewards, such as favorable treatment in avoiding arrest, sentencing, or incarceration. Some have more emotional impetuses, such as playing detective, fear, or survival. In addition, some informants merely inform to manipulate the system. Typically, informants have multiple motivations and expect some sort of benefit.

Given the status of most informants and their motivations, one might logically assume that the information they provide carries no guarantee or even any indicia of reliability.[7] Nevertheless, police, prosecutors, and triers of fact (judges and jurors) rarely question informants' motivations. Evidence of the institutionalized failure to question their reliability is clear in the federal sentencing guidelines, which state that the main avenue to receiving lenient consideration is to provide assistance as an informant (Gould 1993).[8]

The Position of Law Enforcement

Generally, there are two ways of approaching the problem of informant misconduct and abuse: conventionalists assume that informants are vital and necessary to our criminal justice system (Farris 1988; Harney and Cross 1968), while realists assume they are problematic and their use should be curtailed (Moore 1983; Reuter 1983).[9] Most law enforcement officials are conventionalists. Blinding themselves to the inherent problems with informants, they offer, almost catechismically, anecdotes of convictions made possible only by use of informants. In an effort to categorize the good and isolate the bad, supporters distinguish between coerced and voluntary informants and between rewarded and unrewarded ones. They parse the rewards as well, separating tangible from intangible, distinguishing monetary from property, and separately categorizing charging and sentencing considerations.

Information lies at the heart of the system's informant dependency, and law enforcement uses it in a variety of ways and relies on it to varying degrees. Officials may want information to stay in the know (no reliance), commence an investigation (some reliance), bolster a case (significant reliance), or make a case (complete reliance). As public and political pressures to solve or resolve a case mount, law enforcement officials extend their reliance on informant information to the highest degree. For example, complete reliance arises when officers use jailhouse informants, who typically present law enforcement with a complete case in the form of the accused's confession but also bring the most baggage: they have a high motivation for fabrication and little, if any, incentive to tell the truth.

The Role of the Judicial System

"Courts have countenanced the use of informers from time immemorial; in cases of conspiracy, or in other cases when the crime consists of preparing for another crime, it is usually necessary to rely on them or upon accomplices because the criminals will almost certainly proceed covertly" (*United States v. Dennis* 1950: 224). Like law enforcement, the courts also tend to take a conventionalist approach to informants. Court doctrine sets the guidelines and limits for law enforcement behavior; thus, the law enforcement behavior just described falls within the court limits concerning informants. In fact, judicial treatment of informants contributes to protection of the confidentiality and security of their use.

Courts apply two doctrines when addressing informants: assumption of risk and handler distancing. "The thrust of the assumption of risk doctrine is the principle that the Constitution will not protect individuals who unknowingly divulge incriminating information to informants or undercover law enforcement officials" (Zimmerman 1994: 105). Thus, courts do not exhibit any initial concern for informant misconduct and are much more likely to blame the victim.

From the assumption of risk doctrine, courts have developed a second informant jurisprudence, known as handler distancing (Zimmerman 1994). Like assumption of risk, handler distancing developed in the context of challenges to law enforcement practices in criminal cases. Here, courts separate the conduct of the informant from that of the handler. Handlers, then, are not held accountable for—are not even linked to—the misconduct of their informants. "Court analysis generally focuses on the defendant (not the informant), the constitutional right at issue, and the relief requested. These foci insulate the law enforcement arrangement with the informant, avoid consideration of the linkage between the two, and offer no recognition of, insight into, or relief from the broader problems of informant misconduct and mishandling" (Zimmerman 1994: 108–9).[10] Through the implementation of these two doctrines, the judiciary fails to rectify abuses happening elsewhere in the system, instead allowing them to continue and effectively endorsing the continued misuse of informants.

Systemic Pressures

With respect to informants, societal pressure has been institutionalized, bringing law enforcement and informants together on a collision course. The system asserts that informants are most necessary for "invisible crimes"–when there is no victim or the victim is reluctant to complain (Moore 1983; Skolnick 1975). This includes drug crimes, which law enforcement and the public have long considered a serious social problem. Not surprisingly then, statutes criminalizing drugs are also vast repositories of informant rewards (Blumrosen and Nilsen 1998; 28 U.S.C. § 524), and the budgets for informants in these areas of law enforcement are extraordinarily large.[11]

In addition, elected law enforcement officials, particularly prosecutors, sheriffs, and police chiefs, are subject and sensitive to public perceptions of criminal offenses, crime rates, and the timely resolution of cases. These public perceptions, in turn, rest on two key factors: solving crimes and solving them quickly. As societal pressure builds, officials transmit the pressure down the line to other law enforcement personnel, with speed becoming the overriding factor. This concentration of pressure is even greater in high-profile cases.

Therefore, among law enforcement officials, the lure of informants is strong because they save both time and effort. Informant information is readily accessible, typically complete (in terms of identifying persons), and time saving (versus establishing an undercover operation). A jailhouse informant brings together all these factors because the information yields a confession: the most powerful piece of evidence that a prosecutor can use in obtaining a criminal conviction (Leo and Ofshe 1998).

Clearly, strong incentives and motivations for use and misuse exist on both sides of the handler-informant equation. The combination of needs and benefits, external pressure, and ease create the ideal circumstances for use, reward, and toleration of incidental abuses as long as the ultimate outcomes are favorable to law enforcement. But within this tangled web, control is lost, informants predominate, and the innocent will suffer.

Informants Lead to Wrongful Convictions

Criminal justice experts, legislators, and law enforcement officials continually call for informant controls, instructions on tactics and recordkeeping, and orders for stricter corroboration. Yet the literature is replete with evidence that informants regularly "ignore the standards [on not committing crimes], use prohibited methods, lie, believe that the handler has granted them immunity, and feel as if they have 'grown a badge'" (Zimmerman 1994: 143; Marx 1988). Similarly, handlers routinely view informants' disregard for the rules and law enforcement's blindness to it as simply a cost of doing business.[12]

The tales of informant misconduct and mishandling are long and numerous. In many cases, these abuses have proven to be the critical element that ensnares an innocent person in the criminal justice system. Emblematic is the story of Marion Pruett who, as a jailhouse informant, pinned an inmate's murder on another, was released as a result of his testimony, and went on to commit a string of bank robberies and murders only to be reincarcerated, at which time he admitted that he had committed the original murder that had led to his release (Trott 1996). More prodigious is the situation in the Los Angeles County Jail, where Leslie White was so accomplished at fabricating the confessions of other inmates that he demonstrated his methods on television during *60 Minutes* and later revealed an in-prison "school" where more experienced inmates taught recently incarcerated prisoners how to create the confessions of others (Zimmerman 1994).

The following, more detailed examples offer insight into how both informant and handler misconduct can lead to the conviction of innocent individuals. These cases are divided into four categories: police fabrication of informants, police mishandling of informants, prosecutorial mishandling of informants, and the use of jailhouse informants. All typically involve heinous crimes or high-profile cases in which the systemic pressure to arrest and convict is at its peak.

Police Fabrication of Informants

Police have been accused of fabricating informants to bolster warrant applications (Curriden 1995a). According to one former FBI agent, in the 1960s bureau agents were creative at finding names when an inspection of the informant files loomed. To identify informants they had allegedly used in the past, agents took names from grave markers, janitors, bartenders, and newspaper delivery men. "This was standard practice for most agents" (Swearingen 1995: 54). One agent used to call sitting in a bar drinking Cutty Sark "contacting his informant" (Swearingen 1995: 54).[13] After the Watts riots in 1965, FBI director J. Edgar Hoover wanted every agent in Los Angeles to have a ghetto informant. In response, agents promptly invented informants and filled out the appropriate paperwork (Swearingen 1995: 68).

The case of the Ford Heights Four is an example of how police fabricate and manipulate informants to solve high-profile cases as quickly as possible. In 1978, a white couple was abducted in Homewood, a predominately white Chicago suburb. The woman was subsequently discovered raped and murdered and the man found murdered in a townhouse in Ford Heights, a predominately African-American suburb of Chicago. In response to public pressures to solve this heinous crime, local law enforcement officials used false informant testimony to fabricate a murder case against four innocent men, who spent many years on trial, in jail, and on death row before finally being found innocent and exonerated. During the initial investigation, law enforcement officials received an anonymous informant tip that the possible offenders drove a red Toyota, a beige Toyota, and a yellow Vega. As a result, the police questioned Dennis Williams, Verneal Jimerson, Kenneth Adams, and Willie Raines, the owners and occupants of these vehicles. Each lived in the Ford Heights area, was a working man who had graduated from high school, and, with one exception, had no prior criminal record (Taylor 1999).

As the investigation continued, the racial aspect of the case was publicized, and law enforcement officials increased the pressure on the suspects and witnesses. They identified the informant as Charles McCraney, who also lived in the neighborhood. Under pressure, McCraney told investigators that the vehicles had been in front of the townhouse during the early morning hours when the murders occurred. Investigators then redoubled their questioning of the suspects, subjecting them to racial abuse, threats, and physical violence, including the repeated beating of Williams. All of the suspects maintained their innocence (Taylor 1999).

McCraney's information continued to merge slowly with the facts needed in the case. He claimed that the cars were parked in front of the townhouse between one and three o'clock in the morning. (The murders occurred after 2:30 A.M.) He stated that he saw a group of men running from the area of the cars into the townhouse. He further told police that he then heard one shot come from the townhouse. The judge specifically relied on this statement in finding probable cause to hold Williams, Adams, and Raines. Jimerson was not yet criminally charged. Investigators, however, failed to explore the alterations and inconsistencies that appeared in McCraney's statements, including his claim that he had heard only one shot (ballistics reports showed five) and the fact that he was obviously adding facts with every repetition of his story to make it coincide with what was known to the police (Taylor 1999).

Before the trial, McCraney was given a financial stipend to relocate. At the trial, he positively identified Williams, Adams, and Raines as the three people who had left the cars and entered the townhouse. He continued to place the events in the proper time frame for the murders. As a result of this as well as other evidence, Williams, Raines, and Adams were convicted, with Williams sentenced to death, Raines sentenced to life, and Adams sentenced to seventy-five years. All three men appealed (Taylor 1999).

While the appeal was pending, private investigations by the men's families as well as reporters and journalism students began to uncover conflicting facts, many of which law enforcement officials had known but ignored. Meanwhile, the convictions of Williams and Raines were overturned because both men had been represented by the same counsel. Adams's conviction, however, was affirmed, and a new indictment was handed down against Jimerson. On retrial, Williams, Raines, and Jimerson were convicted, with Williams and Jimerson receiving death sentences and Raines receiving a life sentence. On appeal, all of the convictions were affirmed. Jimerson, however, sought post-conviction relief and was granted a new trial (Taylor 1999).

Until this time, law enforcement officials had not located any ballistics evidence linking any of the four with the crime. Private investigators learned that, early in the investigation, officials had received information implicating four other persons who had been driving a Buick Electra 225. According to the same source, these suspects had discussed a robbery on the night of the murders, had obtained a .38 caliber weapon for the robbery (the same caliber involved in the murders), and had disposed of the weapon after the crime. Persistent private investigation gradually yielded a wealth of new information, including the fact that the police had ignored this other evidence, confessions to the crime by two of the other suspects, and DNA tests that linked one of the other suspects and ruled out all of the Ford Heights Four (Taylor 1999).

The four were released and filed civil cases against the law enforcement officials who had targeted them. During the investigation related to the civil suits brought by Williams, Jimerson, Raines, and Adams, their attorneys located documents as well as McCraney himself and learned much more about his relationship with the law enforcement handlers and how it had been instrumental in procuring the conviction of the innocent men. First, counsels for the four found that the sheriff's investigators had maintained "working" or "street" files on the cases (which included information related to the cases) but did not provide these files to the defense as required by law, even though they contained evidence favorable to the four men. One document in these files related an interview with Sherry McCraney, then informant McCraney's wife. At the time of the initial investigation, she told investigators that she had seen people on the street and heard a shot fired but that all of this activity had occurred before 12:50 A.M., too early to be related to the murders under investigation. Furthermore,

Charles McCraney had related this same series of events to the police. The information was consistent with Williams's and Adams's alibis and firmly established a time frame earlier than the murders. Moreover, Charles McCraney had given a signed statement, but that document as well as any notes relating to it were not in the files (Taylor 1999). Thus, existing and missing documentation clearly identified the shift in McCraney's informant information from reality to law enforcement necessity once he was under the complete control of the handlers and exposed the subsequent coverup of that shift.

Depositions of the prosecutors revealed that McCraney had told them he was "sure" that he had heard a gunshot around 12:30 A.M. (two hours before the earliest time for the murders) and that he only heard one gunshot (as opposed to at least five involved in the actual murders). Counsel for the sheriffs then turned over a document in which McCraney had been interviewed at the time of the investigation and had stated that he "saw no faces" (despite his trial testimony identifying three of the four). The attorneys for the four then located McCraney for a deposition. McCraney admitted that he had supplied the information, asserted that he could not remember whether it was accurate, and verified that he was given five thousand dollars by the prosecution for his testimony (Taylor 1999).

McCraney's testimony had been critical in commencing and maintaining the criminal investigation and prosecution of the Ford Heights Four. The obvious inconsistencies and lapses in credibility should have veered law enforcement officials away from Williams, Adams, Raines, and Jimerson as suspects, especially when credible evidence identified another set of perpetrators, with physical evidence (ballistics and DNA) linking them to the crime. Yet law enforcement officials took McCraney's informant testimony and molded it to fit their needs, which eventually led to the convictions of four innocent men. The civil case brought by the four against law enforcement officials resulted in the single largest civil rights settlement to date: 36 million dollars (Taylor 1999).

Police Mishandling of Informants

In addition to fabricating or shaping informant testimony, police handlers have often actively encouraged illegal informant activity. Without handler abuses, such misconduct would either not have occurred or not occurred to this degree.

The Cleveland Postal Workers. During the late 1980s and early 1990s, the postal inspectors in Cleveland hired several informants to infiltrate the postal workers and find narcotics crimes. During 1992, these informants were given more than $240,000 to purchase drugs, and as a result framed many innocent people. The informants used friends to create audiotape recordings of the alleged drug buys. Only when prosecutors realized that tapes supposedly of the same suspects contained different voices and that some suspects had no criminal records and strong alibis did they begin to investigate the informants. One of these, Willie Kemp, had become an informant after a robbery arrest; and he, like some other informants, was "renting fancy cars, living in pricey condos, wearing expensive clothes and hosting parties" (Curriden 1995b: A25). Using a confidential list provided by law enforcement agents, the informants had apparently learned which postal employees had signed up for substance abuse counseling and then targeted those individuals. Many of these innocent people were convicted and suffered enormously before the truth was revealed. The informants, including Kemp, were eventually convicted (Curriden 1995b).

COINTELPRO and Informants. During the 1960s and 1970s, the FBI's counterintelligence program, COINTELPRO, targeted, to a large degree, black organizations and other groups critical of the government, ostensibly to prevent violence and neutralize the groups. To this end, the FBI and local law enforcement officials used informants to infiltrate these groups and try to discredit them, disrupt them, and ultimately cause them to disband. Thus, the FBI actively encouraged local law enforcement agencies to use informants in whatever way and by whatever means necessary to achieve these results. In these instances, the informants served more as agents provocateurs, inciting numerous acts of violence rather than supplying information about crimes.

These acts of violence were committed or facilitated by informants with the encouragement, support, and complicity of their FBI handlers and included specific murders (Donner 1990; Swearingen 1995). One informant planted an informant report in Stokely Carmichael's car, leading the Black Panthers to order a hit on him. As a result, he left the United States for an extended period of time (Swearingen 1995:82).[14]

In Chicago, the local FBI enlisted informant William O'Neal, who was incarcerated at the time, and instructed him to join the Black Panther Party (BPP) and supply information. O'Neal became the local chief of security for the BPP and served as the catalyst within the organization for FBI disruption—for example, inciting dissension between the BPP and the Blackstone Rangers and between the BPP and the Vice Lords to prevent mergers of the groups. O'Neal received a monthly salary ranging from $100 to $500 for his informant work (*Hampton v. Hanrahan* 1979).

As tensions built between the BPP and local law enforcement, the state's attorney and local police determined to raid BPP leader Fred Hampton's apartment. O'Neal gave them a detailed floor plan of the apartment and detailed information about it. This floor plan was then used to plan a raid intended to murder all of the Panthers in the house. Based on O'Neal's information, the state's attorney sought and obtained a search warrant for the apartment. Raiders were armed with a machine gun, a semi-automatic weapon, a sawed-off shotgun, and other weapons. During the raid, law enforcement officials killed Hampton and Mark Clark and injured numerous others in the apartment.

A civil lawsuit was brought on behalf of the deceased and by the injured, alleging that law enforcement officials and O'Neal had conspired to murder and injure as many of the occupants as possible. At the civil trial, the plaintiffs' ballistics expert testified that only one of the numerous shot shells came from a weapon seized from the apartment. After the raid, O'Neal's handler sought and received both a bonus and future pay for O'Neal based on the fact that he provided information critical to the raid that was not available from any other source (Swearingen 1995: 88–89; *Hampton v. Hanrahan* 1979: 606–8).

Prosecutorial Mishandling of Informants

All too often, prosecutors knowingly use "despicable . . . characters" as some, or the only, witnesses in their cases (Trott 1996: 1386). In one case, prosecutors called twenty-seven informants to testify (1388). The prosecutorial role can take several forms. For example, prosecutors can proceed to trial knowing that their informant witness will not testify truthfully. While police can limit investigations and information passed along to prosecutors, prosecutors have the power to drop charges and are typically the ones who will testify on an informant's behalf regarding issues of sentence reduction in exchange for cooperation. Numerous instances of prosecutorial mishandling of informants have allowed untruthful informant testimony to permeate the criminal justice system and have led to wrongful convictions (Zimmerman 1994: 98–99). The following example illustrates the potential damage of prosecutorial mishandling of informants.

In their zeal to convict members of the El Rukn street gang, prosecutors in the U.S. Attorney's office in Chicago coddled and catered to the needs and desires of several in-custody gang members turned informants (Zimmerman 1994: 97). Prosecutors allowed these witnesses, who were being held in the Metropolitan Correction Center, to have numerous unauthorized privileges, including private contact visits with their wives and girlfriends during which sexual relations occurred (*United States v. Boyd* 1993). During these visits, witnesses also received and ingested illegal drugs, facilitated by prosecutors who permitted the witnesses to have the contraband (Ex Lax) necessary to pass the drugs through their bodies (*United States v. Boyd* 1993).

Furthermore, prosecutors suppressed drug test results, interceded on witnesses' behalves in the jail, and were aware that witnesses and a prosecution paralegal were engaging in sexually explicit telephone conversations (*United States v. Burnside* 1993). They also provided the witnesses with money, gifts, and access to government telephone lines (*United States v. Boyd* 1993; *United States v. Burnside* 1993). None of this information was disclosed to the criminal defense attorneys before or at the trials in which the witnesses testified. The prosecutions resulted in the convictions of other El Rukn gang members (Zimmerman 1994: 98).

The Use of Jailhouse Informants

Jailhouse informants are exploited by many handlers, including police, jailers, and prosecutors. This relationship is often a win-win situation for both handlers and informants, providing a neatly tailored confession for the handler and, very often, a desirable reward for the informant. These "made to order" confessions are enticing to handlers and provide devastatingly effective evidence in court. With one of these jailhouse confessions in hand, police frequently fail to pursue other leads (that could lead to other suspects), and prosecutors play down or choose to ignore contradictory evidence. Triers of fact tend to believe confession evidence, even when offered by a jailhouse snitch; and such evidence is difficult to undermine without a recantation of the testimony.

Guy Paul Morin. In 1985, Guy Paul Morin was arrested and charged with the murder of a little girl. He was held without bail in the Whitby, Ontario, jail. During this time, two jailhouse informants, Robert Dean May and Mr. X, came forward claiming that they had heard Morin confess to the crime. May told law enforcement authorities that Morin, who was his cellmate at the time, had confessed to him that he had "killed that little girl." Mr. X, who was jailed in an adjoining cell, asserted that he overheard this confession (Kaufman 1998; Weinberg 1998). This was "the only direct evidence of Mr. Morin's guilt" (Kaufman 1998: 546).

Both May and Mr. X approached law enforcement authorities the day after the alleged confession and stated that they had had a feeling that "something" was going to happen (Kaufman 1998: 415). Both were facing serious charges (May had assaulted a jailer and attempted to escape, and X was charged with criminal sexual assault) and told the police that they could give them "anything" regarding Morin (Kaufman 1998: 418, 420). Both May and X, however, insisted on a deal in exchange for their testimony. Later both admitted that they had talked to each other after the alleged confession and before contacting the authorities.

At Morin's first trial, both May and Mr. X testified for the Crown, each stating that he expected a benefit for his testimony and repeating the alleged confession (Weinberg 1998). Morin was convicted, but his conviction was reversed on appeal. At the second trial, both May and Mr. X again testified. This time, however, each testified in response to specific inquiries by the prosecutor that he was "voluntarily" testifying, had turned down an offer to be excused from testifying, and, by implication, would receive no benefits from his testimony (Kaufman 1998: 548; Weinberg 1998). Each then testified to Morin's alleged confession.

Morin was subsequently found to be innocent of the crime because of DNA evidence and was released from prison.[15] The Crown's handling of his case led to an inquiry into its practices and procedures, including the handling of the informants (Kaufman 1998). These proceedings made patently clear that May and X had lied and had deep motivations to lie and that the Crown had grossly mishandled them. For instance, May had tried to escape on several occasions and had also feigned mental illness with the goal of being transferred to facilitate an escape attempt. Only after these failures did he come forward with the alleged confession. During a police interview, May stated that he would give them "anything you want to hear" (Kaufman 1998: 418). During that same conversation, he made it very clear that he wanted and expected something in exchange, preferably "a reduced sentence or [to] get out of here before I give them any information" (Kaufman

1998: 418). Likewise, Mr. X was willing to give "anything" in exchange for his freedom (Kaufman 1998: 420). Both stated that they would be willing to testify against others as well. The prosecutors accepted these testimonies with little, if any, doubt, facilitating them by conferring benefits on the informants.

Before the first trial, several charges against May were dropped (including escape and assault on a jailer), and he received a dramatically lower sentence on the remaining charges (Kaufman 1998). Within a week after the first trial and because of the intervention of his handlers, May was released on parole (Kaufman 1998). Subsequently, he contacted local authorities regarding new criminal charges in another province, and the Crown gave him some assistance (Kaufman 1998).

Mr. X also sought benefits before the first trial; however, even with handler assistance, his attempt for release was unsuccessful (Kaufman 1998). After Morin's first trial, the Crown refused to assist X regarding his sentencing, asserting that his testimony had not been useful (Kaufman 1998). After his testimony at the second trial, however, X faced another criminal charge. He contacted prosecutors, who interceded and facilitated a reduction in the penalty (Kaufman 1998).

The prosecution should have been wary of May and X, whose proclivity to lie was readily apparent. At the second trial, the defense introduced the testimony of a psychometrist, a physician, and a psychiatrist, all of whom agreed that May was a liar. In particular, the psychometrist testified that May was a pathological liar; the physician testified that "it was extremely difficult to ferret out what was the truth and what was untrue"; and the psychiatrist testified that May had no ability to resist lying (Kaufman 1998: 407–9). A psychiatrist testified that Mr. X also suffered from a proclivity to lie. The bottom line in Morin's case is that the Crown had a weak case against Morin. May's and Mr. X's testimony filled a gaping hole in that case, and the prosecution willingly accepted the questionable testimony and advanced the informants' willingness to perjure themselves by offering benefits in exchange for the testimony.

Rolando Cruz. In 1983, Rolando Cruz was charged with the rape and murder of a twelve-year-old suburban girl. The crime was brutal, the community was outraged, law enforcement had no direct physical evidence, and the sheriff was in a close reelection campaign. Although the evidence was shaky, including a purported dream statement in which Cruz allegedly dreamt the facts of the crime, the prosecution went forward with the case against him and his alleged accomplices, Stephen Buckley and Alejandro Hernandez.

To bolster the case, the prosecution found and used informant testimony to support Cruz's alleged confession. Armindo Marquez, a jailed repeat offender serving time for burglary, testified to Cruz's jailhouse statements. A prosecutor also testified that Marquez had not received anything from prosecutors, although in fact he had received the minimum sentence in exchange for his testimony (Frisbie 1999; Frisbie and Garrett 1998: 78–79).[16]

Specifically, the jailhouse informant testimony was tailored to the prosecution's theory of the case: that the three defendants had intended to burglarize the house and ended up abducting, raping, and murdering the girl. Also at the first trial, jailhouse informant Arthur Burrell testified that, while incarcerated, Cruz sent him a letter asserting that the town in which the murder took place was a good place to commit burglaries. Burrell received, at the prosecutor's behest, a very light sentence (Frisbie 1999). Although Cruz was convicted and sentenced to death, his conviction was reversed on appeal.[17]

Before the second trial, the prosecution learned that another man, Brian Dugan, was the actual perpetrator of the abduction, rape, and murder, although he refused to confess without immunity from the death penalty. Reeling from this monumental discovery, the prosecution decided not to abandon its case against Cruz. Instead, it merely altered its theory of the case, asserting that Dugan had committed the murder but that Cruz had confessed that he and Hernandez had been present at the time. At the second trial, the prosecution presented several informants to support this new theory. Once again, the state offered no physical evidence directly linking Cruz to the crime.

Informant Dan Fowler testified that Cruz had told him he was "involved" in, but did not commit, the murder. While this testimony was consistent with the prosecution's new theory of the case, it was inconsistent with Fowler's prior grand jury testimony in which he had stated that Cruz had told him that he (Cruz) knew who was involved and planned to testify against those people (*People v. Cruz* 1994).

Stephen Ford, a jailhouse informant, testified that Cruz had told him that he had "kind of killed" a girl, but Ford was also impeached. At the first trial, Ford had testified that he was unsure about Cruz's statement to him. Further, he denied receiving any benefit for his testimony yet admitted that he had received a light sentence for several burglary charges and that numerous other burglary charges had been dropped within two weeks of his reporting his conversations with Cruz to local law enforcement officials (*People v. Cruz* 1994).

Jailhouse informant Robert Turner, a convicted murderer and sex offender, also testified against Cruz. Turner's testimonial greatly supported this new prosecution theory, directly contradicting the theory put forward in the first trial. Turner testified that Cruz had told him about the abduction, rape, and murder and that he, Hernandez, and "someone named Dugan" had killed the girl. Turner's appeal was pending at the time of his testimony, and he testified that he was not offered and expected no benefits for his testimony. The defense presented two other death row inmates who testified that Turner had talked to them about how to create the confessions of other inmates as a way to get off death row. Turner had also offered testimony against seven other death row inmates. After Cruz's trial, a prosecutor testified on Turner's behalf when he attempted to overturn his death sentence (Frisbie and Garrett 1998: 176–77; see also Frisbie 1999 and *People v. Cruz* 1994).

Cruz was again convicted and sentenced to death; but on appeal, the conviction was again reversed. After DNA testing established that Dugan was the rapist, still another jailhouse informant came forward claiming that Cruz had admitted to being present at the time of the murder. Ultimately, at a third trial, in light of other law enforcement misconduct, the charges against Cruz were dropped, and he was freed (Frisbie and Garrett 1998).

Conclusion

Criminal justice handlers frequently misuse their informants, which has resulted in the conviction of numerous innocent individuals. Police and prosecutors often accept informant information with little thought about its reliability or the credibility of the informant. They, in fact, encourage informant misuse and misconduct by rewarding these informants regardless of the validity of their information. This incorrect and self-serving information can lead handlers and triers of fact to overlook important evidence that may counter what the informant has provided and thus result in a wrongful conviction. Neither the courts nor the law enforcement officials who use informants seem willing or able to contain informant excesses, although the lives of Rolando Cruz, Guy Paul Morin, the Ford Heights Four, and many others have been permanently altered through informant misconduct or mishandling.

The costs of informant misconduct and mishandling are readily apparent. Other costs, however, are not so clear and can extend deep into the fabric of our society. This chapter has neither recounted nor identified the personal cost in terms of those who are wrongly accused but not charged or the wrongly prosecuted but not convicted. Further, the actual monetary costs from these law enforcement activities are staggering, weigh heavily on taxpayers, and keep valuable resources from being allocated to and used for more beneficial work.

The excesses in informant misconduct, government mishandling of informants, and wrongful convictions have also scarred our criminal justice system by fueling an already cynical public attitude toward law enforcement and the judicial system, both of which are supposed to be fair representatives of the public good and arbiters of society's needs and values. Moreover, our legal system has become a complicitous tolerator of deception, further eroding the critical societal values of integrity and loyalty.

Research can and should explore these areas to fully expose and develop all of the harms traceable to informants. To ensure that the road from the jailhouse to the courthouse is not littered with the remains of innocent victims of informant misconduct and mishandling, we must revamp the system of informant use and control and institute new policies, procedures, and jurisprudence.

NOTES

Thanks to Richard Leo and Gary Marx for reading and commenting on an earlier draft of this chapter, to James F. Tozzi and Julie Livergood for research assistance, and to the editors for making this project a wholly satisfying experience.

1. Informants do not include witnesses to crimes, victims of crimes, or others who voluntarily offer information but expect nothing in return.
2. According to the *Oxford English Dictionary* (1989: 442), the first definition of *sycophancy* is "one who is in the trade of lying" ("calumnious accusation"). The first definition of *sycophant,* the noun, is "one of a class of informers" and the second involves lying ("an informer, tale-bearer, malicious accuser, a calumniator, traducer, slanderer"). The first definition of *sycophant,* the verb, is "to slander, calumniate, traduce."
3. The abusive conduct of sycophants and their ability to individually bring "malicious and arbitrary" prosecutions has been likened to the informant power that existed in the reign of terror during the French Revolution (Burckhardt 1998: xxxvi).
4. The approvement process and appeal, as it was termed, required that the accused be charged with and confess to treason or a felony. The accused now became an informant, termed an *approver,* and had to implicate others either as felonious partners or in some other crime. If the approver was found to be lying in any part of that confession or appeal, he or she would

be executed. If the appeal against another was not successful, the approver would also be executed (Zimmerman 1994:153–55).

5. The approver system ended in the fifteenth century and was replaced by the practice of "king's evidence or king's mercy" and the common informer system (Zimmerman 1994: 156, note 437). All three systems were based on the same fundamental principle that an accused can receive a reward for providing information about another's crime.

6. For a more detailed discussion of the Klan, the Los Angeles County Jail, and the World Trade Center bombing, see Zimmerman (1994: 90–99). For a more detailed discussion of the federal government's use of informants to infiltrate legitimate civil rights organizations, see Donner (1990), who examined activities focusing primarily on four major urban centers: Chicago, New York, Los Angeles, and Philadelphia.

7. Two critical indicia of reliability are the voluntarism of the offer of information and the lack of expectation of benefit in return for the offer. Once a person is in custody, voluntarism is absent, and the situation is automatically coercive. Likewise, once in custody, the suspect will seek and expect some consideration in return for the offer of information. Compare this to the situation of an ordinary witness, who is not in custody, has no pending or potential charge, and offers information simply because that is what he or she saw. While questions of reliability may exist here as well (that is, visual acuity, memory, bias, and so on), none of those concerns were brought about by law enforcement presence or systemic imposition into the situation.

8. Federal Rule of Criminal Procedure 35 is the only way by which a federal sentence can be reduced. This rule allows for reduction consideration if, within one year of the sentencing, by motion of the prosecutor, evidence is presented that the convicted informant provided "substantial assistance" in other cases.

9. The conventionalists "are very deferential to the police and believe the confidentiality and security of informants must be maintained at great cost." The realists "examine how law enforcement functions, in reality, to reach goals and set expectations specific to informants" (Zimmerman 1994: 84). For a lengthy analysis of the common ground and differences between conventionalists and realists, see Zimmerman (1994: 83–84, 138–46).

10. For the development of these two doctrines, see Zimmerman (1994: 105–29).

11. For example, in 1988 the Drug Enforcement Administration (DEA) informant budget was between 2 and 4 million dollars; in 1975 the FBI spent 2 million dollars on information and an additional 3.5 million dollars on informants; and in 1981 the New York City Police Department paid $500,000 for informants (Zimmerman 1994:101, n. 83). By 1994, the combined informant budgets of the DEA, FBI, and U.S. Customs Service grew to 87 million dollars (Fitzgerald 1995).

Numerous court decisions uphold informant rewards in drug cases, with few real limitations. Courts have ruled that the receipt of profit from a drug bust does not create a monetary interest that would bias an informant's testimony (*United States v. Cervantes-Pacheco* 1987; found informant reward was not absolute bar to testimony). Courts have also determined that an informant's receipt of a high payment from the proceeds of a bust is not improper so long as the amount or percentage is not specified in advance (*United States v. Shearer* 1986).

12. For examples and citations, see Zimmerman (1994: 143, note 361). For an example of the rationalization that leads an informer from considering him or herself a snitch or traitor to a more legitimate role, see Kipps (1996: 77).

13. Swearingen (1995: 83) later states that approximately 75 percent of the informants in informant programs in the Chicago and Los Angeles FBI offices were "phony."

14. Space does not permit addressing the full breadth of the wrongful acts and convictions that resulted from the FBI abuse and mishandling of informants in this period. For greater detail on FBI exploits, see Donner (1990: 65–289).

15. This came after Morin's second appeal and was the result of a DNA test that excluded him as the perpetrator.

16. At trial, both Marquez and the prosecutor were impeached with the transcript of the informant's sentencing hearing, at which the prosecutor specifically related the informant's assistance to the judge.

17. Cruz's conviction and sentence were reversed primarily because his case was not separated from the trial of Hernandez, who was also convicted and sentenced to death. The court held that many statements by witnesses attributed to one defendant (Hernandez) and introduced to implicate that defendant (Hernandez) were not sufficiently limited so as not to implicate unfairly the other defendant (Cruz) (*People v. Cruz* 1988).

REFERENCES

Armstrong, Ken, and Steve Mills. 2000. "Ryan: 'Until I Can Be Sure' Illinois Is First State to Suspend Death Penalty." *Chicago Tribune,* 1 February. [Internet]

Blumrosen, Eric, and Eva Nilsen. 1998. "Policing for Profit: The Drug War's Hidden Economic Agenda." *University of Chicago Law Review* 65: 35–114.

Burckhardt, Jacob. 1998. *The Greeks and Greek Civilization,* translated by Sheila Stern, edited by Oswyn Murray. New York: St. Martin's.

Curriden, Mark. 1995a. "Behind the Affidavits, Some Informants Are Fiction." *National Law Journal,* 20 February, p. A29.

———. 1995b. "Postal Agents Stamped by Scandal." *National Law Journal,* 27 February, pp. A1, A24–25.

Donner, Frank. 1990. *Protectors of Privilege: Red Squads and Police Repression in Urban America.* Berkeley: University of California Press.

Farris, James R. 1988. "The Confidential Informant: Management and Control." In *Critical Issues in Criminal Investigations,* edited by Michael J. Palmietto, 79–100. 2d ed. Cincinnati: Anderson.

Fitzgerald, Dennis. 1995. "Snitches, Narcs and Making Cases." *Champion* 19 (December): 11–18.

Frisbie, Thomas. 1999. "Snitch Testimony Often a Perfect Fit." *Chicago Sun-Times,* 26 March, p. 24.

Frisbie, Thomas, and Randy Garrett. 1998. *Victims of Justice.* New York: Avon.

Gould, Keri A. 1993. "Turning Rat and Doing Time for Uncharged, Dismissed, or Acquitted Crimes: Do the Federal Sentencing Guidelines Promote Respect for the Law." *New York Law School Journal of Human Rights* 10: 835–75.

Harney, Malachi, and John Cross. 1968. *The Informer in Law Enforcement.* 2d ed. Springfield, Ill.: Thomas.

Kaufman, Fred. 1998. *The Report of the Commission on Proceedings Involving Guy Paul Morin.* Toronto: Publications Ontario.

Kipps, Charles. 1996. *Cop without a Badge: The Extraordinary Undercover Life of Kevin Maher.* New York: Carroll and Graf.

Leo, Richard A., and Richard J. Ofshe. 1998. "The Consequences of False Confessions: Deprivations of Liberty and Miscarriages of Justice in the Age of Psychological Interrogation." *Journal of Criminal Law and Criminology* 88: 429–96.

Marx, Gary T. 1988. *Undercover Police Surveillance in America.* Berkeley: University of California Press.

Moore, Mark H. 1983. "Invisible Offenses: A Challenge to Minimally Intrusive Law Enforcement." In *ABSCAM Ethics: Moral Issues and Deception in Law Enforcement,* edited by Gerald M. Caplan, 17–42. Cambridge, Mass.: Ballinger.

Nippel, Wilfried. 1995. *Public Order in Ancient Rome.* Cambridge: Cambridge University Press.

The Oxford English Dictionary. 1989. Volume 17. Prepared by J. A. Simpson and E.S.C. Weiner. 2d ed. Oxford: Clarendon.

Reinhold, Robert. 1989. "California Shaken over an Informer." *New York Times,* 17 February, p. A1.

Reuter, Peter. 1983. "Licensing Criminals: Police and Informants." In *ABSCAM Ethics: Moral Issues and Deception in Law Enforcement,* edited by Gerald M. Caplan, 100–117. Cambridge, Mass.: Ballinger.

Scheck, Barry, Peter Neufeld, and Jim Dwyer. 2000. *Actual Innocence.* New York: Doubleday.

Skolnick, Jerome H. 1975. *Justice without Trial: Law Enforcement in Democratic Society.* 2d ed. New York: Wiley.

Swearingen, M. Wesley. 1995. *FBI Secrets: An Agent's Exposé.* Boston: South End.

Taylor, G. Flint. 1999. "The Case of the Ford Heights Four." *Police Misconduct and Civil Rights Law Report* 6: 37–46.

Trott, Stephen S. 1996. "Words of Warning for Prosecutors Using Criminals As Witnesses." *Hastings Law Journal* 47: 1381–431.

Weinberg, Martin G. 1998. "Excerpts From: The Commission Report." *Champion* 22 (August): 60–66.

Zimmerman, Clifford S. 1994. "Toward a New Vision of Informants: A History of Abuses and Suggestions for Reform." *Hastings Constitutional Law Quarterly* 22: 81–178.

CASES CITED

Hampton v. Hanrahan, 600 F.2d 600 (1979).
People v. Cruz, 121 Ill.2d 321, 521 N.E.2d 18 (1988).
People v. Cruz, 162 Ill.2d 314, 643 N.E.2d 636 (1994).
United States v. Boyd, 833 F. Supp. 1277 (1993).
United States v. Burnside, 824 F. Supp. 1215 (1993).
United States v. Cervantes-Pacheco, 826 F.2d 310 (1987).
United States v. Dennis, 183 F.2d 201 (1950), *affirmed* 341 U.S. 494 (1951).
United States v. Shearer, 794 F.2d 1545 (1986).
28 U.S.C. § 524.

DIANNE L. MARTIN

4 The Police Role in Wrongful Convictions
An International Comparative Study

*So in some cases the innocent can find themselves
in double jeopardy: where the police, deluding
themselves into believing that a suspect is guilty,
corrupt themselves by taking unlawful steps to
ensure his conviction; and where Appeal Court
judges, deluding themselves into believing the
police are incorruptible, declare convictions to be
safe and satisfactory which clearly are not.*
—Ludovic Kennedy, quoted in
McKee and Franey 1988: i

The concern of British author and activist Ludovic
Kennedy has been expressed recently in one form
or another throughout the common law world, where the problem of
wrongful convictions has been shaking confidence in criminal justice
systems from Australia to the United States.[1] Wrongful convictions
represent a double failure of justice: not only is an innocent person
wronged, but a guilty person is thereby allowed to go free. Moreover,
many of the systemic frailties and failings that result in the conviction of the innocent are identical to the practices that result in a failure to apprehend or prosecute the guilty, such as reliance on stereotypes
and bias rather than objective fact, overconfidence in eyewitness testimony or jailhouse informants, and blind faith in confessions elicited by police. The police investigation is inevitably at the heart of

these miscarriages of justice because the police gather the evidence, identify the prime suspect, and build the case for conviction.

The adversarial system of criminal prosecutions rests on the assumption that built-in checks and balances ensure that only the guilty are convicted. Judicial pronouncements over time and across jurisdictions stress the first rule of criminal justice: convict only the guilty. Procedural safeguards are premised on this rule.[2] Further, the model of *constabulary independence,* which dominates in jurisdictions that follow the British tradition (Canada, Australia, New Zealand, and the United Kingdom), assumes that the police neutrally gather evidence until they have a reasoned belief about guilt and then hand that evidence in the form of a case brief over to prosecutors, who exercise an independent judgment about whether or not the case should be prosecuted—another level of accountability (Zuckerman 1992). According to the American tradition, an office of the district (or state) attorney is actively involved in supervising the investigation, thus somewhat blurring the distinction; but here as well, the assumption of investigative neutrality is maintained.

Nevertheless, an examination of the history of miscarriages of justice casts considerable doubt on this simplistic picture. Those who have studied individual wrongful convictions as well as those who have looked at the phenomena more widely understand how police officers present frail, misleading, and even false evidence to prosecutors, defense counsel, and thus to courts, while almost always asserting—and often believing—that they are simply "doing their job."

Thus, understanding the scope and nature of the police role in wrongful convictions is essential for both eradicating and simply remedying those wrongs. While many researchers have examined police mistakes (biased lineups, informant misuse, the solicitation of false confessions, reliance on poor forensic science, and so on), few have studied the institutional contexts that allow these mistakes to occur and remain unchecked. This chapter focuses on those institutional conditions within police culture that contribute to conviction of the innocent. In addition, it presents an international comparative discussion of the role of the police in wrongful convictions. Drawing on commissioned studies, Royal Commissions and judicial inquiries, as well as criminological literature and decided cases, the chapter offers a meta-analysis of sources from across the common law world, highlighting the importance of the issue both inside and outside of the United States.[3]

Before moving on to those issues, I offer here some general conclusions about wrongful convictions and their causes so as to place police practices into a broader institutional context. In most cases, wrongful convictions are neither aberrations nor difficult to prevent. They typically can be found in one or both of two institutional contexts (which frequently overlap): the pressure to convict in the highly charged and politicized environment generated by high-profile cases; and the willingness to prosecute and convict someone without real scrutiny of the evidence, which can be engendered by stereotypes and bias operating in routine environments. Even when the conduct itself is deliberate—when confessions are improperly obtained or witnesses purposely suborned, for example—the practices are often rationalized as "noble cause corruption": the belief that the ends justify the means and that improper and even dishonest practices are in order (Wood 1997). Commonly, police and others maintain their belief in guilt long after their case has fallen apart and been exposed as a false construction, which demonstrates how deeply ingrained this rationalization may become. For instance, in high-profile cases in which the innocent are convicted, extensive and substantial police misconduct may be practiced to ensure convictions. More routine cases, which may involve sloppy, cynical, callous practices that build a case against the most obvious suspects, are less frequently uncovered, often result in guilty pleas, and are usually excused by heavy caseloads. Both contexts infect police and prosecution services all over the world—an infection that ultimately touches all investigations.

Indeed, it is important to be aware that wrongful convictions are not just a product of the high-profile, pressure-to-convict paradigm so familiar in notorious cases of wrongful conviction, although such cases and their institutional context receive most attention in the literature. Miscarriages of justice, however, are often rooted in the far more common problem of institutional cynicism and neglect—the same old suspects "obviously guilty" of the same old offenses, which require no investigation and never involve a presumption of innocence. These cases, dubbed "target practice" among some police officers to emphasize their routine nature, demonstrate a culture and climate that promotes cutting corners and worse. Indeed, in the words of the commissioners investigating the wrongful conviction of a Canadian aboriginal man, Donald Marshall, Jr., the errors in such routine cases "could have and should have been prevented if persons involved in the criminal justice system had carried out their duties in a professional and/

or competent manner" (Hickman et al. 1989: 275). That is, if the existing rules and standards of competent practice, as they are commonly understood, had been met, the innocent would not have been convicted, and the guilty would not have escaped.

It is clear that certain types of cases are more likely to result in wrongful conviction than others because they are based on evidence readily susceptible to error (eyewitness testimony, confessions, jailhouse informants, speculative or subjective science, and so on). Cases from all jurisdictions demonstrate that, in circumstances of heightened public pressure for arrest and conviction, one or more of these mechanisms that can result in wrongful convictions are more likely to occur, thereby causing a miscarriage of justice. This likelihood is magnified when there is appreciable bias against the accused on the basis of race or other identifiable characteristics. The factors that lead to failures in these cases, however, also contribute to a climate of cynicism and carelessness about the investigation, prosecution, defense, and judgment of criminal cases generally, which itself produces wrongful convictions. Cynicism about even the possibility of innocence and carelessness about procedural and substantive safeguards in cases where "we know he's guilty" are as likely to cause a wrongful conviction as the most extraordinary levels of public pressure to obtain a conviction.

The Scope of the Problem

The problem of the conviction of the innocent is not unique to any one jurisdiction but has occurred, and is occurring, throughout the common law world. In each jurisdiction, criminal justice actors and consumers both tend to assume that the substantive laws and procedures they rely on are eminently fair—even are the best in the world—or that problems with the administration of justice are unique to their own system. The evidence, however, points to the contrary. Similarities among the cases of wrongful conviction in Canada, the United States, the United Kingdom, and Australia are far greater than the differences that local social, doctrinal, and procedural variations produce.

Estimates of the frequency of wrongful convictions, however defined, range widely.[4] In the 1980s the British section of the International Commission of Jurists estimated that fifteen cases of wrongful conviction occurred each year in the United Kingdom. Some surveys of defense lawyers suggest the rate is 20 percent of convictions in contested trials, although that figure is not the result of a systematic study and the actual number may well be lower (Huff et al. 1996). More recently in England, an unsettling number of wrongful convictions has been exposed, including cases involving the Maguire Seven, the Birmingham Six, the Guilford Four, the Tottenham Three, and the Cardiff Three. The court of appeal has also posthumously quashed the convictions of two men executed in the 1950s: Derek Bentley and Mahmoud Mattan. Nevertheless, these notorious cases represent only a small portion of the occasions in which justice has miscarried in England and Wales. The Justice Society, an English organization whose objectives include upholding the rule of law and preserving fundamental liberties, detailed the occurrence of wrongful convictions in England and Wales in a 1994 report titled *Remedying Miscarriages of Justice*. The report identified thirty-seven cases between 1980 and 1987 involving forty-nine persons referred to the court of appeal by the home secretary after fresh evidence cast doubt on the safety of their convictions. In that same period, the home secretary paid compensation to sixty persons who were wrongly convicted.

In the wake of this wave of miscarriages of justice, the United Kingdom established in March 1997 an independent commission to review claims of wrongful convictions. Known as the Criminal Cases Review Commission (CCRC), the group assumed the function, formerly performed by the Home Office, of reviewing post-appellate claims of wrongful conviction in England, Wales, and Northern Ireland to determine which, if any, were sufficiently suspect to warrant their referral to the relevant court of appeal. According to its first annual report, the CCRC referred twelve doubtful verdicts to a court of appeal in its first year of operation. Before the commission's second anniversary, a Canadian newspaper reported that, in total, the CCRC had referred thirty-four cases to a court of appeal and that, "of the seven referrals heard to date, six resulted in quashed convictions and exoneration" (Lett 1999: A9; see also CCRC 1998).

While there is no way to find an empirically satisfactory answer to the question of the frequency of wrongful convictions, it is clear that their incidence is higher than would occur if the phenomenon were merely a matter of inevitable aberration. Recent studies and inquiries in the United States, England, and Australia continue to uncover cases of wrongful conviction; and all of them identify systemic and institutional factors, many of which involve policing practices, that strongly suggest significant numbers of other cases as yet unredressed or unidentified (Kaufman 1998; Radelet et al. 1992; *Royal Commission on Criminal Justice* 1991; Wood 1997).

Moreover, the answer to the question about the number of wrongful convictions and the scope of the problem is not simply empirical but rests on the assumptions one brings to criminal justice questions more generally. At one extreme is a deep concern about preserving faith in the integrity of the criminal prosecution process or resisting increases in due process safeguards and mechanisms. If one assumes that focusing on errors will impair faith in the process and has a high rate of belief in the apparatuses of criminal justice, one will find considerable comfort in the fact that a relatively small percentage of the total number of cases turn out to be wrongful convictions. Such people will describe these cases as the inevitable errors of a human system and portray them as a price worth paying in the interests of efficiency and effectiveness. In the same vein, efficient, effective investigative techniques (unhampered by outmoded due process safeguards) will be promoted as the best means to reduce the already small number of miscarriages of justice (Cassell 1998). If, on the other hand, one views the integrity of the system as requiring real (as contrasted with apparent) fairness, the occurrence of any wrongful convictions will be of concern. This position is frequently associated with advocacy for increased procedural safeguards and more accountability measures for police misconduct (Martin 1998; Packer 1968).

The two positions may be closer than their rhetoric suggests. It is not surprising that actual numbers of miscarriages of justice are relatively low considering the small number of cases in the system in which factual guilt is actually at issue. Most cases involve people who are known to each other and to the system and are resolved through plea negotiations. Fewer than 15 percent of all charges proceed to a contested trial, and of that percentage, a much smaller number involve cases in which factual guilt is at issue. Most of the disputes concern matters of justification, such as self-defense or consent, or of intention or state of mind rather than the identity of the perpetrator or whether a crime has occurred at all. True "who done it" or "what happened" crimes are relatively rare. On the other hand, a disturbing number of these "who done it" cases have been wrongly decided. Although their actual percentage among all criminal charges is low, these are the crimes by which the justice system is measured. The crimes of the serial rapist and killer or the more common but equally troubling crimes of stranger against stranger terrify us and make us cry out for resolution—any resolution. A significant error rate in resolving these crimes becomes even more disturbing if, as this research suggests, the miscarriages of justice that occur with these cases are often the result of systemic and institutional errors at the hands of the police (Zuckerman 1992).

Thus, those who seek to promote faith in the system because it makes few errors are not asking the necessary questions about why this is so. Those who seek greater traditional due process safeguards as a means to prevent miscarriages of justice, such as access to lawyers during interrogations, may also be failing to ask why miscarriages occur. We must instead look to the quality of the evidence and the reliability of the conviction obtained by existing investigative practices and within dominant police cultures rather than artificially bolster or rhetorically damn them for other purposes. In other words, investigations must search for the truth, not simply for convictions.

The Institutional Context: Predisposing Factors

Most wrongful convictions demonstrate at least one of three common predisposing circumstances: (1) the case placed significant pressure on authorities to resolve with a conviction, (2) the accused was a marginalized outsider, or (3) the case rested on suspect or inherently unreliable evidence. Many involve all three. Indeed, when all of these predisposing factors are present, a retrospective analysis makes a wrongful conviction appear almost inevitable. These predisposing conditions allow for the police mistakes commonly found in wrongful conviction cases to occur without redress. Within these contexts, police are more likely to overlook the initial reluctance of an eyewitness, to pressure a defendant into a false confession, to believe a jailhouse snitch, or to sway expert scientific testimony.

The paradigmatic case of wrongful conviction begins with a heinous unsolved crime and pits an unpopular or minority accused, assisted by an inadequate defense, against a determined prosecution zealously seeking a conviction to resolve community concern. Little evidence is available, but police are able to gather enough to warrant a trial. A trial culminating in a conviction restores order, and the case is over. We know about these cases and this pattern because they receive the most public attention, particularly in jurisdictions in which commissions of inquiry are used to determine what went wrong.

In fact, a less dramatic but equally troubling version of this paradigm

may account for a much larger number of cases of wrongful conviction. In these low-profile cases, the pressure to convict is generated
from pressures of work and routine stereotypical reasoning and involve
standard cases to which no one pays close attention. Indeed, apart from
the level of public pressure to solve high-profile cases, the factors associated with miscarriages of justice in more routine cases—cynicism,
apathy, institutionally corrupt practices in which everyone goes through
the motions—also involve a marginalized accused. This marginalization
may, in fact, serve as the rationale for the subsequent improper conduct. It is a form of dehumanization and distancing that is itself a social product generated out of racialization, class location or other
stereotyping, or deliberate demonization. In any case, it appears to be
essential to the "convict at all cost" mentality that permits the opera-
tional practices and mistakes that result in wrongful convictions. When
an accused in such a case is inadequately assisted by an inadequate
defense or none at all, the outcome may be almost inevitable.

Pressure to Convict: The Odious Crime

In high-profile cases or in any case that has sub-
stantial pressure to produce a resolution, a "convict at all costs" climate exists. This was clearly the case in the Irish Republican Army
(IRA) pub bombing cases in England in the 1970s. Scores of people
died when the IRA planted bombs in pubs frequented by off-duty British soldiers, a terror tactic that provoked extraordinary public fear and
anger. Three cities were involved in what became three separate wrongful prosecutions: Guilford and Birmingham, where bombs were deto-
nated; and Manchester, where an entire family, the Maguires, was
wrongly convicted of having supplied the explosives. The police
rounded up hundreds of young Irish men and women, particularly
those who were leaving England in the days after the bombings or who
had any connection to the IRA. They subjected them to intense questioning, looking for names. Ultimately, suspects were identified, almost at random, from the pressured informants and brought in for
further investigation. The Guilford Four and the Birmingham Six, as
these suspects became known, were subjected to lengthy and abusive
interrogations until false confessions were finally signed (composed
in advance by the police); and police forensics experts were thereaf-
ter convinced to offer misleading opinions about matters such as gunshot residue tests.

Popular books (McKee and Franey 1988; Mullin 1990), a very popular film (*In the Name of the Father*), and a Royal Commission (*Royal Commission on Criminal Justice* 1991), among others, have examined what went wrong; but all acknowledge that police were responding to a pressure to convict with what one senior police official called "noble cause corruption." Conduct explained in this way may include everything from disregard for due process safeguards, to overt pressure on witnesses to give evidence that will support the conviction of the selected suspect, to falsification of evidence, all in the name of securing a conviction of someone police have decided is guilty. Such cases are found in all jurisdictions, often in the most high-profile crimes of their day as well as the most publicized miscarriages of justice.

Marginalized Accused: The Odious Suspect

Noble cause corruption is neither an inevitable nor even a common result of the pressure to resolve a case that is troubling the community. Nor does it exist in isolation. A marginalized suspect who can be made to bear public fear and loathing is a necessary element of most cases of wrongful conviction. The rationalization that the "ends may justify the means" rests on the assumption that the police have found, and the state is prosecuting, the right person. Because this is not necessarily the case, such rationalization can lead to the freedom of the guilty, both through the conviction of an innocent person and through the release of a factually guilty person when corruption is discovered and leads to appellate reversal. The same rationalization also facilitates miscarriages of justice when the accused is an outsider to the dominant community, reinforcing existing bias and reaffirming the status quo. Again, the IRA cases exemplify this point. The Irish immigrant to England is a stereotypical outsider— untrusted, denigrated, racialized. In the pub bombing cases, almost anyone Irish with even a faint possibility of a connection to either the IRA or the locations where the bombs went off, became first a suspect, then an accused, and finally a convicted innocent. In the United States, racialization, particularly of African Americans, is an even more potent force in generalizing a suspect into the accused who is then convicted; and this situation is common in Canada as well, particularly in charges involving alleged aboriginal offenders.

The case of Willie Nepoose is typical of a relatively low-profile case in which a marginal, racialized accused is convicted almost routinely. Nepoose was an aboriginal drifter, an alcoholic with a long record of convictions for minor crimes, who in 1987 was convicted of second-degree murder in Alberta. Although no physical evidence connected him to the murder, Nepoose was implicated by two women who testified that they saw him commit the crime. The women had given a series of inconsistent statements to police and were also alcoholics lacking credibility, but their evidence was enough. The defense alibi—that Nepoose was drinking in a hotel with his brothers—was rejected after the Crown called evidence that no one was registered at the hotel under the name Nepoose on the day in question. After all appeals were exhausted, new evidence was found that resulted in his release: a phone bill was discovered that proved he was not at the scene of the crime but at the hotel with his brothers, as he had originally testified. Other fresh evidence included a recantation by the key prosecution witness, who admitted to lying on the stand and stated that she did not see Nepoose on the night of the murder. A welfare check was then disclosed, showing that she was not present at the time of the murder—evidence that had been withheld from the defense. The police also withheld from both the prosecution and the defense inconsistent statements made by the other prosecution witness and the fact that she could not pick out the deceased from a photo lineup.[5]

The three most famous Canadian cases of wrongful conviction (the cases of Marshall, Morin, and Milgaard) all share this quality. Donald Marshall, Jr., was an aboriginal teenager known to police who was wrongly convicted of murdering his friend, a black youth named Sandy Seale. Police jumped to the conclusion that Marshall was the killer, even though Marshall, wounded by the real killer, had flagged down police to get help for himself and his friend. The police did not want to believe that a middle-aged white man had killed the boy (which turned out to be the case). To ensure that their version succeeded, the police did not bother to investigate the crime scene or search for witnesses. Instead, they pressured teenage witnesses and withheld important information from the defense and the courts. In a racially charged community, no more evidence was needed.

David Milgaard was a drug-using teenage hippie heading to Saskatoon with two friends when Gail Miller, a young nursing assistant, was raped and murdered on a bitterly cold winter night. The case was high profile; and when another drug-using teenager implicated Milgaard during police questioning about another matter (a common occurrence), police quickly built a case based on the evidence of Milgaard's friends and on a rambling, drug-induced statement by Milgaard himself. It took twenty-three years of constant pressure from and reinvestigation by his mother Joyce, the New Jersey–based Centurion Ministries, and others to finally unravel the conviction (Karp and Rosner 1991). Approximately six years after Milgaard's release from prison, DNA testing confirmed his innocence and implicated another man; and in November 1999, a serial rapist named Larry Fisher, who was living just blocks away from the murder scene, was convicted of Gail Miller's murder. While police had known about Fisher and the seven similar rapes and knife attacks he had committed, the prosecution ensured that the defense never learned of his existence. A commission of inquiry into David Milgaard's wrongful conviction is expected.

A related process may involve the demonization of someone not obviously marginal—as, for example, in the Ontario case of the wrongful conviction of Guy Paul Morin for the murder of eight-year-old Christine Jessop. A neighbor of the murdered girl, Morin (and his family, by necessary implication) became cast in the role of outsider even though he and his family members were law-abiding and productive members of the community. Police began describing him as "weird" because he played the clarinet and kept bees, among other rationalizations. Family members were also described as suspect because they repaired old cars in the backyard and socialized together. Morin became first a target and then an obsession as a case was built against him out of nothing. The media, the prosecution, and the courts were all captivated by the implicit designation "outsider," and a conviction was ultimately obtained—at a second trial. Without the exceptional effort of teams of defense counsel (in both trials) and a growing unease in the community about the case, Morin's innocence might never have been established. Moreover, it is still impossible to know whether he would have been freed without DNA, which came on the eve of his appeal from the verdict in the second trial (Kaufman 1998; Makin 1998).

Unreliable Evidence

Each of the cases just discussed represents a situation in which police settled on a guilty party who was a marginalized member of the community. The police relied on a form of tunnel vision whereby the guilt of the suspect was assumed and evidence manipulated through the use of a number of questionable practices to prove that guilt.

But whether or not a case is high profile, the risk of a wrongful conviction is substantially increased when the prosecution's case rests primarily on sources of evidence that are unreliable and susceptible to police pressure, such as circumstantial evidence generally, eyewitness evidence, jailhouse informant evidence, confessions, and speculative or fragile forensic evidence. Here, the role of the police in generating the evidence is only half of the equation. The other half rests on the role of the police and their high status within the administration of justice. Each of these categories of evidence relies for its probative force on the acceptance of the credibility of the witness, which in turn relies on an underlying generalization. The reasoning is "if X, then Y": assuming that the witness, X, is accurate and truthful, then Y is the man. That reasoning requires further, often unarticulated reasoning steps about the accuracy of the witness, which often amounts to the generalization that the police have arrested the correct suspect. The circularity of this reasoning is rarely made explicit but is frequently used.

This cycle is, without a doubt, a factor in wrongful convictions based on mistaken eyewitness evidence. Despite a plethora of celebrated cases of mistaken identification, eyewitness evidence carries an intuitive force that is difficult to challenge (Connors et al. 1996; Loftus 1980). The significance of the police role is reinforced by experience with the jailhouse or in-custody informant. Although evidence from a fellow prisoner who claims to have received the accused's confession to the crime and agrees to testify in exchange for some benefit is inherently and intuitively unreliable, police around the world present such evidence to prosecutors, and juries accept it. This type of evidence has been a factor in a significant number of wrongful convictions; indeed, it is almost a hallmark of the weak prosecution case. In some high-profile cases, such evidence was all that was produced in court. While a suspect's confession is as persuasive as eyewitness identification or informant information, here, too, police practices can generate false confessions from innocent men and women (Gudjonsson 1993). The conclusion is difficult to avoid. Unreliable evidence becomes transformed into something persuasive by the operation of two forces: the need to convict at any cost, and a belief that the police will only bring the guilty to trial.

Police Practices and Wrongful Convictions

Stereotypes—particularly those based on racism, sexism, and class bias—work to both wrongly exclude and wrongly include suspects in an investigation (Ericson 1993; Shearing 1981), not only because the police share the biases of the community but also because they tend to strenuously resist their eradication (Martin 1993; Shearing 1981). Moreover, police training and experience tend to reinforce stereotypes. Patrol work, in particular, is designed to identify who or what doesn't fit, whether it is a black youth in a white neighborhood or some other shorthand picture of "what should be there" (Ericson 1993). Detective work, on the other hand, stereotypes familiarity and is frequently an exercise in locating and processing "typical" offenders who have committed the same crime many times before (Ericson 1993; McConville 1992; McConville et al. 1991). Police investigators often do not have the skills needed to uncover initially unknown offenders and thus fall back on stereotypes, with the result that cases without obvious offenders suffer from both over- and under-inclusion. This should not be surprising. In a pressure-to-convict climate that urges a rush to judgment, where this pressure is compounded by occupational pride and pressure to get a result, the certainty and swiftness of stereotyped reasoning is very appealing and frequently results in the targeting of marginalized individuals. Once a conclusion is reached, all subsequent evidence, reliable or not, is used to strengthen it. Thus, the filter through which the evidence is viewed is of utmost importance. This filter is manifested primarily in two ways: through influencing witnesses to conform to a prosecution theory; and through direct police error in obtaining, processing, and presenting evidence for the trial itself. The cases analyzed here demonstrate both of these mechanisms, which occur with surprising consistency across the jurisdictions examined.

Influence on Witnesses

Police influence and participate in witness error in two ways: by failing to detect it when a witness first offers it (whether motivated by the witness's own agenda or unconsciously induced by police), or by deliberately forcing or encouraging a witness to change his or her testimony. Police failure to detect witness error is often (although not always) a product of tunnel vision: if the misleading evidence fits police theory or biases, it may not be rigorously examined. In the case of police-induced error, the most common explanation is "the ends justify the means," or that the witness's "improvement" is acceptable because the police know that the accused is, in fact, guilty (Ericson 1993; Martin 1993; McConville et al. 1991; Zuckerman 1992).

The report of Justice Fred Kaufman (1998) into the wrongful conviction of Guy Paul Morin provides a chillingly exhaustive portrayal of just such a series of events. Some witnesses eagerly changed their evidence with only slight police encouragement, while others were interviewed repeatedly until they gave the "right" evidence. Police used more serious pressure to obtain incriminating evidence from teenage witnesses in the Milgaard and Marshall cases. Similar examples are found in all jurisdictions.

Direct Police Misconduct

Police also participate more directly in producing wrongful convictions. Because of their initial and essentially exclusive access to the evidence and the accused in custody, officers have relatively easy opportunities to tamper with or plant evidence, such as planting fingerprints (easy with Scotch tape), trace evidence (alleged to have occurred in the IRA pub bombing case), drugs, and weapons. They also have the means and the opportunity to destroy or ignore potentially exculpatory evidence, coerce witnesses, and illegally extort confessions. Police stations are closed institutions with few, if any, outsider eyes scrutinizing conduct, and within this world there are ample opportunities to improperly obtain and manipulate evidence and then manage the internal documentation (the paper trail) so that the misconduct is difficult to detect.

Examples of this type of misconduct can be found all over the world. In Australia's now infamous "dingo baby case," police misconduct coupled with distorted and unreliable forensic evidence were woven together to support the prosecution theory, thus mistakenly dubbing a tragically accidental child death as murder (*Royal Commission of Inquiry into Chamberlain Convictions* 1987). In Canada, overt police misconduct and corruption were ultimately revealed as the source of Rejean Hinse's wrongful conviction, but perjury has been a factor in others as well—notably, the cases of Nepoose and Morin (Kaufman 1998).[6] In the United Kingdom, the most well-developed illustrations of severe and deliberate police misconduct in obtaining confessions appear in the IRA cases, but they are not the only ones. The cases of Anthony Paris and Stefan Kiszko, in particular, document a litany of police abuse of power and false testimony to cover it up.[7] As the court of appeals concluded in the case of the Birmingham Six, "the police lied" (Conlon 1991).

Conclusion

While this record is troubling, we must note that it is often the police who uncover and remedy wrongful convictions, or prevent them from happening in the first place. The issue here is not so much a matter of police bashing as a call to ensure scrupulous professionalism and a high ethical standard in all branches of law enforcement, particularly the investigative branch. This may involve no more than ensuring that the standard of investigations actually meets the expectation. It may be too much to expect the public not to feel relief when the media report an arrest, particularly in a high-profile case, and thus to believe that they already know who the guilty person is. As Herbert Packer (1968: 160–61) notes, "if there is confidence in the reliability of informal administrative fact-finding activities that take place in the early stages of the criminal process, the remaining stages of the process [trial, appeals] can be relatively perfunctory."

The ultimate challenge is to be morally ethical and intellectually honest during investigations, scrupulously fair during trials, and, above all, humble enough to admit error. Anyone can make a mistake; the evil lies in refusing to admit it. The history of wrongful convictions is littered with stubborn and wicked refusals to admit error. Now that we are no longer innocent about the risks or ignorant of our frailties, one can hope that the future will be different.

NOTES

I am grateful for the assistance of Mara Green and the students enrolled in the Innocence Project of Osgoode Hall Law School, York University, Toronto, Ontario. This chapter is based on research developed for the Inquiry into Proceedings against Guy Paul Morin, submitted 17 November 1997.

1. Jurisdictions operating under the civil tradition also have cases of wrongful conviction, but their study has proved to be beyond the scope of this inquiry. Generally, see Wegg-Prosser (1982: 205–23) and "Remedies for Wrongful Convictions: Review of s.690" (1998).
2. As far back as 1470, Sir John Fortescue (1949: 63), then chief justice of the King's Bench, wrote that he "should, indeed, prefer twenty guilty men to escape death through mercy, than one innocent to be condemned unjustly." More recently, Justice Deane of the High Court of Australia in *Van der Meer v. R.* (1988: 31) eloquently affirmed:

   The complementary direct objectives of the administration of the criminal law are the conviction and punishment of the guilty and the acquittal of the innocent. The frailty of all human institutions precludes the complete achievement of both. That being so, there is inevitable tension between them. In the context of such tension, the entrenched and guiding thesis of the criminal law . . . is that the second objective is incomparably more important than the first; that the searing injustice and consequential social injury which is involved when the law turns upon itself and convicts an innocent person far outweigh the failure of justice and the consequential social injury involved when the processes of the law proclaim the innocence of a guilty one.

3. The most recent Canadian investigation of the causes of wrongful conviction may be found in the report of Justice Fred Kaufman (1998) on the inquiry into the case of Guy Paul Morin. Morin had been convicted (after two bitterly contested trials) of the rape-murder of eight-year-old Christine Jessop, his neighbor, in Queensville, Ontario. He was ultimately exonerated through DNA profiling, and a commission of inquiry was established to determine the cause of the wrongful conviction and make recommendations to avoid the same errors in the future. Ten years earlier, the exposure of the wrongful conviction of a Micmac youth, Donald Marshall, Jr., generated a similarly wide-ranging and significant inquiry (Hickman et al. 1989).

In the United Kingdom, a recent Royal Commission considered the phenomenon after wrongful conviction scandals, initially arising out of the IRA pub bombing cases of the 1970s, rocked the justice system (Justice Society 1994; *Royal Commission on Criminal Justice* 1991). Australia has a similar record. While there have been no studies into their national prevalence, the commission headed by Justice James Roland T. Wood (1997), established in 1994 to inquire into corruption in the New South Wales police force, disclosed thirty-five claims of wrongful conviction that were still under active investigation in November 1997. In regard to Australia's most notorious wrongful conviction, the "dingo baby case" (immortalized in a film starring Meryl Streep), see the *Royal Commission of Inquiry into Chamberlain Convictions* (1987); and *Re Conviction of Chamberlain* (1988).

4. Here, the term is used to refer to cases of the conviction of a factually innocent person—the wrong person convicted when the issue was "who done it"—and cases of the conviction of a person for a crime when, in fact, no crime occurred, which has happened in deaths mistakenly categorized as homicides. The miscarriages of justice that may occur when a defense, such as self-defense or insanity, is involved have not been included.

5. See the following newspaper articles: "Similarities," 1991; "Nepoose Takes Huge Step," 1992; "Court Sets Nepoose Free," 1992; "Indian Free," 1992; and RCMP to Review," 1992. See also *R. v. Nepoose* (1988, 1992).

6. Hinse was convicted of a gang-related robbery in 1964. He became a suspect when he attempted to sell his car to a leader of the gang that had committed the robbery. This gang member had been test-driving Hinse's car when he was stopped by the police before the robbery. Once Hinse was a suspect, the police approached him and asked him to participate in a photo lineup. The victims picked Hinse out of the photo lineup and then identified him at trial in an in-dock identification (a Canadian phrase used to describe a witness identification made while the offender is in the prisoner's box in court; understood to be a misleading way to conduct an identification procedure). Hinse was released on parole after spending nine years in prison. In 1990, a police reinvestigation revealed that

two officers had perjured themselves on the stand to convict Hinse. They had an interest in the outcome because the real robbers were friends of the police. The investigation also found that the pretrial lineup procedures were grossly improper. A hat, similar to the hats used by the gang members in the robbery, was placed on Hinse for the lineup, but not on the others' heads, to ensure the misidentification. See the following newspaper articles: "Compensation Sought," 1997; "Laval Man Cleared," 1997; "Emotional Hinse," 1997; "Portrait," 1997; "Hinse Seeks $5 Million," 1997; "Quebec Man," 1997; and "Anger Ends," 1997. See also *R. v. Hinse* (1994, 1995, 1997).

7. The case of Anthony Paris and his codefendants Yusuf Abdullahi and Stephen Wayne Miller, known as the Cardiff Three, and the case of Stefan Ivan Kiszko were quashed by the English court of appeal, and acquittals were entered when confession evidence that was central to their convictions was found to be completely unreliable. In Paris's case, a coerced and unreliable confession from Miller, implicating Paris, was improperly used as a basis for his conviction for the murder of a prostitute named Lynette White. In Kiszko's case, an immature and physically fragile man was convicted of the murder of eleven-year-old Lesley Molseed. Kiszko's case is particularly troubling. Medical evidence provided to the court of appeal revealed that semen found on the little girl's body could not have been produced by Kiszko, who was incapable of producing sperm (*R. v. Kiszko* 1992; *R. v. Paris, Abdullahi, and Miller* 1992).

REFERENCES

"Anger Ends for Man Who Was Wrongly Convicted." 1997. *Vancouver Sun,* 23 January. [Internet]

Cassell, Paul. 1998. "Protecting the Innocent from False Confessions and Lost Confessions—And from *Miranda.*" *Journal of Criminal Law and Criminology* 88: 497–556.

"Compensation Sought." 1997. *Globe and Mail,* 23 January, p. A3.

Conlon, Gerry. 1991. *Proved Innocent.* London: Penguin.

Connors, Edward, Thomas Lundregan, Neal Miller, and Tom McEwen. 1996. *Convicted by Juries, Exonerated by Science: Case Studies in the Use of DNA Evidence to Establish Innocence after Trial.* Washington, D.C.: National Institute of Justice.

"Court Sets Nepoose Free." 1992. *Calgary Star,* 10 March. [Internet]

Criminal Cases Review Commission (CCRC). 1998. "Press Release: CCRC Receives 1,380 Applications in its First Year," 21 July.

"Emotional Hinse Savours Acquittal." 1997. *Montreal Gazette,* 23 January. [Internet]

Ericson, Richard V. 1993. *Making Crime: A Study of Detective Work.* Toronto: University of Toronto Press.

Fortescue, John. 1949. *De Laudibus Legum Angliae,* edited and translated by S. B. Chimes. Cambridge: Cambridge University Press.

Gudjonsson, Gisli. 1993. *The Psychology of Interrogations, Confessions, and Testimony.* Chichester, U.K.: Wiley.

Hickman, T. Alexander, Lawrence Poitras, and Gregory Evans. 1989. *Royal Commission on the Donald Marshall, Jr. Prosecution.* Vol. 1. Halifax, Nova Scotia: Royal Commission.

"Hinse Seeks $5 Million in Damages." 1997. *Montreal Gazette,* 5 February, p. A4.

Huff, C. Ronald, Arye Rattner, and Edward Sagarin. 1996. *Convicted but Innocent: Wrongful Conviction and Public Policy*. Thousand Oaks, Calif.: Sage.

"Indian Free after 6-Year Battle." 1992. *Toronto Star,* 10 March. [Internet]

Justice Society. 1994. *Remedying Miscarriages of Justice*. London: Justice Society.

Karp, Carl, and Cecil Rosner. 1991. *When Justice Fails: The David Milgaard Story*. Toronto: McClelland and Stewart.

Kaufman, Fred. 1998. *The Report of the Commission on Proceedings Involving Guy Paul Morin*. Toronto: Publications Ontario.

"Laval Man Cleared after 35 Years." 1997. *Montreal Gazette,* 22 January, p. A10.

Lett, Dan. 1999. "Ultimate Miscarriage." *Winnipeg Free Press,* 25 February, p. A9.

Loftus, Elizabeth F. 1980. "Psychological Aspects of Courtroom Testimony." *Annals of the New York Academy of Sciences* 347: 27–37.

Makin, Kirk. 1998. *Redrum the Innocent: The Guy Paul Morin Story*. Toronto: Penguin.

Martin, Dianne L. 1993. "Organizing for Change: A Community Law Response to Police Misconduct." *Hastings Women's Law Journal* 4: 131–74

———. 1998. "Retribution Revisited: A Reconsideration of Feminist Criminal Law Reform Strategies." *Osgoode Hall Law Journal* 36: 151–88

McConville, Mike. 1992. "Videotaping Interrogations: Police Behaviour On and Off Camera." *Criminal Law Review* (August): 532–48.

McConville, Mike, Andrew Sanders, and Roger Leng. 1991. *The Case for the Prosecution: Police Suspects and the Construction of Criminality*. London: Routledge.

McKee, Grant, and Ross Franey. 1988. *Time Bomb: Irish Bombers, English Justice, and the Guilford Four*. London: Bloomsbury.

Mullin, Chris. 1990. *Error of Judgment: The Truth about the Birmingham Bombings*. Dublin: Poolbeg.

"Nepoose Takes Huge Step toward Freedom." 1992. *Calgary Star,* 2 March. [Internet]

Packer, Herbert. 1968. *The Limits of the Criminal Sanction*. Stanford, Calif.: Stanford University Press.

"Portrait of the Perfect Victim." 1997. *Montreal Gazette,* 1 February. [Internet]

"Quebec Man Wins 30 Year Long Fight." 1997. *Vancouver Sun,* 22 January. [Internet]

Radelet, Michael L., Hugo Adam Bedau, and Constance E. Putnam. 1992. *In Spite of Innocence*. Boston: Northeastern University Press.

"RCMP to Review Nepoose Case." 1992. *Toronto Star,* 18 March. [Internet]

"Remedies for Wrongful Convictions: Review of s.690." 1998. Canada: Department of Justice.

The Royal Commission on Criminal Justice. 1991. London: Home Office.

The Royal Commission of Inquiry into Chamberlain Convictions. 1987. Northern Territories: Australian Government Printer.

Shearing, Clifford D. 1981. *Organizational Police Deviance: Its Structure and Control*. Toronto: Butterworths.

"Similarities Seen in Cases against Natives." 1991. *Calgary Star,* 23 February. [Internet]

Wegg-Prosser, Charles. 1982. *Compensation for Wrongful Imprisonment*. London: Justice Society.

Wood, James Roland T. 1997. *The Royal Commission into the New South Wales Police Service*. Sydney: Government of New South Wales.

Zuckerman, A.A.S. 1992. "Miscarriages of Justice—A Root Treatment." *Criminal Law Review* (May): 323–45.

CASES CITED

R. v. Hinse, 24 W.C.B. (3d) 130 (Que.C.A. 1994).

R. v. Hinse, 29 W.C.B. (2d) 88 (S.C.C. 1995).

R. v. Hinse, W.C.B. (2d) 201 (S.C.C. 1997).

R. v. Kiszko, unreported (released 15 February, 1992).

R. v. Nepoose, 46 C.C.C. (3d) 421 (Alta.C.A. 1988).

R. v. Nepoose, 71 C.C.C. (3d) 419 (Alta.C.A. 1992).

R. v. Paris, Abdullahi, and Miller, 97 Cr.App.R. 99 (1992).

Re Conviction of Chamberlain, 93 F.L.R. 239 (1988).

Van der Meer v. R., 82 A.L.R. 10 (H.C. 1988).

The Social Characteristics of the Wrongly Convicted

WILLIAM M. HOLMES

5 | Who Are the Wrongly Convicted on Death Row?

The wrongful conviction issue lies at the core of the current debate over the death penalty. As evidence mounts revealing the causes and growing prevalence of wrongful convictions, especially in regard to death row cases, national calls have increased for a moratorium on the use of the death penalty (Death Penalty Information Center 2000). In early 2000, Illinois's governor George Ryan responded by implementing a moratorium on executions in his state: since the reinstitution of the death penalty in Illinois more than two decades ago, thirteen men on death row have been declared wrongly convicted and released (Armstrong and Mills 2000; Death Penalty Information Center 2000).

No judicial remedy is available to someone who has been wrongly executed; there is no way to undo the mistake. Until recently, wrongful convictions and executions were thought to be rare (Carrington 1978; Gross 1996). Numerous recent studies, however, indicate that this is not the case. Radelet et al. (1992) list 416 miscarriages of justice between 1900 and 1990 (see also Bedau and Radelet 1987). Many of these were individuals on death row, including twenty-three who were actually executed. Gross (1987) found 136 misidentifications of offenders alone, and Rattner (1988) also documented a number of erroneous convictions. Thus, mistakes in conviction in capital cases are far from rare. Given the finality of execution, not to mention the violation of human rights if the executed individual is innocent, it is important to learn who the wrongly convicted individuals released from state death rows are as well as examine the process that put them on death row to begin with. Only by fully understanding how such mistakes were made can we take effective preventative measures.

To date, the vast majority of the research on wrongful convictions has explored the flaws and failures in the legal process that have led to the conviction of innocent people (see Fisher 1993; Givelber 1997; Gross 1987, 1996; Huff et al. 1996; Radelet et al. 1992; Zimmerman 1994). Little systematic study, however, has focused on the social structure of these cases (Black 1989)—the social characteristics (social class, race, ethnicity, marital status, and so on) of the alleged offenders, victims, witnesses, and other case participants. While it is certainly important to understand the legal mistakes that lead to a wrongful conviction, it is also important to realize that these mistakes do not occur in a social vacuum and are not randomly distributed throughout the population of defendants. Certain defendants with particular social characteristics are more at risk for a wrongful conviction than others are. By analyzing the social characteristics of defendants whom the law has determined to be innocent and therefore has released from death row, this chapter takes a first step toward filling a void in the research.

Defining Wrongful Conviction

What is a wrongful conviction? As defined by other studies, the wrongfulness of a conviction may apply either to the process leading to the conviction or to the person who is ultimately convicted (and possibly sentenced to death) for a crime he or she did not commit. For example, studies by Radelet et al. (1992), Gross (1987), and Rattner (1988) have focused on convictions of people who are actually innocent. Such a conviction may or may not follow proper procedure but convicts the wrong person.

Before moving on with the analysis in this chapter, I must clarify my definition of *wrongful conviction*. For my purposes, it is important to distinguish between someone who is illegally convicted and someone who is wrongfully convicted. A person illegally convicted may or may not have actually done the crime for which he or she is charged, but a grievous legal defect in the process leads to his or her conviction. An appellate court has ruled that it was illegal to have convicted the prisoner given the defects of the trial process. For example, if police planted evidence against the defendant or the judge failed to instruct the jury to ignore hearsay testimony that had been excluded, this could be a fault critical to the issue of conviction. In such cases, a question is asked: "Is there a reasonable chance that the defendant would not have been convicted if the defect had not occurred?" If the outcome of the trial is likely to have been affected, the defect is regarded as grievous, and the conviction illegal. Defects that are unlikely to have affected the outcome of the case are not regarded as grievous and are not usually grounds for overturning the conviction.

Almost any constitutional violation is regarded as a grievous defect. Denying a defendant access to an attorney, a speedy trial, due process, equal protection, a jury of one's peers, and other constitutional guarantees can overturn a capital conviction because they are regarded as essential to the system of American justice. Such convictions are illegal because they are grievously defective; the defendant has been denied basic rights. It is difficult or impossible to know if true guilt or an appropriate sentence has been established if the process leading to them has been fundamentally defective.

Some of those whose illegal convictions are overturned are actually innocent. In the context of this study, these are the individuals who have been wrongfully convicted. When convictions are overturned, they are usually returned to the court of original jurisdiction (the original trial court) to be considered for retrial. Before retrial, the prosecuting attorney may decide that the evidence seen in the light of the appellate review may not justify a retrial and drop all charges. Alternatively, a retrial may occur, and the defendant may be found not guilty. In either case, a person sentenced to death will have been found legally innocent.

The U.S. Supreme Court has not unequivocally ruled that an innocent person has a constitutional right to challenge a conviction. In the case of *Sawyer v. Whitley* (1992), the Court ruled that if new evidence has a reasonable chance in a new trial of producing a verdict of innocent and if no state avenue for appeal is available, only then can a person's claim of innocence be used to overturn a capital conviction (Duffett 1993). The Court has rejected the principle that newly discovered facts showing innocence, per se, are sufficient to prompt federal review. In *Herrera v. Collins* (1993), however, it did allow that a "truly persuasive demonstration of actual innocence" would make an execution unconstitutional (Tanner 1994). The burden is on the defendant in the appeal to establish that he or she has a reasonable chance of proving innocence. The appeal must rest on compelling new evidence unavailable at the time of the original trial and must be "truly persuasive." In other words, the claim of innocence alone is not enough to rule that the person has been wrongfully convicted.

The analysis here focuses primarily on wrongful convictions to capital sentences for people whose wrongful convictions were determined by judicial review: cases overturned by appellate courts and sent back to the trial court, only to have the charges dropped by the prosecutor or the defendant found not guilty on retrial. This does not include all possible wrongful convictions. It excludes those where innocent persons were sentenced to death by a court process not ruled to be legally defective, some of whom were executed. It also excludes innocent persons given retrials who were falsely convicted during their retrial. The number of such persons excluded by this process is subject to considerable dispute. There is little doubt, however, that those who are identified in this study using these criteria are legally innocent and meet the standard for wrongful convictions. One might speculate that guilty persons were found innocent on retrial, but only unsubstantiated, anecdotal stories support such claims: no evidence indicates that guilty persons go free on retrial more often than innocent persons are again found guilty.

Methodology

To examine the defendants who have been wrongly convicted and released from capital sentences (that is, death row), this chapter relies on the "Prisoners on Death Row" data base from the U.S. Bureau of Justice Statistics (U.S. Department of Justice 1993). Covering the period between 1970 and 1992, this data base contains information about more than 6,200 individuals in prison with a capital sentence—a census of all capital prisoners in state and federal prisons during this time. Some of these states do not currently have capital punishment. The data base has information on changes in the convictions or sentences of inmates and the primary reason for those changes, including whether the conviction or sentence was found illegal on appeal as well as the final disposition of the overturned cases.

The data provide information about the proportion of capital convictions and sentences that have been found illegal: cases that have been overturned on appeal because of legal flaws in the trial or sentencing process. The data also document the final outcomes of these overturned cases, thereby providing information about which of these illegal convictions were actually wrongful convictions. The measure of wrongful conviction used here is a conservative measure: it includes cases in which the original conviction or sentence was overturned in a court of law and the person was found not guilty on retrial as well as those in which the charges were dropped without retrial. The data also provide information about the characteristics of the offenders in these cases. These data are available on the Internet from the National Criminal Justice Data Archive of the Institute for Social Research at the University of Michigan (U.S. Department of Justice 1997).

The data have been recoded so that those people executed during this period are included in the "not wrongful" category since they were not proven wrongful under the strict requirements of this analysis. Although studies by Bedau and Radelet (1987) and others (Gross 1987; Radelet et al. 1992) provide strong evidence that some of those executed were probably innocent, it is beyond the scope of this chapter to identify such cases in the "Prisoners on Death Row" data series and recode them as "innocent but executed." The percentages of wrongful convictions reported here, therefore, are lower bounds for the actual rate of wrongful convictions of people on death row.

Findings

These findings provide information about the prevalence of wrongful convictions and identify the social characteristics associated with an increased risk of sending the legally innocent to death row. Nevertheless, to place the discussion of the wrongly convicted into context, we briefly review here basic descriptive information about the general population of death row inmates and those illegally convicted and sentenced.

Prisoners on Death Row

Prisoners sentenced to death are primarily single males who are non-Hispanic and not well educated and who have been convicted for murder (see table 5.1). A majority are white (55.9 percent), although whites are underrepresented in comparison to their percentages in the national population on the whole. African Americans are disproportionately overrepresented on death row (42.6 percent). Men comprise 98 percent of those on death row, reflecting a long tradition in which few women are sentenced to death. Nearly three-fourths of the prisoners are single (including divorced, widowed, and never married). Hispanics are 6 percent of this population. Only 8 percent have some college education. Nearly half have not graduated from

Table 5.1 Profile of Prisoners on Death Row

CHARACTERISTIC	NUMBER	PERCENT
Sex		
Male	6,114	98.2
Female	114	1.8
Race		
White	3,484	55.9
Black	2,654	42.6
Native American	44	0.7
Asian or Pacific Islander	30	0.5
Other	16	0.3
Marital status		
Married	1,671	26.8
Separated/divorced	1,178	18.9
Widowed	164	2.6
Never married	2,766	44.4
Hispanic origin		
Hispanic	369	5.9
Non-Hispanic	4,623	74.2
Unknown	559	19.9
Education		
Less than high school	3,026	48.6
High school graduate or GED	1,744	28.0
Some college	396	6.4
College graduate	98	1.6
Unknown	964	15.5
Most serious offense		
Murder	6,125	98.3
Rape	56	0.9
Kidnapping	34	0.5
Other	13	0.2

The total number of cases equals 6,228.
Source: Holmes (1999).

high school, and almost all of those sentenced to death are charged with murder (98.3 percent). A few have been charged with crimes such as receiving stolen property, burglary, or robbery. These results are consistent with what has been reported about current death row inmates (U.S. Department of Justice 1998).

Illegal Convictions and Sentences

Table 5.2 summarizes the number of convictions and sentences overturned because of grievous legal defects. For all of the offenders who were under capital sentences during this period, more than 40 percent were found to have been illegally convicted or sentenced in their first trial (2,510 individuals from 1970 to 1992).

Table 5.2 Illegal Convictions and Sentences to Capital Punishment

	CONVICTION ILLEGAL (PERCENT)	SENTENCE ILLEGAL (PERCENT)	CONVICTION AND SENTENCE ILLEGAL (PERCENT)	TOTAL ILLEGAL (PERCENT)	TOTAL NOT ILLEGAL (PERCENT)	TOTAL SENTENCED (NUMBER)
Alaska	0.3	14.4	30.4	45.2	54.8	299
Arizona	10.4	22.5	8.7	41.6	58.4	231
Arkansas	0.0	36.8	10.5	47.4	52.6	95
California	7.8	19.7	3.4	30.9	69.1	669
Colorado	37.5	25.0	0.0	62.5	37.5	16
Connecticut	0.0	44.4	0.0	44.4	55.6	9
Delaware	25.7	17.1	2.9	45.7	54.3	35
District of Columbia	0.0	33.3	0.0	33.3	66.7	3
Florida	0.3	31.5	12.6	44.3	55.7	787
Georgia	1.7	37.5	14.6	53.8	46.2	288
Idaho	2.9	25.7	8.6	37.1	62.9	35
Illinois	0.4	24.3	8.8	33.5	66.5	272
Indiana	8.6	24.7	7.5	40.9	59.1	93
Kansas	0.0	100.0	0.0	100.0	0.0	2
Kentucky	0.0	31.7	26.8	58.5	41.5	82
Louisiana	5.3	40.2	5.8	51.3	48.7	189
Maryland	1.7	50.0	18.3	70.0	30.0	60
Maine	0.0	52.6	0.0	52.6	47.4	19
Mississippi	0.7	44.9	15.0	60.5	39.5	147
Missouri	0.0	7.1	11.4	18.6	81.4	140
Montana	0.0	23.1	15.4	38.5	61.5	13
Nebraska	0.0	18.2	13.6	31.8	68.2	22
Nevada	0.0	14.5	6.4	20.9	79.1	110
New Jersey	2.2	33.3	17.8	53.3	46.7	45
New Mexico	32.0	16.0	20.0	68.0	32.0	25
New York	37.5	62.5	0.0	100.0	0.0	8
North Carolina	28.5	24.3	11.1	63.9	36.1	432
Ohio	32.6	7.4	3.4	43.3	56.7	298
Oklahoma	14.2	17.5	15.7	47.4	52.6	268
Oregon	6.1	51.0	2.0	59.2	40.8	49
Pennsylvania	4.6	15.2	6.7	26.5	73.5	283
Rhode Island	100.0	0.0	0.0	100.0	0.0	2
South Carolina	18.9	17.6	12.8	49.3	50.7	148
South Dakota	0.0	0.0	0.0	0.0	100.0	2
Tennessee	19.1	17.9	4.0	41.0	59.0	173
Texas	0.0	3.6	15.2	18.8	81.2	697
Utah	0.0	25.0	8.3	33.3	66.7	24
Virginia	0.0	7.3	54.5	11.8	88.2	110
Washington	20.7	34.5	13.4	58.6	41.4	29
Wyoming	50.0	20.0	10.0	80.0	20.0	10
Federal	11.1	0.0	0.0	11.1	88.9	9
Total	7.7	21.6	11.0	40.3	59.6	6,228

Source: Holmes (1999).

South Dakota (with two death row prisoners) is the only state without any convictions or sentences found illegal. Sixteen states have more than 50 percent of their capital prisoners with illegal convictions or sentences. In three states (Kansas, New York, and Rhode Island), all of the prisoners with death sentences have illegal convictions or sentences. At the federal level, one in nine prisoners with a death sentence is a result of an illegal conviction.

Wrongful Convictions

Of the 2,510 people with illegal convictions, 688 had their overturned convictions ordered for retrial. (The remaining illegal convictions were cases sent back to the trial court for resentencing.) In 445 cases, the result of the retrial order has not yet been determined. Of the remaining 243 individuals with a known retrial result, 16 were found not guilty, and 42 had all charges dropped against them. Thus, 58 (23.9 percent) of the 243 individuals that had a retrial disposition are legally innocent (see table 5.3). More than one in five of the prisoners on death row who have an illegal conviction and a retrial determination have been wrongfully convicted of the crime for which they had been sentenced to death. If this rate of innocence applies to the rest of the prisoners on death row awaiting retrial, more than 106 wrongfully convicted individuals will have been among the prisoners on death row during this period, prisoners whose innocence will have been established by official legal proceedings.

Wrongful convictions were found in nearly two-thirds of the states that had retrial orders (60 percent). In four states, all of the cases sent for retrial were found to be wrongful convictions (Indiana, Montana, Nevada, and New Mexico). Among the high-execution states, practice does not produce perfection. Among California, Florida, Georgia, and Texas, the rate of wrongful convictions among the illegally convicted ranges from 10 percent (Texas) to 42 percent (Florida).

Correlates of Wrongful Convictions

Crosstabulation is used to examine whether the prisoner characteristics are associated with having a wrongful conviction. It focuses primarily on inmates' sex, race, Hispanic background, marital status, education, and the seriousness of the crime for which they were convicted at their first trial. The seriousness of the offense was recoded to combine all less serious offenses into one category because there were so few cases. Since the findings reported are popu-

Table 5.3 *Capital Punishment Retrial Results*

STATE	GUILTY ON RETRIAL (PERCENT)	NOT GUILTY OR CHARGES DROPPED (PERCENT)	WRONGFUL CAPITAL CONVICTIONS (NUMBER)	TOTAL RETRIAL WITH KNOWN RESULTS (NUMBER)
Alaska	84.2	15.8	3	19
Arizona	60.0	40.0	2	5
Arkansas	100.0	0.0	0	2
California	62.5	37.5	3	8
Delaware	100.0	0.0	0	1
Florida	58.1	41.9	18	43
Georgia	83.3	16.7	2	12
Idaho	100.0	0.0	0	3
Illinois	89.0	11.0	1	5
Indiana	0.0	100.0	2	2
Kentucky	100.0	0.0	0	9
Louisiana	100.0	0.0	0	6
Maryland	100.0	0.0	0	6
Mississippi	100.0	0.0	0	7
Missouri	100.0	0.0	0	2
Montana	0.0	100.0	1	1
Nebraska	50.0	50.0	1	2
Nevada	0.0	100.0	2	2
New Mexico	0.0	100.0	4	4
North Carolina	52.9	49.1	8	17
Ohio	87.5	12.5	1	8
Oklahoma	77.8	22.2	4	18
Pennsylvania	75.0	25.0	1	4
South Carolina	88.9	11.1	1	9
Tennessee	100.0	0.0	0	5
Texas	89.7	10.3	4	39
Utah	100.0	0.0	0	1
Virginia	100.0	0.0	0	3
Total	76.1	23.9	58	243

Note: Results are for states that have had capital cases sent for retrial.

lation parameters for the time period in question, no significance tests are reported. All group differences are actual population differences. All of the factors examined show differences between groups at risk of wrongful convictions (see table 5.4).

Men are much more likely to have been wrongfully convicted than women are. Almost all of the cases in which the retrial disposition is known involve men, and more than one in five have been found to be wrongful convictions. Of the two women whose retrial disposition is known, neither has been found innocent.

Striking differences also emerge between racial and ethnic groups

Table 5.4 Correlates of Wrongful Convictions

CORRELATE	WRONGFUL CONVICTION (PERCENT)	NUMBER
Sex		
Males	22.5	236
Females	0.0	2
Race		
White	19.4	139
Black	25.5	94
Native American	25.0	4
Asian/Pacific Islander	100.0	1
Hispanic background		
Hispanic	35.7	14
Not Hispanic	17.3	179
Marital status		
Married	28.6	77
Separated/divorced	20.6	34
Widowed	11.8	9
Never married	19.8	101
Education		
Less than high school	16.5	133
High school graduate or GED	28.3	53
Some college	35.7	14
College graduate	33.3	6
Most serious offense		
Murder	20.4	230
Rape	71.4	7
Burglary	100.0	1

Note: The total number for each set of characteristics does not add to 243 (the total number of illegal convictions with a known retrial result) because of missing data.

at risk for wrongful convictions. Among Asian Americans, the sole known retrial disposition found the man innocent. Among African Americans and Native Americans, 25 percent have been found to be wrongful convictions. Blacks are 31 percent more likely than whites to have a wrongful result. Hispanics are more likely than non-Hispanics to have had a wrongful conviction on retrial. Their rate of wrongful initial result is twice that of non-Hispanics. This result for wrongful convictions of Hispanics is opposite to that for illegal convictions as reported in Holmes (1999). In other words, Hispanics may be less likely to have an illegal conviction, but when it occurs, the risk of a wrongful result is high.

Being married, separated, or divorced is a significant risk factor in having a wrongful conviction among those sent for retrial. Those

Table 5.5 *General Linear Model Correlates of Wrongful Convictions*

VARIABLE	SUM OF SQUARES	DEGREES OF FREEDOM	MEAN SQUARE	F	SIGNIFICANCE
Corrected model	14.111	3	4.704	7.8	.000
Intercept	0.003	1	0.003	<0.1	.941
Murder versus not murder	1.045	1	1.045	1.7	.191
Education	1.887	1	1.887	3.1	.079
Hispanic	6.839	1	6.839	11.3	.001
Error	121.811	201	0.606		
Total	172.000	205			

Note: R-squared=0.104; adjusted R-squared=0.090

who are married are determined to be legally innocent in 28.6 percent of the cases, separated or divorced 20.6 percent. Those never married have nearly as many wrongful convictions (19.8 percent); widowed far fewer (11.8 percent).

Education has a substantial positive relationship with the risk of a wrongful conviction. Those who have less than a high school education have a 50 percent lower risk of a wrongful result than those who are college graduates. A clear and consistent pattern reveals that the less education one has, the less likely one's conviction will be a wrongful result. This pattern for wrongful convictions by education is the reverse of that reported for illegal convictions and sentences in Holmes (1999). It appears that the better educated are less likely to have an illegal conviction or sentence initially but are more likely to be found innocent after the case is sent for retrial.

Finally, results vary depending on the seriousness of the offense for which the defendant originally was convicted. For any charge other than murder, the vast majority of all convictions were found to be wrongful when retried—approximately three out of four. Given that nearly all of the nonmurder capital convictions during this period were overturned for grievous legal defects (Holmes 1999), trials for offenses other than murder are nearly certain to result in wrongful convictions.

Overlapping Influences

It is likely that some of these correlates of a wrongful court outcome are related to each other. If so, the effects of these variables overlap. To further explore the association between these factors and a wrongful disposition, I must control for the effects of the other variables. Therefore, these correlates were entered into a general linear model (GLM) estimation in which a dichotomous variable— wrongful result versus not—was treated as a dummy dependent variable. All of the correlates were treated as factors in the model except for education, which is treated as a covariate. Weaker correlates were identified by deciding that the significance of the F-test for their effects had to be greater than 0.20. This criteria excluded variables with less than a 10 percentage point difference between groups. Using a GLM approach in this case is intended purely to explore relationships and is not a rigorous model estimation.

When a simple model is estimated that excludes interactive effects, differences continue between groups in the rate of wrongful convictions, except for race (see table 5.5). The specific parameter values of this exploratory model are not as meaningful as the fact that most of these variables continue to be associated with wrongful conviction even after controlling for the other correlates. The relationships between the seriousness of the offense, marital status, education, Hispanic background, and wrongful conviction appear to be separate, independent effects. The stronger association of Hispanic background with a wrongful disposition could be influenced by systematic missing data on the ethnic background of offenders. For nearly 20 percent of the offenders, the data do not show whether or not they are Hispanic. The next highest correlate, education, raises questions about whether the less educated—and, presumably, the poor— are more likely to fail in their legal appeal and be convicted on retrial.

Discussion

More than 20 percent of all prisoners sentenced to death row as a result of an illegal conviction or sentence who are sent for retrial are also wrongfully convicted. Approximately 8 percent of the total number of individuals sentenced to death are subsequently found legally innocent on review. This could be as many as 500 of the more than 6,200 prisoners currently awaiting execution.

Wrongful convictions in capital cases are not a result of random chance or bad luck. Systematic differences among death row inmates who are wrongly convicted appear to be related both to the social characteristics of the offender and the seriousness of the offense for which they are convicted.

In particular, Hispanics are at much higher risk of wrongful conviction than are non-Hispanics. This may be related to the high level of poverty among Hispanics living in the United States, which may prevent them, on the whole, from being able to afford the type of legal expertise necessary to effectively investigate and defend against a capital charge. Social class and access to resources may also help explain why more highly educated defendants are more likely to be able to prove their innocence on retrial. Although the additional resources that generally come with higher levels of education do not seem to have protected these individuals from the initial wrongful conviction, they may have come into play during the retrial to support a more complete investigation and fervent defense of their case.

Finally, it is important to note that the seriousness of the offense for which the inmate initially was convicted also influences the likelihood of a wrongful conviction. Only a few of the capital convictions were for crimes other than murder. Of the convictions for these crimes that were found to be illegal and sent for retrial, a full three-fourths were determined to be wrongfully convicted. Given that murder trials tend to attract more law and more resources than do trials for less serious offenses, it is not entirely surprising that more mistakes are made and more wrongful convictions result from the trials involving these less serious crimes. This finding is particularly interesting given that the majority of wrongful conviction cases involving death row inmates that capture the national spotlight are murder cases.

Conclusion

Three conclusions seem reasonable based on these findings. First, it is clear that a significant percentage of prisoners sentenced to death are found to be legally innocent—wrongly convicted. Miscarriages of justice, then, are not rare but occur with relative frequency. There is no reason to believe that courts are any better at correcting their mistakes than they are at preventing them to begin with; therefore, it is quite possible that innocent people have been executed in the past and will be in the future, if no significant reform is forthcoming.

Second, certain types of defendants are at higher risk of being wrongfully convicted in a capital case than others are. The social structure of the case does influence the likelihood that a wrongful result will occur. These initial findings point to the need to further examine how the social characteristics of the case participants affect the risk that an innocent person will be convicted. Future studies need to examine the characteristics of other parties in the case (in addition to the defendant), the relationships among the parties, and the interaction of these social characteristics with the legal processing of the case.

Finally, further research will be needed to determine whether the risk of wrongful convictions can be reduced by reforms that have been proposed for handling capital cases, such as using lawyers certified for capital cases and reducing the time and grounds allowed for appeal. The changes that have currently been proposed do not, however, seem specifically directed to affect the possible influences identified here. This chapter reveals that the adjudication of death penalty cases is influenced, to some extent, by factors unrelated to the legal processing of the case. Until the officials in the criminal justice system realize that the death penalty (and the risk of a wrongful conviction) is distributed unequally according to the social characteristics of those involved in a case, the impact of reforms aimed at improving the legal handling of capital cases will be limited at best.

REFERENCES

Armstrong, Ken, and Steve Mills. 2000. "Ryan: 'Until I Can Be Sure' Illinois Is First State to Suspend Death Penalty." *Chicago Tribune,* 1 February. [Internet]

Bedau, Hugo Adam, and Michael L. Radelet. 1987. "Miscarriages of Justice in Potentially Capital Cases." *Stanford Law Review* 40: 21–179.

Black, Donald. 1989. *Sociological Justice.* New York: Oxford University Press.

Carrington, Frank. 1978. *Neither Cruel nor Unusual.* New Rochelle, N.Y.: Arlington House.

Death Penalty Information Center. 2000. Available at http://www.essential.org/dpic/.

Duffett, Lisa R. 1993. "Habeas Corpus and Actual Innocence of the Death Sentence after *Sawyer v. Whitley*: Another Nail into the Coffin of State Capital Defendants." *Case Western Reserve Law Review* 44: 121–56.

Fisher, Stanley Z. 1993. "'Just the Facts, Ma'am': Lying and the Omission of Exculpatory Evidence in Police Reports." *New England Law Review* 28: 1–62.

Givelber, Daniel. 1997. "Meaningless Acquittals, Meaningful Convictions: Do We Reliably Acquit the Innocent?" *Rutgers Law Review* 49: 1317–96.

Gross, Samuel R. 1987. "Loss of Innocence: Eyewitness Identification and Proof of Guilt." *Journal of Legal Studies* 16: 395–405.

———. 1996. "The Risks of Death: Why Erroneous Convictions Are Common in Capital Cases." *Buffalo Law Review* 44: 469–500.

Holmes, William M. 1999. "Illegal Convictions and Sentences to Capital Punishment." *Criminal Justice Policy Review* 10: 103–14.

Huff, C. Ronald, Arye Rattner, and Edward Sagarin. 1996. *Convicted but Innocent: Wrongful Conviction and Public Policy.* Thousand Oaks, Calif.: Sage.

Radelet, Michael L., Hugo Adam Bedau, and Constance E. Putnam. 1992. *In Spite of Innocence.* Boston: Northeastern University Press.

Rattner, Arye. 1988. "Convicted but Innocent: Wrongful Conviction and the Criminal Justice System." *Law and Human Behavior* 12: 283–93.

Tanner, Phaedra. 1994. "*Herrera v. Collins*: Assuming the Constitution Prohibits the Execution of an Innocent Person, Is the Needle Worth the Search?" *Utah Law Review* 45: 253–317.

U.S. Department of Justice, Bureau of Justice Statistics. 1993. "Capital Punishment, 1992." Washington, D.C.: U.S. Department of Justice.

———. 1997. "Capital Punishment in the United States, 1973–1995." [Computer file]. Compiled by U.S. Department of Commerce, Bureau of the Census. ICPSR ed. Ann Arbor, Mich.: Inter-university Consortium for Political and Social Research.

———. 1998. "Capital Punishment, 1997." Washington, D.C.: U.S. Department of Justice.

Zimmerman, Clifford S. 1994. "Toward a New Vision of Informants: A History of Abuses and Suggestions for Reform." *Hastings Constitutional Law Quarterly* 22: 81–178.

CASES CITED

Herrera v. Collins, 506 U.S. 390 (1993).
Sawyer v. Whitley, 505 U.S. 333 (1992).

KAREN F. PARKER
MARI A. DEWEES
MICHAEL L. RADELET

6

Racial Bias and the Conviction of the Innocent

Throughout the twentieth century, the issue of racial disparities in the criminal justice system has attracted the attention of criminologists. Scholars have studied race and ethnic differences in the frequency of criminal behavior and in arrests by police, adjudication by prosecutors, decisions by jurors, and sentencing by judges. These scholars are now beginning to turn their attention to a new avenue of research: the study of miscarriages of justice. Despite the relative recency of research into this area, ample evidence reveals that the racial and ethnic disparities found in other areas of the criminal justice system also are found among those cases in which innocent people are erroneously convicted. In this chapter, we review studies that provide evidence of the relationship between racial bias and miscarriages of justice. We follow this discussion by identifying different explanations that address why these two issues are interrelated. It is important, however, to place that discussion in a larger context by briefly reviewing the role that race and ethnicity play in the criminal justice system in general.

Racial Bias and the Criminal Justice System

Blacks compose 12.9 percent of the American population (U.S. Department of Commerce 1999: 14). Yet at the end of 1998, blacks accounted for 49.4 percent of the 1.3 million residents of American jails and prisons (U.S. Department of Justice 1999: 9). This proportion has risen slightly (from 48.6 percent in 1990), indicating that recent increases in prison populations disproportionately affect blacks. In fact, between 1990 and 1997 the number of prisoners serving sentences of more than one year increased substantially: 54 percent for white males and 61 percent for black males. Given these increases, the end of 1997 found more black males than white males in American state and federal prisons (U.S. Department of Justice 1999: 9).

This overrepresentation of blacks in U.S. prisons is partially attributable to higher rates of arrest for conventional crimes (Silberman 1978). Tonry (1995: 49), for example, found that blacks made up 44.8 percent of violent crime arrestees in 1991. In a study of 1992 arrest rates, Walker et al. (1996: 39) concluded that blacks were arrested at a rate two and a half times higher than that predicted by their representation in the general population.

Other studies found that, once arrested, black and other minority defendants fare worse in the criminal justice system than their white counterparts do. In a Los Angeles study, Spohn et al. (1987) examined prosecutors' decisions to reject or dismiss charges. Hispanic males emerged as the group with the highest rate of full prosecution (42 percent), followed by blacks (39 percent), and then white males at 26 percent. Other studies have also found racial and ethnic disparities in the area of prosecutorial discretion specifically (for example, Barnes and Kingsnorth 1996; Radelet and Pierce 1985).

Studies examining only cases of convicted felons continue to document racial disparities in sentencing; the bulk of this work has found that people of color receive more severe sentences than whites do. For example, in a study of persons arrested and charged with a single drug felony in Sacramento County, California, between 1987 and 1989, Barnes and Kingsnorth (1996) found that blacks were more likely than Hispanics and whites to receive a prison term. Additionally, among those sentenced to prison, both blacks and Hispanics served longer terms than whites did. These findings mirror those of Spohn et al. (1981–82) who, when controlling for multiple legal and extralegal variables that affect sentencing decisions, found that black males convicted of felonies had higher incarceration rates than white males did. Another key finding in the Spohn et al. study was judges' treatment of borderline cases (where the judge has the option of imposing either a lengthy probation sentence or a short prison term), in which blacks received prison terms more often than whites did. Racial disparities in sentencing have been well established in other studies as well (such as Hagan and Bumiller 1983; Kramer and Steffensmeier 1993; Spohn 1990; Spohn and Cederblom 1991).

Evidence of racial disparities also appears in the administration of the death penalty in the United States. Death sentences have always been disproportionately applied to blacks, other minorities, and the poor (Bowers 1984). While evidence of racial bias in executions has been found for as long as the death penalty has been used, particularly in rape cases (Wolfgang and Reidel 1973), researchers continue to find strong and consistent evidence of racial bias in death sentences today. In early 2000, 3,670 prisoners were on U.S. death rows; 46.3 percent were white, 42.9 percent were black, and 10.8 percent were other minorities (NAACP Legal Defense Fund 2000). Several recent studies find that race—especially the race of the victim—remains a strong predictor of who has been sentenced to death during the past twenty-five years (Baldus et al. 1990; Gross and Mauro 1989; Radelet 1981; Radelet and Pierce 1985, 1991). In a 1990 review of twenty-eight studies that examined the correlation between race and death sentencing in the United States since 1972, the U.S. General Accounting Agency (1990: 6) concluded: "the synthesis [of the twenty-eight studies reviewed] supports a strong race of victim influence. The race of offender influence is not as clear-cut and varies across a number of dimensions. Although there are limitations to the studies' methodologies, they are of sufficient quality to support the syntheses findings." These disparate rates carry over to those prisoners who enter American execution chambers. Of the 625 prisoners executed in the United States between 1976 and 1 April 2000, 35.5 percent were black, and 82 percent were executed for killing white victims (NAACP Legal Defense Fund 2000).

Race and Innocence

While there is abundant evidence of racial disparities in arrests, pretrial decisions, sentencing, and the administration of the death penalty, criminologists have given far less attention to the subject of miscarriages of justice. Nevertheless, four major studies on wrongful convictions have been published during the past fifteen years, and each shows that the racial disparities found elsewhere in the criminal justice system also appear in the conviction of the innocent.

Bedau and Radelet (1987) have assembled the most extensive data base on cases of wrongful conviction in American history. Their work compiles information on 350 cases of wrongful convictions across American jurisdictions during the twentieth century (including the year 1900): 326 cases in which the defendant was convicted of homicide, and 24 in which an innocent defendant was sentenced to death for rape. Of the 139 cases in which the defendant was wrongly sentenced to death, Bedau and Radelet (1987: 72) provide twenty-three case examples where defendants were executed despite substantial doubts about their guilt. They found that, among the 350 cases, some 40 percent involved black defendants. This finding led them to conclude that "the risk of a miscarriage of justice falls disproportionately on blacks when compared to their representation in the population, but not in comparison to their arrest rates" (39). In their subsequent publication, *In Spite of Innocence,* the inventory of cases involving wrongful conviction grew from 350 to well over 400 (Radelet et al. 1992).

Huff et al. (1996) have constructed a second data base on wrongful convictions, including 205 erroneous convictions for felonies—not solely rape and homicide cases as in the Bedau-Radelet data base. Unfortunately, Huff et al. do not give information that can be used to identify their cases, so reanalysis or replication is not possible. Nor do they report the precise racial breakdown of the wrongly convicted. Nonetheless, from their own reading of the cases, the authors find significant racial disparities: "Many convicted innocents are white, some are even middle-class, but a disproportionate number are black or Hispanic" (Huff et al. 1996: 80).

The third data base consists of the cases of eighty-seven women and men who have been released from U.S. death rows since 1970 due to doubts about their guilt. This compilation was originally assembled by Bedau and Radelet (Radelet et al. 1996), who published descriptions of sixty-eight of these cases. In their examination of these cases, they found that 45.6 percent of the defendants were white, 41.2 percent black, and 13.2 percent other minorities (963). Importantly, the proportion of blacks in this study is highly consistent with the proportion of blacks (40 percent) found by Bedau and Radelet (1987) in their earlier study of 350 wrongful convictions. These data are now regularly updated by the Death Penalty Information Center, and current figures are published on their website (Death Penalty Information Center 2000). Information generated on the eighty-seven cases in this data set in mid-2000 indicates that the proportion of minorities, specifically blacks, facing wrongful execution is growing. That is, of those released from death rows because of innocence by May 2000, forty-one of the defendants were black (47.1 percent), thirty-five were white (40.2 percent), and eleven (12.6 percent) were of other minority backgrounds (nine Latinos, one Native American, and one Jordanian).

The final data base on the wrongly convicted was complied by Barry Scheck and Peter Neufeld of the Innocence Project at Cardozo Law School (Scheck et al. 2000). While this data base is similar to the population studied by Huff et al. (1996) because these data include erroneous convictions for any type of felony, Scheck et al. focus on cases in which prisoners have been exonerated by DNA evidence (sixty-two cases in total). Of this group, their data indicate that 29 percent were white, 57 percent were black, and the racial characteristics of 3 percent were unknown (Scheck et al. 2000: 267).

It is also likely that, among those wrongly convicted of felonies, black defendants are significantly less likely than white defendants to be vindicated. Gross (1996: 497) identified three main factors that typically work in cases in which the wrongfully convicted are successful in clearing their names: the attention a wrongly convicted defendant receives from outside the prison walls, a confession by the true perpetrator, and the timely intervention of Lady Luck. These factors may correlate with race. For example, wrongly convicted white defendants and their families may be better able than their black counterparts to convince outsiders to help reinvestigate their cases. Journalists may be more sympathetic to a letter from a white prisoner alleging wrongful conviction than to a similar letter from a black prisoner. This differential access to resources that lead to vindication further exacerbates the racial differences in wrongful convictions.

Case Studies

Statistical patterns alone do not capture the painful stories of innocent defendants who have been railroaded to prison and even to death row. Nor do statistics fully depict the large role that race can play in how cases involving minorities are handled. To convey how race operates in wrongful convictions, we describe two cases in which innocent black defendants were convicted and sentenced to death.

Anthony Ray Peek

Anthony Ray Peek was on death row in Florida from 1978 until 1987, convicted of first-degree murder (Radelet et al. 1992: 337–38). The only evidence directly linking him to the crime were his fingerprints, which were found on the (white) victim's car. The conviction came despite Peek's claim that he had discovered the abandoned car the day after the murder, when he had opened the car door to look inside, and despite witnesses who supported his alibi testimony that at the time of the murder he was asleep at a nearby halfway house, where he lived. On appeal, the conviction was affirmed by the state supreme court. In 1983, the trial judge granted a new trial because an expert's testimony concerning hair identification evidence was shown to be false. In 1984 at retrial (during which the judge, in an off-the-bench comment to attorneys, referred to Peek's family as "niggers"), Peek was again convicted and sentenced to death. On appeal in 1986, the state supreme court again ordered a new trial, this time because Peek's previous conviction for an unrelated rape was inappropriately introduced at his second trial. In 1987, at his third trial, Peek was acquitted.

When the state supreme court ordered the second new trial for Peek in 1986, the justices noted that the trial judge had used the "n" word to refer to Peek's family. The court added insult to injury by stating, "Trial judges not only must be impartial in their own minds, but also must convey the image of impartiality to the parties and the public. Judges must make sure that their statements, both on and off the bench, are proper and do not convey an image of prejudice or bias to any person or any segment of the community" (*Peek v. State* 1986: 56). In short, the image was the problem, not the overt racism that the judge's comment revealed, much less the system of judicial election that allowed this judge to sit on the bench.

Clarence Lee Brandley

Clarence Lee Brandley was on death row in Texas from 1981 to 1990. He was convicted of and sentenced to death for the 1980 rape-murder of a sixteen-year-old white high school student. The murder occurred at a high school where Brandley was employed as a custodian and responsible for supervising several white co-workers. Under intense public pressure to find the killer, the police arrested Brandley on circumstantial evidence six days after the crime. An investigating police officer at the scene thought that either Brandley or a white co-worker had committed the murder and stated "One of you two is going to hang for this." And then, turning to Brandley, he added, "Since you're the nigger, you're elected" (Radelet et al. 1992: 121).

Both the grand jury that indicted Brandley and the petit jury that sat in his trial were all white. His first trial resulted in a hung jury when one juror held out for acquittal; Brandley was convicted in a second, racially charged, trial. By early 1982, evidence began to emerge suggesting police and prosecutorial misconduct. Critical hair samples and photos collected by the police were missing. Nonetheless, Brandley's conviction and death sentence were upheld on appeal in 1985.

In 1986, a woman approached the prosecutor claiming that her former husband, James D. Robinson (white), had confessed to the killing, but the prosecutor refused to act on the information. She then approached Brandley's defense lawyer. At a 1986 hearing (granted because of concerns about the missing evidence), she testified, as did one of the white janitors under Brandley's supervision. This janitor recanted his trial testimony and implicated another janitor, Gary Acreman. Despite this and additional information bearing on his innocence, Brandley's request for a new trial was denied. A new execution date was set. Public knowledge of and protest against Brandley's wrongful conviction became widespread. James McCloskey and Centurion Ministries, well known for providing investigative resources to the wrongfully convicted, became involved in the case. This led to one of the other janitors accusing both Acreman and Robinson of being the actual killers. The Department of Justice and the FBI became involved, hearings were held, and further misconduct was uncovered. Finally, in 1989 a new trial was granted. In January 1990, Brandley was released on bail, and nine months later all charges against him were dismissed. No person affiliated with the police or prosecutorial teams involved in the miscarriage was ever disciplined.

Theoretical Explanations

Why are minorities in general, and blacks in particular, disproportionately represented among those who have been wrongfully convicted in the U.S. justice system? Explanations are available at both the individual and structural levels.

Individual Explanations

Individual explanations of racial disparities in miscarriages of justice focus on the behavior and traits of both defendants and victims as well as those of officials and citizens involved in erroneous convictions. At least four overlapping and interrelated types of individual explanations can be postulated.

Racism. As in the two case studies we have presented, the disproportionate victimization of blacks in miscarriages of justice is in part a function of overtly racist behavior. This racism can be intentional, as exposed in the overt use of the "n" word, but it can also be unintentional, as when officials subconsciously discount the integrity or veracity of the defendant and those who help bolster his or her case for innocence (for example, when black alibi witnesses are discounted).

Cross-Racial Identification. Blacks are more likely to be victimized by erroneous cross-racial identification than are whites. In their research, Huff et al. (1996: 66) found that erroneous eyewitness identification (usually given in good faith) is the leading cause of erroneous convictions, although Bedau and Radelet, who studied mainly homicide cases (where, by definition, the victim is dead and cannot testify), found that the leading cause of error was perjury by prosecution witnesses (Bedau and Radelet 1987: 60–61). After reviewing research on this issue, Elizabeth Loftus (1979: 136–37), the country's leading student of eyewitness identification, concludes: "It seems to be a fact . . . that people are better at recognizing faces of persons of their own race than a different race."

Stereotyping. In the minds of many whites, people of color are more likely to conform to a criminal stereotype and hence may be at risk of being arrested and convicted on weaker evidence than whites are. One recent example of stereotyping is the case of Amadou Diallo, an unarmed immigrant from West Africa who was gunned down (by forty-one bullets) by New York City police officers on 4 February 1999. After police asked Diallo to stop, he began reaching for his wallet to produce his identification for them. The police, however, thought he was reaching for a gun and opened fire.

Another example of stereotyping can be found in the completion of the self-fulfilling prophecy. Given that blacks are overrepresented in American prison populations, we would expect a higher proportion of blacks than whites among all those arrested to have prior records of felony convictions. Prosecutors, looking at the prior record, may believe that the suspect is the type who fits the stereotype of someone who might commit further felonies and, as a result, discount evidence pointing to a different suspect or to the innocence of the accused. Or prosecutors may ignore their own doubts (no matter how slight) about the evidence in a given case, feeling that if the suspect did not commit the crime for which he or she is suspected, he or she probably committed other crimes that never came to the attention of the authorities. The prior record fits a stereotype that leads to the arrest of the individual, thereby becoming a self-fulfilling prophecy.

Easy Targets. Finally, those who are wrongly convicted are easy targets; and for a variety of reasons, blacks may be easier targets than whites. They are less likely than whites to have access to resources necessary to employ a high-quality defense attorney and other members of a defense team (such as investigators or mental health experts). They may be more likely to be transients and have no roots in the community or less likely to have contacts among established or affluent people with the power, knowledge, and energy necessary to fight an erroneous prosecution. To the extent that blacks, in part because of a relatively lower socioeconomic status, are easier targets than whites, such attributes will contribute to higher rates of wrongful conviction.

Explanations at the individual level tend to concentrate attention on characteristics of the arrested individuals and perceptions of race among jurors, judges, and prosecutors. Crutchfield et al. (1994) argued that such explanations result from a tendency to look at the trees rather than the forest. That is, most research on racial disparities in the criminal justice system only examines one point in the system, such as arrest, prosecution, juror decisions, or sentencing. In contrast, Crutchfield et al. suggest that a structural approach—which allows the racial bias in the criminal justice system to be viewed systemwide, in historical context, and in the broader context of a society in which race matters—may contribute to our understanding of the racial disparities in the criminal justice system.

Structural Explanations

Two explanations for the link between race and wrongful convictions focus on structural dimensions: Blalock's power-threat hypothesis and an urban disadvantage perspective. The first approach considers how an increase in the minority (black) population can lead to attempts among whites to limit the political and economic opportunities of blacks, which in turn leads to differential treatment in the criminal justice system. The second approach positions race in the context of urban areas—residential segregation, poverty, and other types of concentrated disadvantage—and suggests that the treatment of blacks in the criminal justice system mirrors patterns of racial discrimination in society. Overall, these explanations propose that race is built into the structure of our economic, political, and legal institutions and thus contributes to differential opportunities and treatment of racial groups within these institututions.

Blalock's Power-Threat Hypothesis. Hubert Blalock's (1967) theory of minority group relations posits that, as the relative size of the minority group increases, members of the majority group perceive a growing threat to their positions and will take steps to reduce the competition. Blalock argues that the relationship between minority populations and the motivation of the majority group to discriminate assumes two forms: competition over economic resources and power threats. Recognizing that these threats are difficult to disentangle, Blalock postulates that economically produced discrimination will be positively related to minority concentration with a decreasing slope, while discrimination as a result of perceived power threats should be positively related to minority concentration. Central to Blalock's hypothesis is that competition between racial groups causes the conflict between them (Blalock 1967; Blauner 1972; Lieberson 1980).

The idea that conflict forms between racial groups has received widespread attention and support. For example, as minority populations grew in the northern United States due to migration patterns from the south, researchers found that whites' perceptions of blacks as an economic threat flourished; as a result, whites undertook efforts to exclude blacks from better paying jobs and occupations (Blalock 1967; Lieberson 1980). Other studies continue to investigate the ways in which whites respond to the economic and political threat of blacks, whether the threat is real or perceived.

Studies have linked the power-threat hypothesis to racial disparities in income and labor market opportunities (Tienda and Lii 1987) and to the exclusionary employment practices of whites against blacks, leading to higher levels of black unemployment and underemployment (Jaynes and Williams 1989; Kasarda 1983). These studies find that minority groups face systematic exclusion from employment or are relegated to the least desirable jobs, particularly when the proportion of minorities increases (see Tienda and Lii 1987). Lichter (1988), for example, examined racial differences in economic underemployment (involuntary part-time employment and poverty-level wages) from 1970 to 1982 and found that central city black males experienced higher levels of economic underemployment than did their white counterparts, with a widening racial gap over time. Furthermore, consistent with Blalock's approach, the racial disparities in underemployment levels increased with the relative size of the black population (Tigges and Tootle 1993).

The power-threat hypothesis has also gained empirical support in the racial violence literature. In studies of the occurrence of lynching, researchers working from the power-threat perspective have found a direct relationship between the size of the minority population and the lynching rate in the south (Corzine et al. 1983, 1988; Tolnay et al. 1989). For example, Corzine et al. (1988) found that the economic threat to high-paid (white) labor within the farm tenancy system of the post–Civil War south was a strong indicator of rates of black lynching. Olzak's (1987, 1990) research on race riots provides further examples of this link, as does recent research examining the impact of economic and political competition on rates of white-on-black and black-on-white homicide (Jacobs and Wood 1999; Parker and McCall 1999). Overall, these studies suggest that whites perceive blacks as a threat to their dominant position in areas with a high proportion of blacks, thus increasing the likelihood of racial conflict and violence.

Finally, evidence supporting this hypothesis has also been found in the treatment of blacks in the criminal justice system (Myers 1990; Tolnay et al. 1992; Yates 1997). When considering the availability of poor black labor for employers, Myers (1990) found that declines in labor posed a specific threat to cotton-producing landowners, for which the accelerated incarceration of both black and white males compensated. Tolnay et al. (1992) found a link between economic competition and the frequency of legal executions of blacks in the south during two different time periods (1890–1909 and 1910–29).

With this literature in mind, we propose that the power-threat hypothesis can contribute to our understanding of the racial disparities in wrongful convictions. As a result of their economic displacement, minority groups are often unable to protect themselves (see Tienda 1989). Moreover, as some studies have documented, blacks indicate overall levels of distrust and suspicion of white intentions as well as increasing distrust in political and legal institutions that are predominantly white. As Sears and McConahay (1973: 68) state, "[Los Angeles residents] demonstrated the existence in the black community of serious grievances about police brutality, merchant exploitation, agency discrimination, poor service agency performance, local white political officials, and biases in white-managed communications media. . . . Most important, those who felt most aggrieved were exactly those who felt the conventional channels of redress were denied to them." Accordingly, we propose that the higher proportion of blacks who are wrongly convicted may be due to the fact that they are, relative to whites, less able to protect themselves both economically and politically.

Moreover, consistent with this hypothesis, because blacks are perceived as a threat to whites, they face higher conviction rates, even wrongfully, as whites respond to this perceived threat. The erroneous conviction of Clarence Brandley serves as an example in that Brandley (a black man) was supervising white janitors and hence challenging the rural east Texas status quo. This approach suggests that whites perceive blacks as challenging the status quo and implicitly threatening their power, and this belief in turn fosters erroneous convictions. In areas in which whites feel threatened by blacks, they may be more likely to retaliate in a variety of ways through the criminal justice system, such as by creating a climate that is more likely to tolerate erroneous convictions (especially as the size of the black population increases) and voting for guilt (as jurors) in cases with black defendants, even when evidence is weak.

When examining the prevalence of wrongful conviction at a structural level, future research incorporating a power-threat perspective might assess the overall economic and political climate. For example, the presence of black and minority elected officials in political positions could serve as a useful measure of political competition, while the size of the minority population and changes in unemployment rates for whites compared to blacks are possible measures of economic competition. If these measures are found to contribute to the increase in racial disparities in wrongful convictions within a given jurisdiction, researchers will be able to demonstrate support for the power-threat hypothesis; and future research on the relationship between race and wrongful conviction should investigate this possibility.

Urban Disadvantage. Although civil rights legislation made advances toward racial equality in the 1960s (for example, the Fair Housing Act of 1968), researchers continue to find strong patterns of separation, both economically and residentially, of blacks from whites in cities

throughout the United States. These studies clearly suggest that relations between racial groups are influenced by the social and ecological structure in which these groups find themselves. The racial patterns
in cases of wrongful conviction, particularly the finding that blacks
are more likely to be erroneously convicted, are crystallized under these
conditions. That is, these conditions—residential segregation, concentrated poverty, joblessness, and other forms of concentrated disadvantage—reinforce racial disparities in the treatment of minorities in the
criminal justice system, including racial bias in convictions of the
innocent.

Arguments arising primarily from William J. Wilson's seminal book,
The Declining Significance of Race (1978), have suggested that the disadvantages and racial isolation facing minority groups are primarily
due to social class. In the 1970s Wilson was among the first to recognize that poverty had become increasingly concentrated geographically.
In a later work, he (1987) said that poor areas were not only becoming increasingly poverty stricken but also growing in overall number.
Wilson also proposed that economic forces eliminated many jobs for
unskilled minorities and increased the poverty levels among them. This
joblessness was compounded by the rapid deterioration in housing,
schools, recreational facilities, and other community organizations
(Wacquant and Wilson 1989; Wilson 1991). As a result, poorly educated, low-income blacks faced a more disadvantaged residential environment than did the poor of other racial groups. "Poorer blacks are
frequently found in isolated poor urban neighborhoods, poor whites
rarely live in such neighborhoods. . . . In other words, simple comparisons between poor whites and blacks would be confounded with the
fact that poor whites reside in areas that are ecologically and economically very different from poor blacks" (Wilson 1987: 58–60). Studies
continue to find that blacks are especially likely to be segregated, spatially isolated, and poorer than other race and ethnic groups, particularly whites (Denton and Massey 1989; Massey and Denton 1988).
Analyses based on 1980 census data found that blacks remain spatially
isolated and residentially segregated from whites at all levels of economic status, while Hispanics and Asians show clear improvements
as their economic status increases (Massey and Denton 1989).

Accordingly, Massey and his colleagues conclude that black poverty is the outgrowth of persistent racial segregation in metropolitan
cities (Massey and Eggers 1990; Massey et al. 1994). Given poor blacks'
limited options for housing outside economically disadvantaged neigh-

borhoods, the result is an increase in the number of poor blacks moving into already poverty-stricken black neighborhoods. In addition, the
concentration of poverty among blacks in these racially segregated and
highly disadvantaged areas is also on the increase.

What does this literature tell us about the link between race and
miscarriages of justice? While research cited throughout this chapter
has linked race to the operations of the criminal justice system, we
suggest that urban areas where blacks face concentrated disadvantage—
extreme levels of poverty concentration, joblessness, racial isolation,
family disruption, and lack of residential mobility—are places where
the largest racial discrepancies in wrongful convictions are likely to
be found. Jurors, who are primarily white, are more likely to vote for
guilt in cases in which the evidence is weak when the defendant is
seen as "different" and "not like our families and neighbors" and segregated housing increases what we might call the social distance of
race. That is, the link between race and wrongful conviction mirrors
the vast racial disparities and disadvantages in the urban environment
in which these individuals reside. This link may be exacerbated, in
part, by the lack of resources available to minority members to protect themselves from wrongful conviction, such as the lack of highly
skilled attorneys (Bright 1997).

Conclusion

In this chapter, we have reviewed major studies that
provide data on cases of wrongful conviction. These studies offer valuable and detailed information about those who have fallen victim to
the criminal justice system—in particular, the increased risk of wrongful
convictions among blacks and Hispanics. We also offer two case studies
(from the many presented by Radelet et al. [1992]) to reflect the depth
to which race is embedded in the criminal justice system and thus
contributes to the unjust treatment of the innocent.

After a detailed review of previous studies and existing data bases,
we have found consistent evidence that blacks are more likely to be
wrongly convicted and, more specifically, that blacks form between
40 percent (Bedau and Radelet 1987) and 57 percent (Scheck et al.
2000) of the known miscarriages of justice. Given that these estimates
are derived from cases in which miscarriages of justice are eventually
discovered, it is likely that the proportion of blacks and minorities
among the wrongly convicted is even higher, especially since whites
and those with relatively more money, knowledge, power, and

connections are more likely than others to be able to marshal the resources necessary for eventual vindication.

Finally, we have proposed explanations for the racial bias in miscarriages of justice at both the individual and structural levels. Approaches at the individual level focus on how participants in the criminal justice system (court officials, jurors, witnesses, and so on) perceive race and allow the racial attributes of defendants and victims to contribute to the incidents of wrongful conviction. Structural approaches, on the other hand, propose that the effect of race is built into societal institutions (whether economic, political, or legal) and suggest that wrongful convictions are disproportionately found among minorities (particularly blacks) because they lack the political, legal, and economic resources to protect themselves. These approaches, in part, view wrongful conviction as a result of a larger problem. That is, equality in the criminal justice system is not possible until everything else is equal.

REFERENCES

Baldus, David C., George G. Woodworth, and Charles A. Pulaski, Jr. 1990. *Equal Justice and the Death Penalty: A Legal and Empirical Analysis.* Boston: Northeastern University Press.

Barnes, Carole Wolff, and Rodney Kingsnorth. 1996. "Race, Drug, and Criminal Sentencing: Hidden Effects of the Criminal Law." *Journal of Criminal Justice* 24: 39–55.

Bedau, Hugo Adam, and Michael L. Radelet. 1987. "Miscarriages of Justice in Potentially Capital Cases." *Stanford Law Review* 40: 21–179.

Blalock, Hubert M., Jr. 1967. "Status Inconsistency, Social Mobility, Status Integration and Structural Effects." *American Sociological Review* 32: 790–801.

Blauner, Robert. 1972. *Racial Oppression in America.* New York: Harper and Row.

Bowers, William J. 1984. *Legal Homicide: Death As Punishment in America, 1864–1982.* Boston: Northeastern University Press.

Bright, Stephen B. 1997. "Neither Equal nor Just: The Rationing and Denial of Legal Services to the Poor When Life and Liberty Are at Stake." *Annual Survey of American Law* 4: 783–836.

Corzine, Jay, Lin Huff-Corzine, and James C. Creech. 1988. "The Tenant Labor Market and Lynching in the South: A Test of Split Labor Market Theory." *Sociological Inquiry* 58: 261–78.

Corzine, Jay, James Creech, and Lin Corzine. 1983. "Black Concentration and Lynching in the South: Testing Blalock's Power-Threat Hypothesis." *Social Forces* 61: 774–96.

Crutchfield, Robert D., George S. Bridges, and Susan R. Pitchford. 1994. "Analytical and Aggregation Bias in Analysis of Imprisonment: Reconciling Discrepancies in Studies of Racial Disparity." *Journal of Research in Crime and Delinquency* 31: 166–82.

Death Penalty Information Center. 2000. Available at http:/www.essential.org/dpic/.

Denton, Nancy A., and Douglas S. Massey. 1989. "Racial Identity among Caribbean Hispanics: The Effects of Double Minority Status on Racial Segregation." *American Sociological Review* 54: 790–808.

Gross, Samuel R. 1996. "The Risks of Death: Why Erroneous Convictions Are Common in Capital Cases." *Buffalo Law Review* 44: 469–500.

Gross, Samuel R., and Robert Mauro. 1989. *Death and Discrimination: Racial Disparities in Capital Sentencing.* Boston: Northeastern University Press.

Hagan, John, and Kristin Bumiller. 1983. "Making Sense of Sentencing: A Review and Critique of Sentencing Research." In *Research on Sentencing: The Search for Reform,* vol. 2, edited by Alfred Blumstein, Jacqueline Cohen, Susan E. Martin, and Michael H. Tonry, 1–54. Washington, D.C.: National Academy Press.

Huff, C. Ronald, Arye Rattner, and Edward Sagarin. 1996. *Convicted but Innocent: Wrongful Conviction and Public Policy.* Thousand Oaks, Calif.: Sage.

Jacobs, David, and Katherine Wood. 1999. "Interracial Conflict and Interracial Homicide: Do Political and Economic Rivalries Explain White Killings of Blacks or Black Killings of Whites?" *American Journal of Sociology* 105: 157–90.

Jaynes, Gerald D., and Robin M. Williams, Jr. 1989. *A Common Destiny: Blacks and American Society.* Washington, D.C.: National Academy Press.

Kasarda, John D. 1983. "Entry-Level Jobs, Mobility, and Urban Minority Unemployment." *Urban Affairs Quarterly* 19: 21–40.

Kramer, John, and Darrell Steffensmeier. 1993. "Race and Imprisonment Decisions." *Sociological Quarterly* 34: 357–76.

Lichter, Daniel T. 1988. "Racial Differences in Underemployment in American Cities." *American Journal of Sociology* 93: 771–92.

Lieberson, Stanley. 1980. *A Piece of the Pie: Blacks and White Immigrants Since 1880.* Berkeley: University of California Press.

Loftus, Elizabeth F. 1979. *Eyewitness Testimony.* Cambridge: Harvard University Press.

Massey, Douglas S., and Nancy Denton. 1988. "The Dimensions of Residential Segregation." *Social Forces* 67: 281–315.

———. 1989. "Hypersegregation in U.S. Metropolitan Areas: Black and Hispanic Segregation along Five Dimensions." *Demography* 26: 373–91.

Massey, Douglas S., and Mitchell L. Eggers. 1990. "The Ecology of Inequality: Minorities and the Concentration of Poverty, 1970–1980." *American Journal of Sociology* 95: 1153–88.

Massey, Douglas S., Andrew B. Gross, and Kumiko Shibuya. 1994. "Migration, Segregation, and the Geographic Concentration of Poverty." *American Sociological Review* 59: 425–45.

Myers, Martha A. 1990. "Black Threat and Incarceration in Postbellum Georgia." *Social Forces* 69: 373–93.

NAACP Legal Defense Fund. 2000. "Death Row, USA." New York: NAACP Legal Defense Fund, 1 April.

Olzak, Susan. 1987. "Causes of Ethnic Conflict and Protest in Urban America, 1877–1889." *Social Science Research* 16: 185–210.

———. 1990. "The Political Context of Competition: Lynching and Urban Racial Violence." *Social Forces* 69: 395–421.

Parker, Karen F., and Patricia L. McCall. 1999. "Structural Conditions and Racial

Homicide Patterns: A Look at the Multiple Disadvantages in Urban Areas."
Criminology 37: 447–78.

Radelet, Michael L. 1981. "Racial Characteristics and the Imposition of the Death Penalty." *American Sociological Review* 46: 918–27.

Radelet, Michael L., and Glenn L. Pierce. 1985. "Race and Prosecutorial Discretion in Homicide Cases." *Law and Society Review* 19: 587–621.

———. 1991. "Choosing Those Who Will Die: Race and the Death Penalty in Florida." *Florida Law Review* 43: 1–34.

Radelet, Michael L., Hugo Adam Bedau, and Constance E. Putnam. 1992. *In Spite of Innocence*. Boston: Northeastern University Press.

Radelet, Michael L., William S. Lofquist, and Hugo Adam Bedau. 1996. "Prisoners Released from Death Rows Since 1970 Because of Doubts about Their Guilt." *Thomas M. Cooley Law Review* 13: 907–66.

Scheck, Barry, Peter Neufield, and Jim Dwyer. 2000. *Actual Innocence*. New York: Doubleday.

Sears, David O., and John B. McConahay. 1973. *The Politics of Violence: The New Urban Black and the Watts Riot*. Boston: Houghton Mifflin.

Silberman, Charles E. 1978. *Criminal Violence, Criminal Justice*. New York: Random House.

Spohn, Cassia. 1990. "The Sentencing Decisions of Black and White Judges: Expected and Unexpected Similarities." *Law and Society Review* 24: 1197–1216.

Spohn, Cassia, and Jerry Cederblom. 1991. "Race and Disparities in Sentencing: A Test of the Liberation Hypothesis." *Justice Quarterly* 8: 305–27.

Spohn, Cassia, John Gruhl, and Susan Welch. 1981–82. "The Effect of Race on Sentencing: A Re-examination of an Unsettled Question." *Law and Society Review* 16: 71–88.

———. 1987. "The Impact of the Ethnicity and Gender of Defendants on the Decision to Reject or Dismiss Felony Charges." *Criminology* 25: 175–91.

Tienda, Marta. 1989. "Race, Ethnicity and the Portrait of Inequality: Approaching the 1990s." *Sociological Spectrum* 9: 23–52.

Tienda, Marta, and Ding-Tzann Lii. 1987. "Minority Concentration and Earnings Inequality: Blacks, Hispanics, and Asians Compared." *American Journal of Sociology* 93: 141–65.

Tigges, Leann M., and Deborah M. Tootle. 1993. "Underemployment and Racial Competition in Local Labor Markets." *Sociological Quarterly* 34: 279–98.

Tolnay, Stewart E., E. M. Beck, and James L. Massey. 1989. "Black Lynchings: The Power Threat Hypothesis Revisited." *Social Forces* 67: 605–23.

———. 1992. "Black Competition and White Vengeance: Legal Execution of Blacks As Social Control in the Cotton South, 1890–1929." *Social Science Quarterly* 73: 627–44.

Tonry, Michael H. 1995. *Malign Neglect*. New York: Oxford University Press.

U.S. Department of Commerce, Bureau of the Census. 1999. *Statistical Abstract of the United States*. Washington, D.C.: U.S. Department of Commerce.

U.S. Department of Justice, Bureau of Justice Statistics. 1999. "Prisoners in 1998." Washington, D.C.: U.S. Department of Justice.

U.S. General Accounting Agency. 1990. *Death Penalty Sentencing: Research Indicates Pattern of Racial Disparities* (GGD-90–57). Washington, D.C.: U.S. General Accounting Agency.

Wacquant, Loic J. D., and William J. Wilson. 1989. "The Cost of Racial and

Class Exclusion in the Inner City." *Annals of the American Academy of Political and Social Science* 501: 8–25.

Walker, Samuel, Cassia Spohn, and Miriam DeLone. 1996. *The Color of Justice: Race, Ethnicity, and Crime in America.* Belmont, Calif.: Wadsworth.

Wilson, William J. 1978. *The Declining Significance of Race.* Chicago: University of Chicago Press.

———. 1987. *The Truly Disadvantaged: The Inner City, the Underclass, and Public Policy.* Chicago: University of Chicago Press.

———. 1991. "Studying Inner-City Social Dislocations: The Challenge of Public Agenda Research." *American Sociological Review* 56: 1–14.

Wolfgang, Marvin E., and Marc Reidel. 1973. "Race, Judicial Discretion, and the Death Penalty." *Annals of the American Academy of Political and Social Science* 407: 119–33.

Yates, Jeff. 1997. "Racial Incarceration Disparity among States." *Social Science Quarterly* 78: 1001–10.

CASES CITED

Peek v. State, 488 So.2d 52 (1986).

The Faces of the Wrongly Convicted:

Case Studies

MARGARET VANDIVER

7 More Than a Reasonable Doubt

The Trial and Execution of Frank Ewing

The state of Tennessee executed Frank Ewing for rape on 21 May 1919. Ewing had been identified by the victim of the crime; her identification, however, was contradicted by substantial evidence that Ewing was working at a farm some twenty-five miles away when the crime was committed. Although it is not possible, eighty years later, to establish absolutely whether Ewing was innocent or guilty of the crime for which he was executed, a reconstruction of his case reveals more than a reasonable doubt of his guilt.

A mentally impaired black man, Ewing was identified as the perpetrator by a white female victim and was prosecuted, tried, and convicted by a white criminal justice system. Ewing's case appears to suffer from several of the problems commonly noted in contemporary wrongful conviction cases: an overreliance on eyewitness testimony (especially cross-racial eyewitness testimony), a pressured confession from the suspect, and the operation of racial stereotypes and bias. The Ewing case reveals how historically rooted and systemic are the flaws in our system of justice—flaws that can and have led to the conviction and execution of innocent people (see Radelet et al. 1992). To prevent such failures of justice in the future, it is essential to recognize their existence in our past and to examine how they happened.

The Ewing Case in Context

Frank Ewing was one of 125 men executed by the state of Tennessee between 1916 and 1960. Of the ninety men executed for murder, fifty-seven (63 percent) were black; thirty-five men were executed for rape, of whom twenty-nine (83 percent) were black (Bowers 1984: 502–5). In 1915, Tennessee briefly abolished the death penalty for murder, except when committed by a prisoner, but retained capital punishment for rape. The death penalty for murder was reinstated in 1919 (Galliher et al. 1992; White 1965).

During the early twentieth century, there was extreme concern about the rape of white women by black men.[1] Given prevailing racial attitudes, it is not surprising that a white woman's identification of a black man as her attacker outweighed evidence that he had been elsewhere at the time of the crime. What is unusual in Ewing's case is that he had the strong support of alibi witnesses, most of them white, and received concerned legal representation both at trial and on appeal. While the efforts of Ewing's lawyer and witnesses were not enough to save his life, the unusually careful judicial and executive attention he received built a record from which it is possible to reconstruct many of the details of the case.[2]

The Crime and Ewing's Arrest

Frank Ewing was about twenty years old in 1918, when the crime occurred. He lived in Nashville with his mother, Josephine (Josie) Ewing, and his brother, Robert. Ewing had exhibited mental deficiencies all his life (*State v. Ewing* 1918b: 37).

AF, the rape victim, lived a few miles south of Nashville, on Stokes Lane, west of Hillsboro Pike.[3] She and her husband had no children and lived alone in a house set back from Stokes Lane, out of sight of other houses. AF was twenty-five years old at the time of the crime. Her trial testimony indicated that on Monday, 24 June 1918, she was at home alone while her husband worked on a farm he rented, located about three miles from their house (*State v. Ewing* 1918b: 17–19). She testified that at about one o'clock in the afternoon she left the garden where she had been working and went into the house to eat lunch. About an hour later she heard her dogs barking and went out to quiet them. A black man was at her gate, holding a piece of paper in his hand. The man told AF he had a note he could not read and asked her to read it to him. As she took the paper from him, he grabbed her neck with his left hand and showed her a knife that he held in his right hand. He threatened to kill her, forced her into the house, and raped her. Before leaving, he made her promise not to tell what he had done.

When the attacker was out of sight, AF ran to the home of her nearest neighbors, Dr. and Mrs. Bogle. Mrs. Bogle was home at the time. AF was at first too upset to speak. When she had recovered enough to explain what had happened, Mrs. Bogle drove her to the farm where her husband, JF, was working. JF came back with the women and called the police. Later that afternoon, he took his wife to a doctor.

The testimonies of JF and Mrs. Bogle were consistent with the victim's. Mrs. Bogle testified that AF arrived at her house between two and three o'clock, "coming in the back way. She was so excited that for a while she could not talk. Her hair was disheveled and there were bruises or marks on her neck like she had been choked. There was a small scratch on one side of her neck that had bled a little. She was very nervous" (*State v. Ewing* 1918b: 20). JF testified that it was "about two or three o'clock on the 24th day of June" when his wife and Mrs. Bogle arrived at the farm where he was working "and informed me of an assault that had been made upon my wife about an hour previous by a negro brute" (*State v. Ewing* 1918b: 15).

Constable George W. Carter testified that he arrived at the F house about four o'clock on the afternoon of the crime. "Mrs. [F] was very nervous and excited. There were red marks like finger prints on her neck and a slight scratch on one side of her neck. The odor of the negro was still distinct in the front room of the house. The bed was in the south west corner of the front room and the bed showed that it had been lain upon, a dent like a man's knee was noticeable also." Carter testified that bloodhounds were able to follow the attacker's trail east on Stokes Lane but lost it at the Hillsboro Pike (*State v. Ewing* 1918b: 25).

Police "exert[ed] every effort" to find the attacker ("White Woman Victim," 1918: 11). Despite the confident assertion of the *Nashville Banner* ("Negro Assailant," 1918: 5) that "every avenue of escape is now blocked" and "the assailant will be apprehended before night," no one was arrested immediately for the crime. Ewing was arrested some time later on an unrelated charge of stealing a cow in West Nashville. Deputy sheriff Lewis Camp took Ewing from the Nashville jail to the F home.

We drove slowly out through the city and then out the Hillsboro Pike. I had gotten a couple of sandwiches. I asked Ewing . . . if he was hungry, He said he was and I gave him the two sandiwches [*sic*] to eat. He began to eat them like he was very hungry. . . . When the car turned into the lane [leading to the F home] Ewing suddenly choked up and quit eating and seemed distressed. . . . Mr. and Mrs. [F] were standing on the porch watching Ewing and me as we came toward the house from the lane. Mrs. [F] . . . looked at Ewing carefully and said "that is the man, he is the right one, I know his face and his walk." Ewing spoke up and denied being the right man and Mrs. [F] said "You are, I know you [*sic*] voice also." (*State v. Ewing* 1918b: 22–23)

A few days later AF picked Ewing out of a six or seven man lineup at the jail (*State v. Ewing* 1918b: 23).

Evaluating the Evidence
The Case against Ewing

By far the most important piece of evidence against Ewing was the victim's identification of him as her assailant. In her trial testimony, AF described her identification:

The officers at different times later on brought out four or five men for me to identify but I did not do so as I knew they were not the right negro soon as defendant Ewing was brought I recognized him and told my husband I was certain that he was the guilty one. I am positive that he is the man. I examined him closely as he was leaving in order that I might make no mistake. As the officers were approaching the house from the road with the defendant I was standing on the porch with my husband. As the negro approached I recognized him as the man who had ravished me, I knew his rolling walk and his face and general appearance. . . . Some time after I identified the defendant when he was brought out to my home, I went to the jail and picked him out instantly from among a number of negro men. (*State v. Ewing* 1918b: 18–19)

Evidence against Ewing was given by several law enforcement officers as well. Deputy Camp testified about Ewing's behavior when he took him to the F house for identification. In addition, Constable Carter testified:

> After the defendant Ewing was under arrest and in jail I went to his cell in company with Mr. J. B. Miller. I talked to Ewing and asked him to tell the truth about the matter. Ewing denied that he was the man who ravished Mrs. [F]. I asked hum [*sic*] if he knew how the furniture was arranged in that front room and in which corner the bed was situated. He told me that the bed was in the corner away from the door and next to the road. This was the right location for the bed, it being in the south west corner of the room. I asked him if he not not [*sic*] rape Mrs. [F] on that bed. I told him that he ought to tell the truth about it. I did not threaten or abuse him in any way, nor did Mr. Miller or any one else. He then admitted that he ravished Mrs. [F]. (*State v. Ewing* 1918b: 25–26)

John B. Miller, a jailer who accompanied Carter, testified that Ewing at first denied guilt until Miller "told him that he knew that Mrs. [F] had stated that he was the guilty man, and that he had better tell all he knew about the matter. Thereupon Defendant admitted to witness that he was the guolty [*sic*] man. . . . [Ewing told] his movements and all that happened at the home of Mrs. [F] and made a complete confession" (*State v. Ewing* 1918b: 28).

Ewing's Alibi

Although Ewing had strong evidence to support his alibi, the presentation of the alibi at his trial was very weak. Ewing himself made a poor witness (Neil 1919b) and was unable to provide much assistance to his lawyer (West 1919a). The testimony of the most important defense witness, J. M. Summers, was greatly weakened by the circumstances described in the section on Ewing's trial and appeal. Mrs. Summers, whose testimony would have been at least as important as her husband's, was not called as a witness at trial. She finally submitted a handwritten affidavit to the governor, A. H. Roberts, one day before the execution. Another important alibi witness, Robert Taylor, had joined the army and was unavailable to testify at trial (West 1919a). The following is a summary of what is known of Ewing's whereabouts before, during, and after the crime as reconstructed from the available records, primarily trial testimony.

Saturday, 22 June, and Sunday, 23 June 1918. John Douglas, a black man who lived near Hendersonville, testified that Frank Ewing came to his house on Saturday, 22 June, and went to church and Sunday school with the family the next day. Ewing stayed at the Douglas house on Saturday and Sunday nights and left Monday morning to go to Hendersonville to look for work. Douglas said that he remembered the precise dates because his wife was in Nashville on Saturday, 22 June, consulting a doctor. Her visit to the doctor was confirmed by the doctor's records (*State v. Ewing* 1918b: 39–40).

Monday, 24 June. At about ten o'clock in the morning, J. M. Summers saw Frank Ewing sitting on the steps of a store in Hendersonville. Summers was a local farmer, a notary public, and a justice of the peace who had come into town to pick up Robert Taylor, a white man who was working for him. Summers asked Ewing if he was looking for work and took him along with Taylor back to his farm. Once there, Summers asked Ewing to plow corn, but Ewing was unable to do the work. "Defendant had not gone more than 15 or 20 steps before he began plowing up the corn instead of between the rows and witness thereupon in an effort to teach him to plow plowed one round with the mule for him explaining how he should do the work. Defendant, however, was not capable of plowing" (*State v. Ewing* 1918b: 42). Summers recalled in his testimony that Ewing attempted to do the plowing using a mule that was owned by Zebb Dunn. Dunn was not there to do the plowing that week because he was ill (*State v. Ewing* 1918b: 44).

Seeing that Ewing was a failure at plowing, Summers told him to cut weeds. Mr. Summers then went to another part of the farm, and his wife took over supervising Ewing. In her affidavit, Mrs. Summers wrote that she saw "he was ignorant [and] I took the blade and tried to show him how to cut the weeds and still he couldn't do the work satisfactory." At 11:30, the workers ate lunch in Mrs. Summers's kitchen. Frank Ewing ate with Albert Brown and Bud White, whom Mrs. Summers described in her affidavit as "two other small colored boys." After lunch, Frank Ewing and the other two workers were given hoes and sent out to chop weeds "in a smal [*sic*] corn field near the house . . . where I saw him at work all that afternoon" (Summers 1919). The rape of AF occurred south of Nashville, some twenty-five miles away, between two and three o'clock in the afternoon on 24 June.

Tuesday, 25 June, and Wednesday, 26 June. Frank Ewing remained on the Summerses' farm and worked all day Tuesday and then until three or four o'clock on Wednesday afternoon. Mrs. Summers swore in her affidavit that Ewing worked on 24, 25, and 26 June until three or four o'clock: "Then Mr. Summers said to me that he was so ignorant that he was going to pay him and let him go—for he could not use him to any advantage." Mr. Summers paid Ewing his wages, recording the amount and date in his record book, and Ewing "left going out towards Hendersonville" (Summers 1919). Wednesday evening at about dark James McClaud, section foreman for the L & N Railroad, saw Ewing coming along the railroad track in or near Hendersonville. He offered to hire Ewing and paid him in advance an order for one dollar that he could use to buy food (*State v. Ewing* 1918b: 30). Ewing took the order to the grocery in Hendersonville, where R. S. Baker filled it (*State v. Ewing* 1918b: 32).

Thursday, 27 June. Ewing worked all day for McClaud. At the end of the day, McClaud paid him the balance for his work, minus the one dollar advance. McClaud testified that Ewing did not show up for work on Friday (*State v. Ewing* 1918b: 30).

Friday, 28 June, through Monday, 1 July. Walter Pierce, a farmer near Hendersonville, testified for the state that on Friday, 28 June, Ewing came to his farm and worked that day and the next, that "he was trifling and not worth more than his feed." Pierce paid Ewing on Saturday, but Ewing stayed on the farm, eating there, until Monday morning, when Pierce told him to leave (*State v. Ewing* 1918b: 33).

Comparing Claims

The date, time, and place of the attack on AF were definitely established and never disputed. The state and defense disagreed only on Frank Ewing's alibi. Four interpretations of events could support a conclusion that Ewing was guilty of the rape of AF. The simplest and most plausible is the argument that he was not at the Summerses' farm the afternoon of Monday, 24 June, 1918. To reach this conclusion, however, one would have to argue that the dates in the Summerses' record book were incorrect or forged; that both Mr. and Mrs. Summers's memories of the dates were incorrect; that either the dates on Robert Taylor's checks were incorrect or the Summerses' memory of Ewing's arrival during the second week of Taylor's employment was incorrect; and that the testimonies of Albert Brown, John Douglas, Zebb Dunn, James McClaud, R. S. Baker, and Walter Pierce were either incorrect or irrelevant.

Alternatively, one could believe that Ewing was at the farm on 24 June but somehow slipped away from Mrs. Summers's supervision for several hours, stole or borrowed a car, drove twenty-five miles, committed a rape, drove back, returned the car so that its absence was never noted, and resumed his work. Moreover, one must believe that no one noticed his absence or anything odd in his behavior when he returned. Given the unanimous observations of Ewing's limited mental abilities, this possibility can be dismissed as too improbable to deserve serious consideration. A third and thoroughly far-fetched explanation would be that the person who worked for the Summers on 24 June was not Frank Ewing but was pretending to be Frank Ewing, was paid under his name, and so closely resembled Ewing that no one noticed the difference between him and the person on trial. A final explanation, also far-fetched, is that the Summers conspired to conceal Ewing's guilt, forging payroll records and committing perjury to protect a farmworker they barely knew and had dismissed for incompetence.

To conclude that Frank Ewing did *not* rape AF, it is necessary to believe that her confident identification of him as her attacker was incorrect despite the fact that she saw her assailant in broad daylight, reported looking at him carefully, dismissed as incorrect the first four or five suspects brought to her house, and identified Ewing again in a lineup. It is also necessary to question the validity of the confessions that law enforcement officers reported receiving from Ewing.

Ewing's Trial and Appeal

The grand jury met on 22 July 1918 and returned a bill of indictment against Frank Ewing the next day. On 30 July, Ewing pled not guilty, and jurors were selected. The trial was held Wednesday, 31 July, and lasted one day. Ewing was represented at trial by Richard S. West, and the presiding judge was A. B. Neil.

Unfortunately for Frank Ewing, the testimony at trial concerning his alibi was not clear and straightforward. On the morning of the trial, Mr. Summers could not find the memorandum book in which he kept the records of his employees' work dates and what he paid them. Thinking that his testimony and check records for the payment of Robert L. Taylor would suffice, Mr. Summers went to the trial without his memorandum book (*State v. Ewing* 1918b: 48). The check stubs indicated that Summers had paid Robert L. Taylor on Saturday, 22 June, and Saturday, 29 June, 1918. This was consistent with Summers's testimony that Robert Taylor had worked for him for two weeks and that Ewing had come to work on the second Monday of Taylor's employment: that is, Monday, 24 June, the day of the crime. Taylor himself was not available to testify because he had recently joined the army (West 1919a).

According to his trial testimony, Mr. Summers saw Ewing in Hendersonville on the morning of Monday, 24 June, asked him if he were seeking work, and then took him to his farm. Mr. Summers recounted his failed attempt to teach Ewing to plow and testified that he then had Ewing hoe corn and cut weeds. Mr. Summers's memory of the number of days that Ewing had worked for him, however, was incorrect. Summers recalled at trial that Ewing had worked for him the whole week of 24 June: "Witness was positive that defendant worked all of that week from Monday June 24th for him and that he paid him about $3.00 in money when he quit work. While he had a memorandum of the exact amount it had been mislaid and he was unable to put his hands upon it just at the time of this trial" (*State v. Ewing* 1918b: 42).

When the state confronted Summers with the testimony and records of McClaud, Baker, and Pierce as to their contacts with Frank Ewing on Wednesday, Thursday, and Friday of that week, Summers could only say that their records were false (*State v. Ewing* 1918b: 42–43). It is not surprising that the jury accepted the three men's testimony as correct. And since their testimony as to Ewing's whereabouts late in the week contradicted what Summers said, it is not surprising that the jury disregarded Summers's testimony that Ewing was working for him on the day of the crime. It is important to note, however, that no testimony except the victim's contradicted Summers's assertion that Ewing was on his farm working for him on the day and at the time that the crime was committed.

The jury returned a verdict of guilty, and Ewing's attorney immediately filed a motion for a new trial. In a hearing on 10 August, Judge Neil heard testimony on the motion for new trial from J. M. Summers and Albert Brown, who worked for Summers. After the trial, Summers had found his misplaced memorandum book in the pocket of his old coat. Reading it, he discovered that Ewing had indeed been working for him on the day of the crime but that he had left his employment late in the day on Wednesday, 26 June, rather than at the end of the week as Summers had testified. The memorandum book recorded that Ewing had been paid a total of $2.75 for his work and confirmed the dates of payment to Robert Taylor for his two weeks of work (*State v. Ewing* 1918b: 47). Albert Brown also testified in support of the motion for a new trial. He did not know the date of the day that Ewing came to work but did recall that it was a Monday morning and that Ewing came to the farm in a car with Summers and Taylor (*State v. Ewing* 1918b: 49).

The testimony of the three state witnesses, McClaud, Baker, and Pierce, is therefore perfectly consistent with J. M. Summers's written records of Ewing's employment on his farm. Their testimony places Ewing in the Hendersonville area working and looking for work at just the time Summers released him from his employment. In his brief for the Tennessee Supreme Court, Ewing's lawyer Richard West noted:

> The fact that Esquire Summers was mistaken as shown by his memorandum book when he testified in the former trial that he thought the Defendant worked all of that week for him, does not in any way break down his testimony as to the fact that the Defendant Ewing did work for him Monday, Tuesday and Wednesday of that week. In fact his memorandum record offered on motion for a new trial showed that Defendant quit his employment on Wednesday evening, June 26th, and went to the Railroad as testified by the Section Foreman and the Merchant at Hendersonville, who testified for the State. . . . [their testimony] strengthens Esquire Summers's testimony and makes it absolute and conclusive upon the proposition of where Defendant was and what he was doing on Monday, June 24th. (*State v. Ewing* 1918a: 6)

Judge Neil ruled against the defendant on the motion for a new trial and scheduled Ewing's execution for 14 October 1918; however, he granted the defense motion to allow an appeal to the Tennessee Supreme Court, and the execution date was postponed. West's brief to the Tennessee Supreme Court, filed 19 August, mentioned Ewing's mental condition but laid much greater stress on his alibi evidence:

> It is shown conclusively by the proof in the record by disinterested witnesses of unimpeachable character that on this day towit [*sic*]—June 24, 1918, the Defendant was employed by Esquire J. M. Summers. . . . it would have been utterly impos-

sible for him to have committed the crime with which he is charged at a point about twenty-five miles distant, regardless of the positive identification of the lady assaulted and regardless of any alleged confession. . . . And to set aside this alibi and sustain the conviction in this case it could only be done in an absolute disregard of testimony which seems beyond a shadow of doubt to be absolutely accurate, certain and true. (*State v. Ewing* 1918a: 2, 5, 7)

The state's brief argued that Ewing's trial testimony "furnishes every evidence of his shrewdness and cunning" (*Frank Ewing, Colored v. State* 1918: 10). The state first dismissed J. M. Summers's testimony on the motion for new trial by arguing that he must have confused the date of Ewing's employment by one week and then alleged that Summers might have been "willing to fabricate evidence for the purpose of making his former testimony coincide with the testimony which had been given by the State's witnesses" (*Frank Ewing, Colored v. State* 1918: 12–13, 15). The Tennessee Supreme Court upheld Ewing's conviction and sentence and set 7 May as the date of his execution.

Final Efforts on Ewing's Behalf

Even after the court's ruling, substantial efforts were made to save Ewing's life. Attorney Richard West appealed to Governor Roberts to grant executive clemency in the case, arguing both Ewing's mental condition and his alibi evidence. Summers continued his efforts on Ewing's behalf, perhaps feeling that his mistakes during his testimony at trial had contributed to the conviction. He spoke with Ewing's attorney and offered to go and talk to the governor about the case, if the governor wished to see him (West 1919b). Summers also spoke twice with A. B. Neil, the trial judge, who wrote to the governor: "Esquire Summers . . . has some additional corroborating evidence which he wants to submit in behalf of Ewing—and I think he ought to be granted the opportunity to present it. I will say furthermore that Esq. Summers is a splendid man. He is thoroughly convinced that Ewing is innocent, notwithstanding the positive identification of Ewing by the prosecutrix" (Neil 1919a). After a second visit from Summers, Judge Neil wrote to the governor: "Esq. Summers, who is a mighty good citizen, is convinced that this man is not guilty—He has interested himself in the negros [*sic*] behalf because of this belief, and this alone." Judge Neil, however, stated that he had given Ewing "as fair a trial as I knew how" and had no recommendation to make as to whether clemency should be granted (Neil 1919b). Governor Roberts granted Frank Ewing a reprieve on 1 May, postponing the date of execution for two weeks to have time to consider whether to grant clemency ("Condemned Negro," 1919: 5).

The Issue of Ewing's Mental Condition

Although the question of Ewing's guilt was most important, his mental condition also raised concern. Everyone involved in the case recognized that Ewing's level of intelligence was low. His mother, friends, and neighbors noted that his condition had existed even in childhood. An undated petition from "neighbors and friends of Frank Ewing" requested that the governor grant him clemency "for the reason that he is and has been since childhood considered by all of his neighbors and friends to be a weak-minded, half-witted, cracked brain child" ("In the Matter of Pardon," 1919). Ewing's mother testified that her son was a "vwry [sic] illiterate boy and is weak mentallu [sic] and had suffered from his youth by reason of risings in his head, that physicians had not been able to cure. . . . he was easily lead [sic] to make any kind of statement that any person wanted him to make either for or against himself, and that he had been in this condition all his life" (State v. Ewing 1918b: 37). Both Mr. and Mrs. Summers described Frank Ewing's failures as a hired hand because of his inability to perform even the simplest farm work (State v. Ewing 1918b: 42; Summers affidavit 1919). Judge Neil wrote in a letter to the governor: "I regarded him [Frank Ewing] as a man of very low order of intellect" (Neil 1919b).

The governor apparently was concerned to know more about Ewing's mental condition. At his request, Dr. Thomas H. Haines, an alienist (a doctor who treats mental disorders), examined Ewing in the Davidson County Jail on 22 March 1919. Excerpts from Haines's report follow:

> The boy is short and stout. He looks about 20 years of age. His head is small. He has a shuffling gait. He appears to be in good physical condition. He shows himself possessed of more intelligence than his appearance leads one to expect, when he is engaged in conversation.
>
> His memory of events is imperfect. He says he worked for Mr. Summers a month at $2.25 a day. Mr. Summers, after he found his account book, testified in Criminal Court for the

defense that Ewing worked for him three days in June 1918 and the total wages he paid him was \$2.75. . . .

The boy is illeterate [*sic*]. He can write his own first name. But to write Ewing he had to bring out of his pocket a piece of paper on which someone else had written his name. . . .

Of the five absurdities of the Stanford Intelligence Scale for *ten* years, he saw through only one, the body of the girl cut into 18 pieces whom the police thought had killed herself. A ten year old should get four out of the five correct. These tests afford an excellent opportunity for the illiterate and the dullard, who are not feeble-minded to exhibit their native intelligence. Ewing did not seem to have much to exhibit. Likewise on the comprehension questions, he does well on the eight-year level, but cannot cope with the questions for ten-year olds.

Frank Ewing's mental age is about that of an eight year old white child, as reckoned by the Stanford Binet Scale. He did most of the things expected of six, seven, and eight-year olds, so far as they were tried on him. He was tried on nine different tests for nine and ten-year olds, and failed on every one of them.

Making some allowance for the backwardness of his race, it might be reasonable to consider him as of the average intelligence of an eight-and-a-half year old. He is unquestionably of less than medium moron intelligence. It is unreasonable to expect such a child in mind to hew out a course for himself in the complexities of modern life, and have that course of conduct satisfactory to the rest of us.

With this lack of common sense and ability to learn this boy is *crafty and cunning*. . . . The boy cannot be reformed by punishment. He has too little sense. Looking at the situation in a cold logical way, Ewing's life is not of much economic value. He must be kept in custody, all of his life, for the protection of society. From the humanitarian point of view we must recognize it is not a square deal to electrocute one for a crime which his limitation of intelligence makes him unable to understand is anti-social. (Haines 1919)

The governor, however, was not persuaded by Haines's argument for life in prison. On 17 May, he announced his decision to deny clemency and let the execution proceed:

It was represented to the Governor that this young man who is about 21 yrs. of age is too weak mentally to be held responsible for his act, at least that his mentality is so deficient that he should not be executed. The Governor stated that he had had an alienist to make a thorough examination of the man, himself, that he in person had also tested the prisoner's intelligence so far as he was able to do as a non-expert, and that while the prisoner is illiterate and is not of a high order of intelligence, he is crafty, cunning and possesses certain shrewdness which is usually found in the dangerous criminal. The Governor believes he is thoroughly responsible for his act and hence he has stated will not interfere with the judgment of the Supreme Court pronounced in the case, *unless additional evidence is submitted.* (Roberts, n.d.)

Governor Roberts ignored Haines's repeated assertions that Ewing was too deficient mentally to be held responsible but picked up on Haines's remark that he was "crafty and cunning." The governor justified his decision to deny clemency by invoking the "majesty" of the law and referred to enforcement of the law as the "most certain remedy against the disease of mob violence which is too prevalent in this country . . . even to the extent of taking of human life when the interest of society and the ends of justice require it" ("Ewing Electrocution Set," 1919: 4).

An Anonymous Confession

Interestingly, a white man, or someone claiming to be a white man, confessed to the rape of AF. In Governor Roberts's papers on the Ewing case, an unsigned note reads as follows:

May 19, 1919
To Whom it concerns,
i write to let you know that frank ewing is going to die for a crime that i did if [AF] tell the truth she will tell that she got black on her hands where she scratched me i had my face blacked an had on Black Kid gloves. i would give my self up but I got a sister an old father to take care of i felt sorry for the old nigger an thought I would get dirt [?] off of his hands though he may die but God knows hes inocence i am a white man an she knows me well but she didn't know me then if I ever pray it goes for the nigger who died for my crime.

I close hoping he dies brave an he [illegible word] my sympathy. (Anonymous 1919)

This letter seems to have received no official attention or response.

The Last Day

Efforts to save Ewing's life continued even on the day before the execution. Mrs. Summers sent an affidavit to the governor, swearing that Ewing had been on the Summerses' farm and working under her supervision at the time of the crime. The *Nashville Tennessean* ("Negro Is to Pay," 1919: 9) reported:

> All day Tuesday, church leaders, ministers, women and others pleaded with Governor Roberts to stay the hand of the executioner. . . . The Governor spent quite a lot of time in making investigation of this case, hoping that he would be able to find something which would enable him to save the life of the wretch, but he says he can find nothing that will warrant him in doing so. The Governor says the negro is a picture of crime, and the crime of which he has been convicted is the most atrocious and vicious in the whole catalog of crime. Governor Roberts has talked with every witness in the case, has visited the place where the crime was committed, has talked with the victim of the demon's designs, and he says there is no doubt of his guilt, and for him to interfere would be but an excuse for mob violence in such cases hereafter.

Late in the afternoon of 20 May, Ewing was moved from the county jail to the state penitentiary ("Ewing Goes to Pen," 1919: 3).

The Execution

Frank Ewing was executed at a little past six o'clock on the morning of 21 May 1919. The only information about his last night and the execution itself comes from newspaper articles. The local papers reported that Ewing ate a heavy supper and then slept for several hours ("Negro Dies in Electric Chair," 1919: 1; "Frank Ewing Dies," 1919: 6; "Ewing Denies Guilt," 1919: 2). He was visited by Reverend E. N. Caldwell of the First Presbyterian Church, who told the *Nashville Tennessean* ("Ewing Denies Guilt," 1919: 2) that Ewing "prayed several times during the night, each time saying that he was leaving the world an innocent man." A few minutes before the execution,

Reverend Caldwell and C. C. Mansley, secretary of the Board of Charities, asked everyone to leave Ewing so that he could "make a last statement or confession. The negro, however, still stuck to his first statement, that he was innocent of the crime, and met his death without confessing" ("Ewing Denies Guilt," 1919: 2). The *Nashville Banner* ("Frank Ewing Dies," 1919: 6) indicated that Ewing showed no fear of death and walked unaided from his cell to the electric chair. His last reported words were "All that I ask is, please send my body home to my old mother. I will meet her in heaven. Good-bye" ("Ewing Denies Guilt," 1919: 2). Ewing was buried on 22 May in Nashville's Greenwood Cemetery (Greenwood Cemetery 1919).

Discussion

The confused and incomplete presentation of his alibi evidence at trial was not the only, and perhaps not even the greatest, disadvantage that Frank Ewing faced. As a black man accused of rape by a white woman, he confronted a criminal justice system and a society that presumed his guilt at a time and place where "the myth of the black rapist reached pathological proportions" (Hall 1979: 148). The legal system was often unable to contain the hysteria that followed such charges, and black suspects were lynched either before their arrest or after being taken from law enforcement officers. Lynchings were not uncommon in Tennessee (Curriden and Phillips 1999; Tolnay and Beck 1995); just a year before Ewing's arrest, Ell Persons was burned alive in Memphis before a mob of several thousand people ("Thousands Cheered," 1917: 1, 8).

Frank Ewing's mental impairment, which was almost certainly mental retardation, also contributed to his difficulties. Persons with mental retardation face multiple disadvantages in the criminal justice system (Bing 1996: 82–89). Confessions by the retarded are especially problematic and unreliable. Retarded persons frequently answer as they think their questioners wish and are easily manipulated by authorities (Ellis and Luckasson 1985: 431–32). In the early twentieth century south, with the threat of lynching hanging over legal proceedings, it was not difficult to intimidate even mentally competent defendants. Ewing indicated in his trial testimony that he had confessed because he was afraid for his life (*State v. Ewing* 1918b: 35), and this fear was quite reasonable.

The most troubling aspect of the case is the victim's identification of Frank Ewing. Her dismissal of several other suspects and her confidence that Ewing was her attacker indicate that she fully believed she had identified the correct man. Could she have been mistaken? Although eyewitness testimony tends to be persuasive to jurors, recent research indicates that it should be received with great caution; this is particularly true for cross-racial identification (Loftus and Doyle 1997: 86–88). Research indicates that the certainty of eyewitnesses that they are correct is not related to the accuracy of their memories (66–68). To question AF's identification is not to question her sincerity but to acknowledge that there is a real possibility that she was simply wrong.

What would have happened at Frank Ewing's trial if Mr. Summers had not misplaced his record book? What if Robert Taylor had been present to testify that Ewing had come to the farm with him and Summers on 24 June? And what if Mrs. Summers had testified about supervising Ewing all that afternoon? Would the word of the victim have outweighed such strong alibi evidence? The response to these questions can only be speculation. What we know is that the best efforts of Ewing's attorney and his alibi witnesses after trial were not enough to save him from the electric chair. Eighty years after Frank Ewing's execution, the strong probability that he was entirely innocent of the crime for which he died remains a haunting reminder of the fallibility of human justice.

NOTES

I am grateful for the assistance of Julia Rather and Ann Alley, archivists in the Manuscript Room of the Tennessee State Library and Archives, who located documents on Frank Ewing's case. I appreciate Mary Elizabeth Moore's contributions to the research, the information on Tennessee executions provided by Watt Espy, and the comments of James R. Acker, Michael B. Blankenship, Frank Einstein, David Giacopassi, Gordon Haas, Elizabeth Vandiver, and the editors of this volume.

1. Limitations of space prevent even a brief summary of the large and important literature on this point. For classic studies, see Cash (1941), Dollard (1949), Myrdal (1944), NAACP (1969), and Raper (1969). More recent work includes Ayers (1992), Hall (1979), Tolnay and Beck (1995), and Wright (1990).
2. Documents on Frank Ewing's case are located in the Manuscript Room of the Tennessee State Library and Archives in Nashville. Correspondence on the case and documents pertaining to the clemency application and psychological evaluation are located in the Correspondence Files of Governor A. H. Roberts. The legal record is located in the Supreme Court Middle District files; however, no copy of the Tennessee Supreme Court decision was found.
3. Although the victim's name was repeatedly given in contemporary newspaper accounts of the crime, and despite the length of time since the crime, I have chosen to refer to the victim by her initials rather than her full name.

REFERENCES

Anonymous. 1919. Letter. Correspondence files of Governor A. H. Roberts, box 60, file 3. Nashville: Tennessee State Library and Archives, Manuscript Room, 22 May.

Ayers, Edward L. 1992. *The Promise of the New South: Life after Reconstruction*. New York: Oxford University Press.

Bing, Jonathan L. 1996. "Protecting the Mentally Retarded from Capital Punishment: State Efforts Since *Penry* and Recommendations for the Future." *New York University Review of Law and Social Change* 22: 59–151.

Bowers, William J. 1984. *Legal Homicide: Death As Punishment in America, 1864–1982*. Boston: Northeastern University Press.

Cash, Wilbur J. 1941. *The Mind of the South*. New York: Knopf.

"Condemned Negro Gets Short Respite; Governor to Further Consider Ewing's Case." 1919. *Nashville Tennessean*, 1 May, p. 5.

Curriden, Mark, and Leroy Phillips, Jr. 1999. *Contempt of Court: The Turn-of-the-Century Lynching that Launched 100 Years of Federalism*. New York: Faber and Faber.

Dollard, John. 1949. *Caste and Class in a Southern Town*. Garden City, N.Y.: Doubleday.

Ellis, James W., and Ruth A. Luckasson. 1985. "Mentally Retarded Criminal Defendants." *George Washington Law Review* 53: 414–93.

"Ewing Denies Guilt to Last Moment of Life." 1919. *Nashville Tennessean*, 22 May, p. 2.

"Ewing Electrocution Set for Wednesday." 1919. *Nashville Tennessean*, 18 May, p. 4.

"Ewing Goes to Pen to Die in Chair." 1919. *Nashville Banner*, 20 May, p. 3.

"Frank Ewing Dies in Electric Chair." 1919. *Nashville Banner*, 21 May, p. 6.

Galliher, John F., Gregory Ray, and Brent Cook. 1992. "Abolition and Reinstatement of Capital Punishment during the Progressive Era and Early 20th Century." *Journal of Criminal Law and Criminology* 83: 538–76.

Greenwood Cemetery. 1919. Internment records. Nashville.

Haines, Thomas H. 1919. "Report of Mental Examination of Frank Ewing, Colored." Correspondence files of Governor A. H. Roberts, box 60, file 3. Nashville: Tennessee State Library and Archives, Manuscript Room, 22 March.

Hall, Jacqueline Dowd. 1979. *Revolt against Chivalry: Jessie Daniel Ames and the Women's Campaign against Lynching*. New York: Columbia University Press.

"In the Matter of Pardon for Frank Ewing." 1919. Correspondence files of Governor A. H. Roberts, box 60, file 3. Nashville: Tennessee State Library and Archives, Manuscript Room.

Loftus, Elizabeth F., and James M. Doyle. 1997. *Eyewitness Testimony: Civil and Criminal*. 3d ed. Charlottesville, Va.: Lexis Law Publishing.

Myrdal, Gunnar. 1944. *An American Dilemma: The Negro Problem and Modern Democracy*. New York: Harper and Brothers.

National Association for the Advancement of Colored People (NAACP). 1969. *Thirty Years of Lynching in the United States, 1889–1918*. New York: Negro Universities Press.

"Negro Assailant of Woman Sought; Officers Scour County All Night for Perpetrator of Fiendish Crime." 1918. *Nashville Banner*, 25 June, p. 5.

"Negro Dies in Electric Chair Denying Guilt." 1919. *Nashville American*, 21 May, p. 1.

"Negro Is to Pay Death Penalty at Daybreak." 1919. *Nashville Tennessean,* 21 May, p. 9.

Neil, A. B. 1919a. Letter to Governor A. H. Roberts. Correspondence files of Governor A. H. Roberts, box 60, file 3. Nashville: Tennessee State Library and Archives, Manuscript Room, 29 April.

———. 1919b. Letter to Governor A. H. Roberts. Correspondence files of Governor A. H. Roberts, box 60, file 3. Nashville: Tennessee State Library and Archives, Manuscript Room, 19 May.

Radelet, Michael L., Hugo Adam Bedau, and Constance E. Putnam. 1992. *In Spite of Innocence.* Boston: Northeastern University Press.

Raper, Arthur Franklin. 1969. *The Tragedy of Lynching.* New York: Negro Universities Press.

Roberts, A. H. n.d. Untitled statement. Correspondence files of Governor A. H. Roberts, box 60, file 3. Nashville: Tennessee State Library and Archives, Manuscript Room.

Summers, Mrs. J. M. 1919. Affidavit. Correspondence files of Governor A. H. Roberts, box 60, file 3. Nashville: Tennessee State Library and Archives, Manuscript Room, 19 May.

"Thousands Cheered When Negro Burned; Ell Persons Pays Death Penalty for Killing Girl." 1917. *Commercial Appeal,* 23 May, pp. 1, 8.

Tolnay, Stewart E., and E. M. Beck. 1995. *A Festival of Violence: An Analysis of Southern Lynchings, 1882–1930.* Urbana: University of Illinois Press.

West, Richard S. 1919a. Letter to Governor A. H. Roberts. Correspondence files of Governor A. H. Roberts, box 60, file 3. Nashville: Tennessee State Library and Archives, Manuscript Room, 8 April.

———. 1919b. Letter to Governor A. H. Roberts. Correspondence files of Governor A. H. Roberts, box 60, file 3. Nashville: Tennessee State Library and Archives, Manuscript Room, 26 April.

White, Robert H. 1965. "Historical Background re Capital Punishment in Tennessee." *West Tennessee Historical Society Papers* 19: 69–93.

"White Woman Victim of Horrible Crime: Mrs. [AF] Is Brutally Assaulted at Her Home by Negro." 1918. *Nashville Tennessean,* 25 June, p. 11.

Wright, George C. 1990. *Racial Violence in Kentucky, 1865–1940: Lynchings, Mob Rule, and "Legal Lynchings."* Baton Rouge: Louisiana State University Press.

CASES CITED

Frank Ewing, Colored v. State, 1918 [State's Brief]. Davidson Criminal Docket, No. 12, In the Supreme Court of Tennessee. Supreme Court Middle District Files, Manuscript Room, Tennessee State Library and Archives, Nashville.

State v. Ewing, 1918a. Assignments of Error. Tennessee Supreme Court Middle District Files, Manuscript Room, Tennessee State Library and Archives, Nashville.

State v. Ewing, 1918b. Trial transcript and record. Tennessee Supreme Court Middle District Files, Manuscript Room, Tennessee State Library and Archives, Nashville.

JAMES R. ACKER

THOMAS BREWER

EAMONN CUNNINGHAM

ALLISON FITZGERALD

JAMIE FLEXON, JULIE LOMBARD

BARBARA RYN

BIVETTE STODGHILL

8

No Appeal from the Grave

Innocence, Capital Punishment, and the Lessons of History

If men could learn from history, what lessons it might teach us! But passion and party blind our eyes, and the light which experience gives is a lantern on the stern, which shines only on the waves behind us! (Coleridge 1917: 164)

Within New York's long death penalty history lie the cases of eight individuals executed during the twentieth century whom scholars have contended were probably innocent. This chapter recounts the stories of those eight condemned men and the lessons extracted from their cases. Our goal is to bridge the years between the state's early use of the electric chair at Sing Sing Prison and its recent return to capital punishment, this time using lethal injection and promising heightened procedural protections.

The lessons that emerge in this chapter cast grave doubts on the confidence expressed by several New York lawmakers that procedural safeguards will essentially eliminate the risk that innocent people may be executed under the new statute. Laws cannot stamp out prejudices against minority groups, quell the ambitions of overly zealous prosecutors, compel the truth from informants whose testimony is rewarded even while they remain under a cloud of suspicion, render testimony based on eyewitness identification foolproof, or make human beings incapable of error. Because the risk factors evident in the eight cases under review cannot be eradicated through legislation, we find scant reason to be sanguine that erroneous convictions and executions are a vestige of the distant past.

New York's Contemporary Death Penalty Legislation

On 1 September 1995, New York became the thirty-eighth and final state during the twentieth century to reenact capital punishment legislation in the wake of *Furman v. Georgia* (1972), which had declared the death penalty laws of the early 1970s to be constitutionally invalid. By the mid-1960s, support for capital punishment in New York had waned so profoundly that the death penalty was nearly abolished (Acker 1990: 524–25). Nevertheless, the public mood changed dramatically over the next decade (Zimring and Hawkins 1986: 38–45), galvanizing the state legislature to adopt a death penalty law that would withstand constitutional challenge. For eighteen consecutive years, from 1977 through 1994, the New York legislature passed bills aimed at returning the state's death penalty, only to be thwarted by the gubernatorial vetoes of Hugh Carey and Mario Cuomo (Acker 1996: 43). One of Governor George Pataki's first official acts on assuming office in 1995 was to make good on his campaign promise to sign a comprehensive new death penalty act into law.

The contrast between Governor Pataki, an ardent supporter of capital punishment, and Governor Cuomo, a passionate foe of the death penalty, could not have been more pronounced. One of their fundamental disagreements involved the possibility that the death penalty might result in the execution of an innocent person. Governor Pataki's support for capital punishment did not waver even when he was confronted with the plight of his high school friend and former basketball teammate who had been convicted of a savage murder in Queens and sentenced to life imprisonment (the trial judge declared that he wished he could have imposed the death penalty) but who was later exonerated, after serving twenty-eight months in prison, when the real murderer confessed (Berger 1995). In contrast, Governor Cuomo's death penalty veto messages frequently cited the problem of miscarriages of justice in capital cases. When rejecting the legislature's 1986 death penalty bill, he observed: "Nor can we be assured that innocent life would not be taken by this ultimate penalty. The death penalty is an irrevocable act—mistakes cannot be corrected; there is no appeal from the grave. A society that values fundamental human rights cannot tolerate the execution of even one innocent person. Unfortunately, as recent studies have revealed, innocent people have been executed far more often than is commonly believed" (*State of New York Legislative Digest* 1986: 842).

Three years later, in a speech made in anticipation of yet another capital punishment bill veto, Cuomo elaborated on the "recent studies" he had alluded to in his previous comments:

> Think of it: At least 23 people are believed to have been wrongfully executed in the United States since the turn of this century. Twenty-three innocent people officially killed. But it is not called murder.
>
> And tragically, New York State—our great state, the Empire State—holds the record for the greatest number of innocents put to death over the years. We lead all the states in the nation with eight wrongful executions since 1905.
>
> Here are the names of the victims of the State of New York's killings: Charles Becker. Frank Cirofici. Thomas Bambrick. Stephen Grzechowiak. Max Rybarczyk. Everett Appelgate. George Chew Wing. Charles Sberna.
>
> These are real names. These are real people. Like . . . your son. Or your father. Or your mother. Real people who were killed, innocently. (Cuomo 1989: 5–6)

The foundation for Cuomo's remarks was Bedau and Radelet's (1987) monumental research project, which investigated, among other issues, the frequency with which people in the United States since 1900 have been convicted and executed for crimes they did not commit. Among the twenty-three individuals so classified were the eight New Yorkers named by Governor Cuomo (Bedau and Radelet 1987: 73). Bedau and Radelet, whose conclusions have been both criticized (Markman and Cassell 1988) and corroborated (Acker et al. 1998), maintain that their tabulation of twenty-three erroneous executions almost certainly undercounts the true magnitude of this ultimate miscarriage of justice (Bedau and Radelet 1987: 84–86; 1988: 165; Radelet et al. 1992: 271–73). In light of the roughly eighty innocent persons who have been convicted, sentenced to death, and then released from the nation's death rows since *Furman* (Dieter 1997, 1999; Radelet et al. 1996); the numerous incontrovertible near misses (Bedau and Radelet 1987; Pollak 1952; Tabak and Lane 1989: 102–11); wrongful convictions in noncapital cases resulting in incarceration (Huff et al. 1986;

Rattner 1988; Rosenbaum 1990–91); and logical arguments in support of their existence (Gross 1996; Radelet and Bedau 1988), few observers, including many unrelenting proponents of the death penalty (van den Haag 1998: 148), deny that erroneous executions have occurred in this country and will continue to take place.

Before the passage of New York's 1995 death penalty statute, no topic received more prolonged and vigorous debate in the state legislature than did the idea that the law would expose innocent people to the risk of execution (Acker 1996: 202–3). Some legislators dismissed the issue. For example, the principal sponsor of the law in the state senate insisted that "there is no solid evidence that anyone was ever executed [in New York] and found innocent later." He characterized the Bedau and Radelet study as "nonsense" and argued with remarkable aplomb that "under our system, if you are found innocent . . . you are innocent under the law. As I have often said, that doesn't mean you didn't commit the crime" (remarks of state senator Dale Volker, *New York State Senate Death Penalty Debate, 1995* 1995: 1850–51).

Other lawmakers conceded the problem yet concluded that the death penalty bill should be enacted anyway:

> I cannot guarantee the infallibility of human justice. But, we cannot be paralyzed by our inability to guarantee infallibility. . . .
>
> The test is whether or not we are justified in taking the action we propose. What just war can be fought without the knowledge, to a moral certitude, that the mere engaging in the war will result in the innocent killing of people?
>
> Legitimate actions to protect society against predators is justified. (remarks of assemblyman Eric Vitaliano, *New York State Assembly Record of Proceedings* 1995: 14)

> [W]e like to believe that all the safeguards are built in, that the wrong person couldn't get convicted of this crime. There is no ultimate guarantee. I am hopeful and would like to think that the chances in this bill in New York State with our system, are limited, if any.
>
> But one thing I do know, that those 18 people [serial murderer] Art Shawcross killed, as well as many other people . . . would all be alive today if we had this provision in the statue [*sic*]. (remarks of assemblyman Joseph Robach, *New York State Assembly Record of Proceedings* 1995: 44)

For other legislators, however, the risk of executing innocent persons was unacceptable and provided ample justification for defeating the death penalty bill. Noting the irreversibility of capital punishment, one state senator observed: "Saying, 'Oops, we're sorry; we made a mistake' is not enough" (remarks of state senator Martin O'Connor *New York State Senate Death Penalty Debate, 1995* 1995: 1862). Similarly, an assembly representative argued that "the biggest fraud of all is to tell the people of this State that innocent people will not be executed or, if they are, what the hell, it's only once in a while. That, Madam Speaker, is a big fraud and one which I will not participate in" (remarks of assemblyman Martin Luster, *New York State Assembly Record of Proceedings* 1995: 47). While casting his vote, another representative railed:

> In voicing my opposition to this bill, and in aligning myself with the . . . vocal minority of citizens who believe that a bill that would kill innocent citizens is unjust and inhuman and barbaric is not gibber-jabber.
>
> I take solace, though, in knowing . . . that the voices that I've heard, again, is not gibber-jabber, it is the voices of the innocent who already have been killed in this State and we choose not to hear any more of them. (remarks of assemblyman Roger Green, *New York State Assembly Record of Proceedings* 1995: 402)

The Voices of the Innocent?

New York sent 641 people to the electric chair during the twentieth century (Bowers 1984: 458–71). Although its last death sentence was carried out in 1963, New York still ranks third among all states in the number of executions conducted since 1930 (U.S. Department of Justice 1998: 537). The eight New Yorkers identified by Bedau and Radelet (1987) as having been executed in error went to their deaths between 1914 and 1939. We describe their cases here in hopes that, despite the shroud of New York's contemporary death penalty statute, their voices may finally be heard.

Frank Cirofici: Executed 13 April 1914

Frank Cirofici (one of several petty hoodlums of his day known as Dago Frank) was involved in one of New York City's most sensational murders. He was among five people executed for the

July 1912 murder of gangster Herman Rosenthal, who died in a hail of bullets outside a restaurant just two days after his affidavit detailing police graft and corruption was splashed over the front page of the *World*. The alleged mastermind of the Rosenthal murder was New York City police lieutenant Charles Becker, whom Rosenthal named as extorting bribes and kickbacks from gamblers and local businesses in exchange for police protection from arrest and prosecution.

Three of the gunmen involved in Rosenthal's murder died in the electric chair on the same day that Cirofici did: Harry Horowitz (also known as Gyp the Blood), Louis Rosenberg (also known as Lefty Louie), and Jacob Seidenscher (also known as Frank Muller or Whitey Lewis). Just before they were led to the electric chair, Horowitz and Rosenberg both stated that Cirofici had not shot Rosenthal. Sing Sing Prison warden James Clancy reportedly believed in Cirofici's innocence, and his successor, Thomas Mott Osborne, "knew the closest friends of the gunmen [and] stated that these friends all agreed Cirofici had nothing to do with the murder and was not even present when it occurred" (Radelet et al. 1992: 285). For his part, Cirofici maintained that Louie and Gyp had shot Rosenthal and that he had had nothing to do with the killing (Klein 1927; see also Acker et al. 1998).

William Shapiro was the driver of the rented car used by the gunmen in Rosenthal's murder. In his initial account of the incident, he claimed to have slept through the actual shooting. Although Shapiro named two of the three men he transported in the car to the scene of the shooting (neither of whom was Cirofici), he reported that he was not able to identify the third. Only after newspapers reported a tip that Dago Frank was involved and a New York City police commissioner intent on making arrests and reducing publicity presented a single photograph to the chauffeur for identification—Frank Cirofici's—did Shapiro identify him as a participant. Shapiro's indictment for murder was dismissed following his trial testimony (Hynd 1935). The state's other principal witnesses were gangsters who themselves had been implicated in the shooting, all of whom testified in exchange for immunity from prosecution (Acker et al. 1998).

Frank Cirofici was white, twenty-seven years old, and married when he was executed. A former choirboy, he had been convicted of burglary nearly ten years before Herman Rosenthal's murder (Acker et al. 1998; Hearn 1997: 128). His fate was inextricably linked to Charles Becker's, whose alleged involvement in the Rosenthal murder made the case a cause célèbre.

Charles Becker: Executed 30 July 1915

Charles Becker was a twenty-year veteran of the New York City Police Department. He had achieved the rank of lieutenant and headed the department's Strong Arm Unit, a squad charged with ridding the city of criminal gangs, gamblers, and other disruptive elements. Perhaps the first police officer in American history to be executed, Becker was known for his aggressive law enforcement tactics. Some alleged that he was corrupt, demanding protection money from gamblers for not raiding their establishments and taking bribes and kickbacks to fix cases when charges were lodged. As we have said, in an affidavit leaked to the *World* and published on the front page, Herman Rosenthal, a notorious gambler, identified Becker as a crooked cop and a partner in his gambling establishment. Two days later, Rosenthal was gunned down by several assailants in front of the Hotel Metropole in Manhattan. Amid sensational publicity and after two separate trials, Becker was convicted of orchestrating Rosenthal's death. He died in the electric chair for the crime.

The case against Becker was built almost exclusively on the testimony of gangsters who themselves were probably involved in Rosenthal's killing and who secured immunity from prosecution by testifying against Becker and the other men convicted of the murder. In the decision reversing Becker's initial conviction and death sentence, a concurring judge on the New York Court of Appeals charged that the trial "record bristles with inconsistencies and contradictions on the main facts" and characterized the testimony of the prosecution's star witnesses (Bald Jack Rose, Bridgie Webber, Harry Vallon, and Sam Schepps) as "grossly improbable, and . . . related by four men of the vilest character to save their own lives" (*People v. Becker* 1914: 411). The prosecutor in Becker's trial, Charles Whitman, used the case as a springboard to becoming the governor of New York and in that latter capacity denied Becker's appeal for clemency on the eve of his execution.

Becker's conviction after his second trial was produced by the same cast of characters amid a blitz of media publicity (a motion for a change of venue was denied) and rested heavily on corroboration testimony provided by two witnesses, Charles Plitt and James Marshall. Plitt testified after being released from jail and having a pending perjury charge dismissed. He later offered to recant his testimony for a fee, stated that he wanted to change his testimony but feared he would be prosecuted, and on the day that Becker was executed claimed that he had been induced to testify only after being assured by District Attorney Whitman that he would pardon Becker after becoming governor. Marshall recanted his testimony nine months after the trial and admitted to having perjured himself. He subsequently changed his story again and retracted his recantation. More than a year before their execution for Rosenthal's murder, Harry Horowitz (Gyp the Blood) and Louis Rosenberg (Lefty Louie) made jailhouse admissions that "Becker knew nothing about" the murder (Klein 1927: 424). On being led to the electric chair, Frank Cirofici (Dago Frank), who was also executed for the murder although he denied being involved, reportedly told Warden Clancy of Sing Sing Prison that, "so far as I know, Becker had nothing to do with this case" (Klein 1927: 326).

For his own part, Charles Becker declared on his execution day, "I am sacrificed for my friends" (Klein 1927: 399), intimating that others in the New York City Police Department were involved in the web of graft and corruption that had contributed to his own demise. Becker was white, forty-three years old, and married at the time of his execution (Acker et al. 1998; Hearn 1997: 133). The initial surge of 2,000 volts of electricity sent through his body did not kill him. Only after undergoing two additional charges at a higher voltage was Lieutenant Charles Becker pronounced dead more than eight minutes later.

Thomas Bambrick: Executed
7 October 1916

Thomas Bambrick (also known as Thomas O'Neil), a twenty-five-year-old white brick handler employed on New York City's waterfront, was among the estimated 1,000 to 5,000 people crowded into the Manhattan Casino on the night of 24 September 1915 after a parade and festivities sponsored by the McManus Association, a local political organization. Trouble broke out when a rival political faction infiltrated and disrupted the gathering (Hearn 1997: 142). Frank Reilly, a member of the same union to which Bambrick belonged, apparently drew a revolver and shot and wounded a man named Tynan. Three plainclothes police officers in the casino rushed to intervene. As Officer Bishop entered the barroom where the shooting occurred, he was shot in the shoulder and lost consciousness without ascertaining who shot him. Officer George Dapping lunged toward the shooter and received a fatal gunshot wound through the eye. The third policeman, Officer Dowling, who, like Officer Dapping, was unarmed, later positively identified Bambrick as the man who shot and killed Dapping.

Dowling followed Reilly and Bambrick outside the packed casino and tackled Bambrick from behind. Reilly thereupon pulled a gun, pointed it at Dowling's head, and threatened to blow the officer's brains out unless he released Bambrick. Instead of making good on his threat, Reilly vaulted a fence and escaped into the night, remaining a fugitive during Bambrick's trial and eventual execution. After others rushed to assist Dowling, Bambrick cried out, "Don't be trying to stick any gun over on me!" A .32–caliber revolver reportedly pulled from Bambrick's coat pocket matched the caliber of the bullet retrieved from the dead officer's skull. The gun contained two expended and three loaded shells (Acker et al. 1998).

Dowling was the only trial witness to identify Bambrick as the man who had shot Dapping. His testimony was contradicted in several key respects by another prosecution witness (Brady, a Department of Education clerk) who had observed the shooting but was unable to identify the shooter. The testimony of Dowling and Brady differed in crucial respects, such as whether the shooter was running or walking when the fatal shot was fired and what Dowling was doing and where he was standing at the moment when Dapping was shot. Seven other witnesses for both the prosecution and the defense also undermined Dowling's testimony that Bambrick was running from the barroom at the time of the shootings; those other witnesses variously testified that Bambrick was seated at a table or that he was not even present in the barroom and generally corroborated Brady's account of the shooting.

Bambrick maintained his innocence in the slaying of Officer Dapping. His supporters saw him as a stand-up guy who probably knew the identity of the real shooter but refused to divulge it and become known as a squealer (Acker et al. 1998). Warden Osborne of Sing Sing Prison as well as the prison chaplain reportedly were convinced that another man had fired the shots. Said the warden, "It is almost as certain that Bambrick is innocent as that the sun will rise tomorrow" (Radelet et al. 1992: 284).

Stephen Grzechowiak and Max Rybarczyk: Executed 17 July 1930

Stephen Grzechowiak's final words were "Take a good look gentlemen. . . . Keep your eyes open. You are seeing an innocent man die" ("Blue Ribboners," 1930: 1A). He was pronounced dead at 11:06 P.M. on 17 July 1930. Immediately after Grzechowiak's execution, his codefendant, Max Rybarczyk, was strapped into Sing

Sing's electric chair. "I'm an innocent man," said Rybarczyk. "I'm going to leave you in a few minutes" (ibid.). He was pronounced dead
at 11:13 P.M. Last to go to the electric chair that night was a third defendant in the case, Alexander Bogdanoff. Referring to Grzechowiak
and Rybarczyk, Bogdanoff declared, "As I stand before this . . . piece
of furniture, I swear before God that they are innocent" (ibid.). All three
men, who were white and ages thirty-five, thirty, and twenty-five, respectively, had been executed for the July 1929 robbery and murder
of Ferdinand Fechter, a Buffalo restaurateur and payroll clerk (Acker
et al. 1998; Hearn 1997: 183).

Fechter was ambushed by three or four gunmen who feigned a tire
problem with their stolen car and then opened fire on him when he
stopped his own vehicle in front of his house. Fechter had just returned
from a local bank from which he had withdrawn more than $8,000 in
payroll money. Although Buffalo papers trumpeted news of the 27 July
slaying and robbery, during which Fechter was shot seven times in
broad daylight, no arrests were made for nearly six weeks. Then on 7
September, Max (the Goose) Rybarczyk was arrested without incident
at about 4:45 P.M. He was shuttled to a police garage for three hours,
spent approximately five hours in a police car, and was finally taken
to a police station at two o'clock in the morning, roughly nine hours
after his arrest. Police reported that he confessed to the crime the next
day, although he refused to sign a written statement. The newspapers
reported the news of his confession in great detail, even though
Rybarczyk later renounced it and insisted on his innocence.

Stephen Grzechowiak (also known as Big Bob or Bob the Weeper)
and Alexander Bogdanoff (Little Alex) were arrested on 8 September
in a dramatic dawn tear-gas raid in which Buffalo police shattered
twelve windows of the house where the men slept. Grzechowiak was
in bed with his wife, and Bogdanoff was asleep in the same room as
the Grzechowiaks' six-year-old daughter. The *Buffalo Courier-Express*
reported that Grzechowiak confessed "after he had been grilled steadily
in the office of Police Commissioner Higgins more than three hours"
(Curry 1929: 1). The article described how one officer grabbed Grzechowiak "by the back of the neck" to take him for questioning by Chief
John B. Reville.

> [Reville's] booming voice could be heard through the closed
> door, as could the weak answers of the alleged killer. [Grze-
> chowiak] begged for a cigarette. Reville at first refused this

request, and then let him smoke. Reville next painted a vivid word picture of the charred remains of [Grzechowiak] being brought home to his wife, six-year old daughter and his father in a rough box after he had been electrocuted in Sing Sing prison. . . . It was not five minutes later when the story of the Fechter murder began pouring forth from the quivering lips of Grzechowiak. (Curry 1929: 1)

Grzechowiak signed a written confession, although he later proclaimed his innocence and was backed up by several alibi witnesses who testified at his trial.

On 10 September Bogdanoff also supplied a written confession to the robbery and murder. The three men were tried jointly, and their confessions were admitted into evidence, although they differed in several particulars and in some respects were antagonistic. Although identification evidence was presented, it was tenuous and frequently inconsistent. One witness, who initially identified Rybarczyk as the killer who ran off with Fechter's brown paper bag full of money, later testified that he could not recognize Rybarczyk because he could not see the assailant's face.

Two days before their scheduled 3 July 1930 execution, Alex Bogdanoff issued a statement "taking sole blame for the murder and contending that neither Grzechowiak nor Rybarczyk was present when the crime was committed" ("Execution Stay Possible," 1930: 1). Acting governor Herbert Henry Lehman ordered a two-week stay of execution to allow Bogdanoff's claim to be investigated. Refusing to provide the names of the men who, he insisted, actually participated in the crime, Bogdanoff vaguely identified them as Chicago gunmen. The task of investigating this claim was assigned to the same Buffalo police officials and prosecutors who were responsible for securing the confessions and convictions of Grzechowiak and Rybarczyk. On 16 July, the *Buffalo Courier-Express* ("Electric Chair Again," 1930: 11) reported: "Bogdanoff's confession was declared untrue and without foundation in a report to Governor Roosevelt by Walter F. Hofheins, assistant district attorney, who investigated his statements. Detective Sergt. William E. Burns visited Chicago and reported he was unable to obtain any information relating to the Chicago gangsters named in the gang leader's statement."

Stephen Grzechowiak and Max Rybarczyk, along with Alexander Bogdanoff, were executed at Sing Sing Prison on the following day.

Everett Appelgate: Executed 16 July 1936

Everett Appelgate, a white man who was thirty-six years old in 1935, was the vice-commander of the Nassau County American Legion and an investigator for the Veterans' Relief Bureau. He had a spotless record. Appelgate lived in Long Island with his wife, Ada, and their daughter in a home they shared with John and Mary Frances (known as Frances) Creighton and the Creightons' fifteen-year-old daughter, Ruth, and twelve-year-old son. Although such shared living arrangements were common during the Great Depression, they spelled trouble for the families in this case.

Everett Appelgate had an ongoing sexual relationship with fifteen-year-old Ruth Creighton, an affair apparently known to all adult members of the household. Ada Appelgate died on 27 September 1935, a day after ingesting arsenic that had been slipped into her glass of eggnog. Frances Creighton confessed to poisoning Ada and doomed Everett by naming him as her accomplice. Scant additional evidence linked Appelgate to the crime, and he steadfastly maintained his innocence until his death. The jury, thoroughly steeped in the knowledge of Appelgate's scandalous affair with young Ruth Creighton, convicted both defendants of murdering Ada at their joint trial. Everett Appelgate and Frances Creighton were executed moments apart in Sing Sing's electric chair, fewer than ten months after Ada Appelgate died.

Frances Creighton was no stranger to poisoning: she and her husband had previously been tried in New Jersey for the arsenic poisoning of Frances's brother and her father-in-law, although they were acquitted. She disliked Ada Appelgate and wrote a series of bizarre anonymous letters addressed to herself and her husband ordering the Appelgates' eviction from their common home. Ada was also an obstacle to Everett's ability to marry Ruth Creighton, whom Frances may have believed was pregnant. Frances purchased arsenic-based rat poison at a drugstore and had been heard to say that Ada was a nuisance and that she would "like to slip her some rat poison" (*People v. Creighton* 1936: 654). Her confession to the crime left no doubt about her guilt. The only disputed issue was whether Everett also was guilty or had been framed by a vindictive Frances.

Although Everett had driven Frances to the drugstore where she had purchased the rat poison apparently used to kill Ada, he claimed to be under the impression that she was buying corn-removal medicine. Everett had also handed Ada the fatal glass of eggnog, although he maintained he had no inkling that it had been poisoned. Moreover, he resisted having an autopsy performed after Ada's death. Perhaps the most damning evidence the jury heard involved Everett's salacious affair with fifteen-year-old Ruth, which logically could have given him a motive to murder his wife (Markman and Cassell 1988: 135; *People v. Creighton* 1936: 653) and almost certainly cast him in a perverse and reprehensible light in the eyes of the jurors. Nevertheless, except for Frances's condemning accusation, which she once retracted, and the fact that by all accounts she had a deserved reputation for untrustworthiness, the prosecution's case against Everett Appelgate was based on innuendo and speculation rather than hard evidence (Acker et al. 1998; Brown 1958: 103).

George Chew Wing: Executed 10 June 1937

Shortly after midnight following Thanksgiving Day in 1935, four armed intruders burst into a Manhattan apartment used as a gathering point for members of the Tai Pon *tong* (society), one of several intensely loyal informal groups in which recent Chinese immigrants fraternized as they adjusted to life in the United States. The apparent motive was robbery. A melee ensued in which several shots were fired, one fatally wounding fifty-year-old Yip Chow. Although three of the intruders escaped, one, Eng Sho, was captured, beaten by the inhabitants of the apartment, and then turned over to the police. Eng Sho initially denied involvement in the attack, claiming that he had been pushed into the apartment by the fleeing intruders. Later, as a part of an agreement in which he was allowed to plead guilty to second-degree murder and receive a twenty-five-year-to-life prison sentence (and possibly deportation in lieu of serving his sentence), Eng Sho named George Chew Wing and two other men as participants with him in the planned robbery and shooting.

Chew Wing, a thirty-one-year-old man of Chinese descent who had been born in San Francisco, belonged to the Hip Sing society. He had recently shamed Eng Sho by expelling him from the Hip Sing tong for five years because Eng Sho had assaulted another member of the group. Chew Wing's estranged wife testified that Eng Sho and her husband no longer spoke after Eng Sho's suspension from the society. Nevertheless, Eng Sho claimed that Chew Wing had enlisted himself and two other named individuals, neither of whom was ever located, and had planned the robbery that resulted in the fatal shooting. Chew Wing presented an alibi defense at his trial. None of the thirteen people in the raided apartment were able to identify him.

Two other witnesses testified that they had observed Chew Wing running through the hallway outside of the apartment. The first witness's account was severely undermined when a janitor for the apartment complex testified that the hallway could not have been illuminated by a bright light, as the witness had described during his alleged encounter with Chew Wing, because it was not even wired for electricity. The second witness was a frail and elderly man who testified in court while lying in a bed and with the assistance of a physician. He admitted that, when he made his observation, the hallway was not lit, the men he saw were wearing handkerchiefs and running so fast that he had trouble remembering what he saw, and he only knew Chew Wing by seeing him around Chinatown.

A number of irregularities occurred during Chew Wing's trial, including the use of an interpreter who repeatedly embellished the testimony of witnesses as he translated their Chinese into English and who may have been a member of a rival society to the Hip Sing tong to which Chew Wing belonged. Warden Lewis Lawes of Sing Sing Prison came to suspect that Chew Wing had been erroneously convicted (Lawes 1940: 323–26), the victim of perjured testimony and faulty identification evidence. The jury that dispatched Chew Wing to the electric chair deliberated for only thirty minutes (Acker et al. 1998).

Charles Sberna: Executed 5 January 1939

Twenty-nine-year-old Charles Sberna, a first-generation Italian immigrant, and his friend and former prison companion Salvatore Gati, were executed for the murder of police officer John Wilson, who was shot to death as he broke up the attempted robbery of a Manhattan furniture store. Gati undoubtedly was guilty of the crime: his fingerprints were found at the scene, he was identified by three witnesses, and he admitted his participation (*People v. Gati* 1938). Gati also, however, testified that Sberna was not involved in the crime. Sberna's wife and four relatives testified that he was at home, incapacitated by an earache, on the day of the killing. A physician reported issuing Sberna medicine for an ear infection during an office visit he made the day after the shooting, and Sberna had also visited the doctor complaining of ear problems on the day immediately preceding the killing.

Three eyewitnesses linked Sberna to the robbery-murder, although their identifications suffered from serious inconsistencies. The owner of the furniture store that was held up named Sberna only after viewing him at the police station through a peep hole and discussing the description of the robbers with other witnesses. His identification of Sberna as the man who had tied up the store employees was contradicted by the other identifying witnesses and also by Gati, who admitted to playing that role. Another of the eyewitnesses testified that he had caught a three-quarter profile view of Sberna as Sberna raced down the street and glanced into his office, about a minute and a half after another man had dashed down the same route. This witness's testimony was inconsistent with the accounts of others, who swore that the two men ran away within seconds of one another. The third eyewitness, a chauffeur, saw two men running quickly down the street. He testified that he initially had doubts about identifying Sberna as the second of the men and finally admitted that he was not positive that Sberna was one of the men he had seen fleeing the robbery (Acker et al. 1998). Although a blue coat discarded by one of the robbers was laundered at the same cleaning establishment patronized by Sberna, Sberna's wife swore the coat did not belong to her husband, and conflicting testimony was presented about whether or not the coat fit him (Acker et al. 1998).

In Sing Sing, Sberna and Gati met Isidore Zimmerman, who had been sentenced to death for killing a police officer during a 1937 robbery in Manhattan. Eyewitness testimony, in addition to other evidence, had placed Zimmerman at the scene of the crime for which he was to be executed. His life was spared when Governor Lehman commuted his death sentence just two hours before his date with the electric chair. More than two decades later, Zimmerman was exonerated, his conviction was vacated, and he was released from prison. The State of New York awarded him 1 million dollars as compensation for his wrongful conviction (Tabak and Lane 1989: 108; Zimmerman 1964).

Zimmerman came to believe in Sberna's innocence and prevailed on Gati to try to clear Sberna. A meeting between Gati and a homicide detective was arranged. Gati repeated his story that Sberna was not involved in the robbery-murder, although he declined to identify the true perpetrators for fear that his family would be in danger. Although the detective reportedly concurred in the belief that Sberna was innocent, he refused to intervene unless Gati provided the names of the real assailants (Reynolds 1950: 347–57; Sauter and Abend 1979: 77–79). Referring to Sberna, the chaplain at Sing Sing stated, "This is the first time I've ever been positive that an innocent man was going to the chair, and there is nothing I can do about it" (Lawes 1940: 338; see also Bedau and Radelet 1987: 158, note 822).

The Lessons of History

Charles Sberna's execution was carried out in 1939, more than six decades and two generations ago. The executions of the others whose cases have been described date back another quarter century. One of the sponsors of New York's 1995 capital punishment legislation dismissed the stories of Frank Cirofici, Charles Becker, Thomas Bambrick, Stephen Grzechowiak, Max Rybarczyk, Everett Appelgate, George Chew Wing, and Charles Sberna as irrelevant, even "assuming for the purposes of argument" that those men were innocent. Their executions were "conducted prior to the criminal justice protections crafted by the Warren Court era decisions. Drawing conclusions from tales of the executed innocent today would be like drawing conclusions from ox cart accidents to make a point about traffic safety on the [New York State] Thruway" (remarks of assemblyman Eric Vitaliano, *New York State Assembly Record of Proceedings* 1995: 13).

It is impossible, of course, to be certain that any or all of these men, executed long ago, were innocent of the crimes for which they were convicted. We deal with imperfect information and thus with probabilities. It is beyond dispute, however, that the innocent inevitably are at risk of erroneous conviction and execution. No system of criminal justice is infallible. Human beings and their institutions are prone to err. Those truths do not change over time. The causes of ox cart and New York State Thruway accidents undoubtedly do stem from certain commonalities—including driver error, faulty equipment, and simple bad luck—that are not made irrelevant by the passage of time or changing conditions. The cases presented in this chapter strongly suggest that many of the mistakes to which capital cases are susceptible will not be eradicated by due process reforms.

Gruesome murders tend to be highly publicized. They inflame community passions and create corresponding pressures on police and prosecutors for resolution (Gross 1996; Huff et al. 1986). Investigations sometimes focus prematurely, resulting in the apprehension and prosecution of certain likely suspects as other leads and potential lines of inquiry go unexplored (Davies 1991; Rattner 1988). As in many of the cases discussed here, suspects may be identified because they have a criminal past, affiliate with other criminals, have participated in unrelated illicit or immoral conduct, belong to a minority ethnic or racial group, or share other distinguishing characteristics that define them as unpopular social outcasts (Bowers and Pierce 1980; Palacios 1996: 321–24). Witnesses, who are often eager to help bring the guilty to justice, have been known to make mistaken identifications (Bedau and Radelet 1987: 57–61; Gross 1996; Wisotsky 1997). Perjury, whether committed by codefendants who have been granted charging or sentencing consideration, by others to deflect blame from themselves, or for various other reasons, is not uncommon (Bandes 1996; Bedau and Radelet 1987: 60; Gross 1996: 481; Tabak and Lane 1989: 100–102). Confessions can be and have been coerced or fabricated (Gross 1996: 481–88; Leo and Ofshe 1998; Pollak 1952; Schulhofer 1996). Overzealous law enforcement officers and politically ambitious prosecutors sometimes overstep their bounds (Huff et al. 1986: 528–36; Rattner 1988: 289–91; Rosenbaum 1990–91: 809–10). Defense attorneys may be underfunded, overworked, ill-prepared, or just not up to the challenge of handling a capital case (Bedau and Radelet 1987: 57; Huff et al. 1986: 532; Palacios 1996: 319–20).

Mistakes are made, and they may affect innocent people. The irrevocability of capital punishment dramatically magnifies the consequences of erroneous convictions because executions do not allow for second chances. A glimpse into the lives of the men described in this chapter as well as into their alleged crimes and victims helps rescue them from the relative anonymity of being "the eight executed New Yorkers who may have been innocent." To the extent that history can help inform the present and the future, it is vital that the cases of Frank Cirofici, Charles Becker, Thomas Bambrick, Stephen Grzechowiak, Max Rybarczyk, Everett Appelgate, George Chew Wing, and Charles Sberna be remembered and the men personified so that they are not treated simply as "statistical lives" (Glover 1977: 210–13).

Cirofici, Bambrick, Grzechowiak, Rybarczyk, Chew Wing, and Sberna were either recent immigrants or readily identifiable as members of ethnic minority groups. Becker, a renegade cop wreathed in allegations of corruption, was a prime target for a prosecutor whose career was on a trajectory to the governor's mansion and for the prosecution's underworld witnesses whose own necks were on the chopping block. Appelgate's sexual liaison with the fifteen-year-old daughter of his housemates was scandalous and poisoned him in the eyes of a jury. Dubious eyewitness testimony and the self-serving story of a man with a grudge and an incentive to cooperate with the prosecution doomed Chew Wing. Inconsistent eyewitness testimony trumped alibi evidence and a codefendant's insistence that Sberna was not involved in the robbery-murder for which he was executed. The litany of doubts plaguing each of these cases is extensive, defying the brief summaries presented here. And it is enduring.

Contemporary lawmakers might legitimately be asked to consider what good was accomplished by the execution of Cirofici, Becker, Bambrick, Grzechowiak, Rybarczyk, Appelgate, Chew Wing, Sberna, and others duly convicted of capital crimes. Were New York's streets made safer? Did corrections officers enjoy greater protections? Was justice somehow uniquely served? Arguably, the security and ethical equilibrium of the State of New York would not have been unduly compromised had Frank Cirofici and the others been spared the electric chair and instead sentenced to spend their lives in prison. Thus, if mistakes had been made in their cases and later uncovered, those miscarriages of justice could have been corrected, even if not fully repaired. But there is no appeal from the grave.

REFERENCES

Acker, James R. 1990. "New York's Proposed Death Penalty Legislation: Constitutional and Policy Perspectives." *Albany Law Review* 54: 515–616.

———. 1996. "When the Cheering Stopped: An Overview and Analysis of New York's Death Penalty Legislation." *Pace Law Review* 17: 41–227.

Acker, James R., Eamonn Cunningham, Patricia Donovan, Allison Fitzgerald, Jamie Flexon, Julie Lombard, Barbara Ryn, and Bivette Stodghill. 1998. "Gone but Not Forgotten: Investigating the Cases of Eight Executed New Yorkers (1914–1939) Who May Have Been Innocent." Paper presented at the annual meeting of the American Society of Criminology, Washington, D.C., 11–14 November.

Bandes, Susan. 1996. "Simple Murder: A Comment on the Legality of Executing the Innocent." *Buffalo Law Review* 44: 501–25.

Bedau, Hugo Adam, and Michael L. Radelet. 1987. "Miscarriages of Justice in Potentially Capital Cases." *Stanford Law Review* 40: 21–179.

———. 1988. "The Myth of Infallibility: A Reply to Markman and Cassell." *Stanford Law Review* 41: 161–70.

Berger, Joseph. 1995. "Close Call for Pataki's Friend." *Albany Times Union,* 26 February, pp. A1, A7.

"Blue Ribboners Go to Electric Chair Bravely." 1930. *Buffalo Evening News,* 18 July, p. 1.

Bowers, William J. 1984. *Legal Homicide: Death As Punishment in America, 1864–1982.* Boston: Northeastern University Press.

Bowers, William J., and Glenn L. Pierce. 1980. "Arbitrariness and Discrimination under Post-*Furman* Capital Statutes." *Crime and Delinquency* 26: 563–635.

Brown, Wenzell. 1958. *They Died in the Chair.* New York: Holt, Rinehart, and Winston.

Coleridge, Samuel Taylor. 1917. *The Table Talk and Omniana of Samuel Taylor Coleridge.* New York: Oxford University Press.

Cuomo, Mario M. 1989. "Remarks by Governor Mario M. Cuomo, College of St. Rose, St. Joseph's Hall, Albany, New York, Monday, March 20, 1989." Manuscript. Copy on file with authors.

Curry, C. V. 1929. "Max the Goose First of Pair to Tell All under Reville's Fire." *Buffalo Courier-Express,* 10 September, pp. 1, 3.

Davies, Nick. 1991. *White Lies: Rape, Murder, and Justice Texas Style.* New York: Pantheon.

Dieter, Richard C. 1997. *Innocence and the Death Penalty: The Increasing Danger of Executing the Innocent.* Washington, D.C.: Death Penalty Information Center.

———. 1999. *Recent Cases of Innocence and Possible Innocence.* Washington, D.C.: Death Penalty Information Center.

"Electric Chair again Awaiting Blue Ribboners." 1930. *Buffalo Courier-Express,* 16 July, p. 1.

"Execution Stay Possible." 1930. *New York Times,* 3 July, p. 1.

Glover, Jonathan. 1977. *Causing Deaths and Saving Lives.* New York: Penguin.

Gross, Samuel R. 1996. "The Risks of Death: Why Erroneous Convictions Are Common in Capital Cases." *Buffalo Law Review* 44: 469–500.

Hearn, Daniel A. 1997. *Legal Executions in New York State: A Comprehensive Reference, 1639–1963.* Jefferson, N.C.: McFarland.

Huff, C. Ronald, Ayre Rattner, and Edward Sagarin. 1986. "Guilty until Proven Innocent: Wrongful Conviction and Public Policy." *Crime and Delinquency* 32: 518–40.

Hynd, Alan. 1935. "Five Men for One Murder." *Master Detective* (February): 44–45, 55–61.

Klein, Henry H. 1927. *Sacrificed: The Story of Police Lieutenant Charles Becker.* New York: Goldman.

Lawes, Lewis E. 1940. *Meet the Murderer!* New York: Harper.

Leo, Richard A., and Richard J. Ofshe. 1998. "The Consequences of False Confessions: Deprivations of Liberty and Miscarriages of Justice in the Age of Psychological Interrogation." *Journal of Criminal Law and Criminology* 88: 429–96.

Markman, Stephen J., and Paul G. Cassell. 1988. "Protecting the Innocent: A Response to the Bedau-Radelet Study." *Stanford Law Review* 41: 121–60.

New York State Assembly Record of Proceedings. 1995. Albany, 6 March.

New York State Senate Death Penalty Debate, 1995. 1995. Transcript. Albany.

Palacios, Victoria J. 1996. "Faith in Fantasy: The Supreme Court's Reliance on Commutation to Ensure Justice in Death Penalty Cases." *Vanderbilt Law Review* 49: 311–72.

Pollak, Otto. 1952. "The Errors of Justice." *Annals of the American Academy of Political and Social Science* 284: 115–23.

Radelet, Michael L., and Hugo Adam Bedau. 1988. "Fallibility and Finality: Type II Errors and Capital Punishment." In *Challenging Capital Punishment: Legal and Social Science Approaches,* edited by Kenneth C. Haas and James A. Inciardi, 91–112. Newbury Park, Calif.: Sage.

Radelet, Michael L., Hugo Adam Bedau, and Constance E. Putnam. 1992. *In Spite of Innocence.* Boston: Northeastern University Press.

Radelet, Michael L., William S. Lofquist, and Hugo Adam Bedau. 1996. "Prisoners Released from Death Rows Since 1970 because of Doubts about Their Guilt." *Thomas M. Cooley Law Review* 13: 907–66.

Rattner, Ayre. 1988. "Convicted but Innocent: Wrongful Conviction and the Criminal Justice System." *Law and Human Behavior* 12: 283–93.

Reynolds, Quentin. 1950. *Courtroom: The Story of Samuel S. Leibowitz.* New York: Farrar, Straus, and Giroux.

Rosenbaum, Martin I. 1990–91. "Inevitable Error: Wrongful New York State Homicide Convictions, 1965–1988." *New York University Review of Law and Social Change* 18: 807–30.

Sauter, Joseph M., and Sheldon Abend. 1979. *The Guardians: The True Story of the Saints of Dannemora.* New York: Kensington.

Schulhofer, Stephen J. 1996. "*Miranda*'s Practical Effect: Substantial Benefits and Vanishingly Small Social Costs." *Northwestern University Law Review* 90: 500–63.

State of New York Legislative Digest. 1986. Albany: Legislative Bill Drafting Commission.

Tabak, Ronald J., and J. Mark Lane. 1989. "The Execution of Injustice: A Cost and Lack-of-Benefit Analysis of the Death Penalty." *Loyola of Los Angeles Law Review* 23: 59–146.

U.S. Department of Justice, Bureau of Justice Statistics. 1998. *Sourcebook of Criminal Justice Statistics—1997,* edited by Kathleen Maguire and Ann L. Pastore. Washington, D.C.: U.S. Department of Justice.

van den Haag, Ernest. 1998. "Justice, Deterrence, and the Death Penalty." In *America's Experiment with Capital Punishment,* edited by James R. Acker, Robert M. Bohm, and Charles S. Lanier, 139–56. Durham, N.C.: Carolina Academic Press.

Wisotsky, Steven. 1997. "Miscarriages of Justice: Their Causes and Cures." *St. Thomas Law Review* 9: 547–67.

Zimmerman, Isidore. 1964. *Punishment without Crime: The True Story of a Man Who Spent Twenty-Four Years in Prison for a Crime He Did Not Commit.* New York: Potter.

Zimring, Franklin E., and Gordon Hawkins. 1986. *Capital Punishment and the American Agenda.* New York: Cambridge University Press.

CASES CITED

Furman v. Georgia, 408 U.S. 238 (1972).
People v. Becker, 210 N.Y. 274, 104 N.E. 396 (1914).
People v. Creighton, 271 N.Y. 263, 2 N.E.2d 650 (1936).
People v. Gati, 279 N.Y. 631, 18 N.E.2d 35 (1938).

WILLIAM S. LOFQUIST

9 Whodunit?

An Examination of the Production of Wrongful Convictions

The Scene of the Crime

On 4 October 1982, Annette Cooper Johnston, age eighteen, and her fiancé, Todd Schultz, age nineteen, went for a walk in the small town of Logan, in rural southeastern Ohio. They were never again seen alive. Ten days later, police found their torsos floating in a river on the edge of town. Two days after that, their heads, arms, and legs were found buried in a cornfield on the river's edge. Their genitals had been removed and were never conclusively identified. The public was shocked. Gun sales surged. Halloween was canceled. The police were under tremendous pressure to solve these murders. In the days leading up to and in the months immediately following the discovery of the bodies, the specter of drugs, satanism, and sexual abuse loomed over Logan.

Police questioned parents, friends, neighbors, and others who were somehow tied to Annette and Todd. Although no one was arrested for more than eleven months, within a matter of days police focused their investigation on Dale Nolan Johnston, Annette's stepfather. Under police interrogation just after the bodies were found, Johnston confessed to having had sexual contact with his stepdaughter a number of years earlier. He also admitted to a strained relationship with Annette due to her connection to Todd. Further, he consented to a search that produced evidence used to place him in the cornfield. In addition, the FBI's Behavioral Sciences Unit—the now famous "Mindhunters"—developed a profile of the likely killer, who bore an uncanny resemblance to Johnston. With this information, the police obtained warrants for further searches of Johnston's property and, with the evidence collected there, obtained an indictment of him. Johnston was arrested in September 1983. After a two-week trial in January 1984, he was convicted and sentenced to death.

On appeal, however, Johnston's conviction and death sentence were reversed. Critical evidence was deemed inadmissible: (1) a coerced confession regarding his sexual contact with Annette and (2) witness testimony placing him with the two victims near the crime scene—testimony that had been "strengthened" after a police-conducted hypnosis session with the witness. Without this evidence, prosecutors decided not to retry Johnston; he was released from death row in 1990, an innocent man. No one else was ever investigated or arrested for the murders, which remain unsolved. The case is a classic whodunit: a grisly double murder in a small town; the victims young, attractive, and about to begin their lives together; a sexually abusive stepfather; rumors of drugs and police corruption. The whodunit examined in this chapter, however, concerns not the killer of Todd and Annette but the wrongful prosecution and conviction of Dale Johnston.

Theorizing Organizational Wrongdoing

Despite existing research and public scrutiny of wrongful conviction cases, the causes of such cases are undertheorized. If we recognize wrongful convictions as organizational products produced by police and prosecutorial agencies in a manner analogous to corporations' manufacture of unsafe products, we can theorize these cases using the growing and sophisticated literature on organizational wrongdoing (see Ermann and Lundman 1996; Ermann and Rabe 1997; Fisse and Braithwaite 1993; Kelman and Hamilton 1989; Lofquist et al. 1997). Through detailed reconstruction of the Johnston case, this chapter takes on that task.

Historically, organizational wrongdoing has been explained through two different theoretical frameworks (see Lofquist 1997). Rational choice or agency theories emphasize the contributions of individual and organizational planning, external political and economic imperatives, cost-benefit calculations, and financial and career ambitions. In this view, wrongful convictions are produced in a linear fashion by a series of police and prosecutorial decisions likely colored by racial bias, low regard for the targeted suspect, or public or political pressures and directed toward a foreseen and desired end (see Davies 1991; Germond 1996; Gershmann 1993; Lane 1970; Yant 1991).

Organizational process or structure theories approach organizational outcomes as emergent, shaped by the complex interactions of numerous decision makers and their larger environments (see Perrow 1984, 1986). When examining organizational outcomes, one must substantially recontextualize their occurrence and, in so doing, consider how macrolevel forces and microlevel rationality are mediated by the mesolevel organizational contexts in which they are expressed. In this view, wrongful convictions are organizational outcomes linked to premature commitment to a particular suspect, inattention to alternative scenarios due to the operation of "normal science" among investigators, the organizational and legal structures of the criminal justice system, and the lack of resources available to the defense (see also Parloff 1996; Tucker 1997).

Recent research on organizational wrongdoing has elaborated this perspective (Gioia 1992; Lee and Ermann 1999; Yeager 1991). Ermann (1991), for example, has sought to explain how organizations become committed to courses of actions that lead to the production of unsafe products and the concealment of their hazards. His theorizing centers on the concept of escalating commitments, which argues that "motivations to continue developing and selling a product escalate rapidly over time . . . [while] reasons to abandon it accumulate slowly" (Rabe and Ermann 1995: 223). Notably, Ermann explains this process without reference to traditional rational choice motives of greed or career ambitions, focusing instead on organizational dynamics.

The most recent expression of this perspective, and perhaps its signature statement, is Vaughan's (1996) definitive examination of the space shuttle *Challenger* disaster. In this work, she considers, and finds inadequate, the traditional narrative of the disaster, which saw the explosion of the space shuttle as a foreseeable consequence of managerial decisions made against the recommendations of engineers but compelled by economic and political pressures. In its place, she develops an organizational and structural theory that argues that the *Challenger* disaster can be understood as an "incremental descent into poor judgment" (Vaughan 1996: xiii). "No extraordinary actions by individuals explain what happened: no intentional managerial wrongdoing, no rule violations, no conspiracy" (xiv).

More specifically, Vaughan argues that the space shuttle program existed within an environment shaped by political pressures (declining budgets and staffs, declining legitimacy of space flight, and the effort to relegitimize it), engineering culture (belief in redundancy, strength of "normal science"), regulatory oversight, and competitive pressure. These forces led to the emergence of organizational structures and cultures that normalized evidence of design problems and continually renegotiated acceptable limits. Vaughan describes this in a manner remarkably similar to Ermann's concept of escalating commitments when she notes that the incrementalism and repetition that characterize decision making "camouflage from the participants a cumulative directionality that too often is discernible only in hindsight" (119). She arrives at this conclusion after an exhaustive effort to reconstruct the organizational, structural, and cultural contexts in which decisions were made.

The research presented in this chapter fits squarely within this structural approach. Challenging the conventional, rationalistic view that identifiable misconduct serves as a starting point for wrongful convictions, I contend that wrongful convictions are more likely to be produced through the routine operations of flawed systems of police investigations, prosecutorial case making, and death penalty jurisprudence operating within larger social and cultural contexts. Although this vantage point does not deny the existence of bad faith or malicious prosecution, it seeks to present a more comprehensive alternative explanation.

Particularly important are a host of arguments rooted in the dense ethnographic traditions of symbolic interactionism: that the meaning imposed on behavior viewed in hindsight is insensitive to the reality that such meaning is best discerned within the context in which it occurred; that the direction of behavior is highly contingent on factors often deemed irrelevant, if even visible, in hindsight; and that actors impose preexisting frameworks on emergent scenarios. This final point is especially significant. It suggests that legal actors adopt narrative frameworks into which particular crime scenarios are fitted more or less well. These "normal crime" frameworks (Sudnow 1965) shape investigations, assessments of evidence, interpretations of legal rules, and the entire range of decisions in the same way that "normal science" shapes the conduct of engineers (Vaughan 1996).

Before moving on, we should note the significance of this study as it relates to the current death penalty controversy. The death penalty is the most procedurally encumbered area of American criminal law. Its use necessarily involves a bifurcated trial and multiple appeals, rarities in other areas of criminal law. It therefore involves prosecutors, judges, and defense lawyers in active and open presentation of evidence, police and defense investigators, and expert witnesses, all operating under the watchful gaze of the media (at least in those times and places where capital prosecutions are deemed newsworthy). This enormous scope of law and the great number of legal actors involved may lead one to conclude that arrests, prosecutions, and convictions in these cases are particularly "good" in a legal sense—that is, less influenced by social conditions, financial considerations, cultural concerns, or the whole host of extralegal factors that otherwise affect legal decision making. To the contrary, however, a compelling argument has been made for precisely the opposite conclusion (Gross 1996): that capital-case processing has features that are likely to increase the occurrence of wrongful convictions.

In this chapter, I focus on explaining how the police, prosecutors, and judges involved in investigating and trying Dale Johnston's case produced a wrongful conviction despite, or perhaps because of, these legal, social, and cultural contexts. Although the argument that wrongful convictions and executions are so infrequent as to be freakish once relegated such research to the margins of the death penalty debate, a growing body of empirical evidence showing the frequency of wrongful convictions has led many to reconsider this position (Bedau and Radelet 1987; Dieter 1997; Huff et al. 1996; Radelet et al. 1992, 1996). Even death penalty advocates have conceded the importance of wrongful convictions in the debate (Markman and Cassell 1988). A recent national conference on the subject, followed in quick succession by a series of nationally profiled wrongful convictions, has made this issue central to contemporary discussions of the death penalty.[1]

Methodology: Reconstructing the Scene of the "Crime"

Research of the sort undertaken in this chapter requires careful reconstruction of the contexts in which decisions were made, which in turn requires examination of numerous sources of information. I scrutinized newspaper accounts of the crime and case as well as newspaper reports relevant to the broader social, cultural, and criminal justice contexts of the case.[2] I also examined the entire official record of the case, including the trial transcript, each written judicial opinion, and dozens of pre- and post-trial motions and affidavits.[3] It was notably more difficult to discuss the case with the involved parties—attorneys, judges, police, witnesses, reporters. Events such as this one, which divide and even disgrace a small town and call into question the job performance of the entire range of criminal justice professionals, make those involved in the case reluctant to talk. This reluctance is compounded by the fact that the case remains unresolved and that Dale Johnston was never formally exonerated. (Formal exoneration by criminal justice officials is a rare occurrence among wrongful conviction cases.) This legal limbo means that parties to the case may refuse to discuss a formally ongoing investigation.

Despite these problems, some individuals were quite forthcoming in their discussions with me and have provided essential insights into the case and its larger contexts. Although their names and contributions are openly acknowledged in some places, more often these individuals asked that their identities be protected. It remains important to acknowledge that the picture drawn here is incomplete. Nevertheless, I believe that my inferences are warranted by information available in the written record and from the numerous interviews I was able to conduct. All conclusions drawn from outside the written record are based on corroboration from at least two sources.

What Happened? Searching for Clues

The search for Annette Cooper Johnston and Todd Schultz was slowed by the fact that they were adults, known to be contemplating marriage, and known to have an interest in leaving Logan. Although they were reported missing to police only hours after they were last seen leaving Todd's mother's house on 4 October, a police investigation did not begin until 14 October; and police found their torsos several hours later. By then, friends and neighbors had been searching for days; police undertook the search only under pressure from the victims' families. The torsos were found floating in the Hocking River within the town of Logan. Two days later, their arms, legs, and heads were found buried in the cornfield bordering the river, just outside the town limits.[4] The coroner concluded that the cause of death in each case was gunshot wounds; multiple stab wounds were also found and were determined to have occurred after death. Todd's body experienced considerably more violence than did Annette's.

The Investigation: Forensic Science and Escalating Commitment

Initially, police believed that the killings occurred in the cornfield. Preliminary speculation focused on a "psychopathic loner." Within days, however, both Todd's parents and Annette's friends reported to police that Annette had told them she had been sexually molested by her stepfather, and attention turned to Dale Johnston. Over the course of the next several months, this version of events, portraying Johnston as a sexually abusive and jealous stepfather, was bolstered by a series of contributions from forensic science. Three pieces of evidence—hypnotically refreshed witness statements placing Johnston near the cornfield, a bootprint placing Johnston in the cornfield, and a profile of the likely offender—formed the core of the state's case against him, despite the fact that each piece of evidence turned out to be seriously flawed. Discerning the circumstances and motives surrounding the development of these items of evidence lies at the core of theorizing this wrongful conviction. Was the evidence manufactured to create guilt, or was it "discovered" as part of a thorough, albeit cumulatively misdirected, police investigation?

After going to the police station on 21 October 1982 to provide evidence he thought might be helpful in the investigation, Dale Johnston was held by police and interrogated for more than six hours. Reports from Sandra Schultz, Todd's mother, that Annette had confided to her about the sexual relationship with her stepfather and her fear of him, precipitated the interrogation. During this interrogation, which became so heated and coercive that investigator Herman Henry of the Ohio Bureau of Investigation and Identification left in protest of police tactics, Johnston is alleged to have confessed to sexual contact with Annette when she was younger and to the possession of nude photos of her. He also expressed his dislike for Todd Schultz and Todd's relationship with Annette. Further, he consented to a search of his property. This search was conducted immediately, in the last hours of that evening, and led to the seizure of several items of evidence—notably, Dale Johnston's cowboy boots.

This "confession" provided a strong boost to the state's case; it served as a kernel of truth, offered by the primary suspect himself, around which a larger case could be built. Because there are no audio or video recordings, we cannot know precisely what was said. In his subsequent statements, as well as in his wife's statements, Johnston admitted that his family practiced nudism, that he possessed nude photos of Annette, and that he sometimes became aroused in her presence. Nevertheless, he denied sexual contact with her, stating that his earlier confession was coerced. Yet within the highly charged environment of Logan and broader cultural concern about the sexual abuse of children, many interpreted these statements as an admission to an ongoing abusive sexual relationship—as if Johnston had confessed to the allegations of Sandy Schultz and others.

During this same period, as part of a routine canvass of the area, police interviewed Steven R. Rine, a Logan resident and a Schultz family friend. In a series of interviews between 23 October and 3 November, Rine related to police that on the afternoon of 4 October he had seen a vehicle bearing some similarity to one owned by Dale Johnston in Logan within easy walking distance of the cornfield. Johnston denied having been in Logan that afternoon. Rine also related having seen a middle-aged man driving this car yelling at a younger man and woman and forcing them into the car. This initial, very tentative, report to police was followed by police-conducted hypnotic sessions on 11 and 16 November, during which Rine identified the car as a perfect match for Johnston's, the man as a perfect match for Johnston, and the younger people as Todd and Annette, whom he had met briefly a week before their deaths.

Reports from a forensic anthropologist further strengthened the state's case by matching Johnston's boot to bootprints found in the cornfield. Reports from a forensic meteorologist corroborated this finding by suggesting that the condition of the bootprint matched the weather conditions with respect to rainfall and fallen leaves between the time of the murders and the discovery of the bootprint more than two weeks later. These reports supported the state's theory, placing Johnston in the cornfield very near the time of Todd and Annette's disappearance.

Throughout the winter and spring of 1983, the investigation proceeded with surprisingly few developments or disclosures beyond those of October 1982. Although their investigation clearly focused on Johnston, the police told reporters they had no suspects or major clues. In May 1983, the FBI profile of the likely suspect, which Logan police had requested in late October 1982, was given to investigators. It suggested that the offender knew the victims, "had a long term sexual involvement with the female, and also a resentment of a possible sexual relationship which may have existed between the victims," and "killed them at a location some distance from the final location of burial." More specifically, the offender was described as a "white male in his mid to late forties . . . who prefers outdoor work and self-employment." The profile suggested that he had "been divorced and remarried." Finally, the offender was described as underachieving and antisocial, with little formal education and a history of personal and job failures.

At the time of the murders, Johnston was a forty-nine-year-old self-employed contractor living on a farm with his second wife and two stepdaughters.

With this information and evidence, the police came to believe that the murders and dismemberments occurred some miles away, on Johnston's farm. Evidence to the contrary did exist at this time, including eyewitness testimony that Todd and Annette were alive in Logan after being sighted by Rine, that gunshots were heard in the cornfield that evening, and that a man other than Johnston was seen following Todd and Annette, as well as problems with the state's theory of the case.[5] This evidence, however, was overwhelmed by the strength of the sexual history evidence, the narrative power attached to it, and the evidence developed pursuant to it. Contradictory evidence was normalized, witnesses were deemed unreliable, and gunshots in a rural area were deemed unremarkable.

Within weeks, police obtained warrants for two more searches of Johnston's property, including all buildings and a strip mine. These searches produced bloodstained building materials and carpets, feedbags, bullets, shoes matching those worn by Annette on the day of the murders, and a personal check. This evidence was used to elaborate the official version of events: Dale Johnston went to Logan on 4 October (as confirmed by the personal check to a Logan business) with his wife and other stepdaughter, Michelle; forced Todd and Annette into his car (as witnessed by Steven Rine); returned to his farm; shot, stabbed, and dismembered Todd and Annette (as confirmed by the bloody carpets and building materials and the matching-caliber bullets); stuffed them into feedbags; and returned to Logan to dispose of their bodies.

A grand jury was convened in September 1983. Over the course of several days of witness testimony, the state portrayed Johnston as a pathologically jealous stepfather engaged in long-term sexual abuse of his stepdaughter. He was indicted by a nine-to-zero vote on two counts of aggravated murder with death penalty specifications and was arrested later that same day, 29 September. With little likelihood of gaining a change of venue from a town in which his arrest was met with jubilant celebration and a special edition of the *Logan Daily News,* Johnston opted for a bench trial by a three-judge panel.[6] At the forthcoming trial, Hocking County prosecutor Christopher Veidt and assistant prosecutor Frederick Mong would try Johnston. For his defense, he retained the services of Columbus attorneys Thomas Tyack and Robert Suhr, both experienced capital defense attorneys. The judges were James Stilwell, Joseph Cirigliano, and Michael Corrigan. In the meantime, as a result of threats to his safety, Johnston was relocated to the Pickaway County Jail to await trial.

The Trial: Constructing a Compelling Narrative

Without an unambiguous confession or corroborated eyewitness testimony, legal wrongdoing is not the product of factual certainty. Rather, it is the product of narrative constructions: efforts by various people to construct a highly credible narrative account. This process of storytelling or narrative construction inevitably relies on popular images, assumptions, and inferences. Factually unique stories are fitted into particular narrative frames ("normal crime" scenarios) in a manner that diminishes their distinctiveness. The trial is a particularly significant location of narrative construction; "the struggle of attorneys to find the best accounts for their clients turns courtroom transcripts into excellent barometers of what is said and thought in a culture at any given moment of time" (Ferguson 1996: 87). In this forum, the power, resonance, and effectiveness of a narrative can overwhelm the facts or logic of a particular case, leading legal decision makers to ratify a narrative that results in a wrongful conviction.

The three-judge panel hearing the case *State v. Johnston* (1984) convened in Hocking County Common Pleas Court on 11 January 1984. The trial lasted for nine days. The primary evidence against Johnston, most of which was admittedly circumstantial, was the bootprint found in the cornfield, the hypnotically refreshed accounts of eyewitness Steven Rine, and accounts by Todd's mother and several of Annette's friends concerning Johnston's sexual improprieties with Annette. Anthropologist Dr. Louise Robbins testified that the bootprint found on the riverbank matched the cowboy boots taken from Johnston's home. Meteorologist Jym Ganahl testified that weather conditions in Logan at the time were consistent with the condition of the bootprint. Steven Rine testified that on 4 October 1982 he observed Johnston arguing with Todd and Annette before forcing them into his car on a Logan street corner. Also significant to the prosecution's case were police accounts of Johnston's interrogation, focusing on his sexual contact with Annette and his anger at Annette's relationship with Todd. All of this evidence was woven together by a narrative depicting Johnston as a jealous, incestuous stepfather.

Before and during the trial, the defense did little to offer an alibi for Johnston or a narrative alternative to the state's version of events. Rather, because there was neither a weapon nor a reliable eyewitness, the defense believed that the state's case was too circumstantial to meet the burden of proof, and focused on challenging this case. More specifically, the defense offered evidence from state police investigator Herman Henry that the crime scene had not been properly preserved and that Johnston had been coerced during his October 1982 interrogation. State criminalists also testified that none of the physical evidence removed from Johnston's property in the two June 1983 searches, including bullets, carpets, clothing fibers, and bloodstains, could be conclusively linked to the crime.

The defense was able to elicit testimony that the footprint so central to the state's case had not been cast until 19 October, fifteen days after the murders and three days after the body parts were discovered. The defense also argued that Dr. Robbins was not an expert in footprint identification, thereby disqualifying her testimony. A defense footprint expert argued that the impression in question was not only not Johnston's bootprint but the print of a bare foot. Most important, defense experts challenged the reliability of hypnotically refreshed testimony, arguing that such a procedure inevitably and irreversibly contaminates memory, making it impossible to distinguish pre- and post-hypnosis memories. The defense also challenged the methodology used in hypnotizing Rine, arguing that it was done by an untrained and biased police officer.

Because the defense did not point toward alternative stories, the media covered the case as a straightforward, although ghastly, murder, suggesting little doubt as to Dale Johnston's guilt until well after the verdict and sentencing. Even though the formal, legal burden of proof rests with the state, the absence of a credible alternative narrative can be viewed as strengthening the state's case. Research suggests that legal decision makers, including prosecutors, judges, and juries, use a story frame (a kind of "normal crime" scenario) to organize information (Greene 1989; Pennington and Hastie 1986). Here, the cultural availability of a stepfather–sexual predator framework served to strengthen the state's case, particularly without an alternative frame. After brief and collegial deliberations among the unanimous judges, Johnston was convicted on 28 January 1984. The verdict was met with public celebration. The sentencing phase of his trial was held in March, and he was sentenced to death after a brief trial on 23 March 1984.

His execution was scheduled for 4 October 1984, the second anniversary of the murders.

Post-conviction Proceedings: Constructing an Alternative Narrative

In the immediate aftermath of the conviction, Johnston's attorneys professed shock and aggressively challenged the prosecution's case and methods. In doing so, they proceeded along two paths: filing the customary appeal of the verdict, while filing a separate appeal for a new trial based on newly discovered evidence. The first appeal challenged the admission of Rine's testimony and other elements of the trial. The second appeal took a more affirmative tack, offering alternative accounts of the events of 4 October 1982. The first alternative, offered in the first of a series of motions for a new trial filed throughout the summer of 1984, appealed to another popular narrative construction of the time—that the murders had been committed by a satanic cult. Subsequent motions presented the affidavits of witnesses able to offer exculpatory testimony and argued that the prosecution had violated discovery rules by withholding the names or statements of these witnesses. With these later motions, the defense quickly abandoned its satanic cult theory and focused on a second alternative scenario—that local resident Kevin "Tex" Meyer had committed the murders. Meyer was a drifter and an experienced butcher and was alleged to be enamored of Annette.

The trial judges heard and denied the first series of motions for a new trial, ruling that the state had complied with discovery requests and that the defense had failed to present any evidence warranting a new trial (*State of Ohio v. Dale Johnston* 1984). The defense then appealed to the Hocking County Court of Appeals, which heard and ruled on each of the two lines of appeal (*State of Ohio v. Dale Johnston* 1986). While upholding the state in its reliance on the expertise of Dr. Louise Robbins and on minor points relating to the search warrants and the grand jury proceedings, the court ruled that Rine's testimony was improper, that discovery rules had been violated, and that sentencing procedures were violated. With these rulings, the court ordered a new trial.

As the cases were working through Ohio's appellate courts, two important developments occurred outside the courtroom. First, while on death row, Dale Johnston recalled what he had been doing in the late afternoon of 4 October 1982; he had heretofore been unable to remember. By looking at a calendar and reconstructing events, he remembered that he had been talking to three men—Ralph Cherry, John Cherry, and John Johnson—who had come to the area to work on the property across the street from his farm. Defense investigators pursued this lead and were able to corroborate this alibi, placing Johnston on his farm eleven miles from Logan at the same time Rine had placed him in Logan. Second, *Akron Beacon Journal* reporter Bill Osinski, who had covered the trial and been troubled by the verdict, conducted an independent investigation, the results of which were published in a series of articles beginning on 27 October 1985. In addition to alleging police and prosecutorial misconduct, Osinski argued that the likely killer was William Wickline, who by then was on death row in Ohio for the August 1982 murder and dismemberment of a couple from Columbus. These murders were six weeks and forty miles removed from the Logan killings.

At the same time, continuing defense investigation further weakened the state's case. The defense produced affidavits of witnesses placing Todd and Annette in the cornfield in the late afternoon of 4 October; these witnesses further reported seeing a man following them in the cornfield and hearing shots and screaming from the direction of the cornfield soon after. The defense also further deposed meteorologist Ganahl, who reversed his earlier testimony and expressed considerable doubt that the footprint in the cornfield was made in early October. Rather, the condition of the print suggested that someone searching for Todd and Annette had made it.

In its appeal, the prosecution countered by challenging the veracity and timing of these new defense disclosures and presenting additional witnesses of its own. Most notable was Kevin Scudder, a former cellmate of Johnston's in the Pickaway County Jail, who stated that Johnston had confessed to him that he had killed Todd and Annette.

On 5 October 1988, the Ohio Supreme Court affirmed the appellate court decision in support of a new trial (*State v. Johnston* 1988). More specifically, the Supreme Court used this case to establish guidelines for hypnotically induced testimony and held that Rine's testimony met none of these guidelines. The court also ruled that the prosecution had withheld exculpatory information from the defense. The case was then remanded to Hocking County and granted a change of venue to Franklin County. The presiding judge then ruled that Rine's testimony would be inadmissible at the second trial and that the interrogation of Johnston was inadmissible due to police violations of Johnston's rights under the Fifth and Fourteenth Amendments.

Although the prosecution appealed these rulings, the Franklin County Court of Appeals upheld the rulings on 10 May 1990 (*State v. Johnston* 1990). On 11 May, the prosecution announced that it lacked the evidence to proceed with a second trial; all charges against Johnston were withdrawn, and he was released from custody that same day.

Whodunit? Investigating the Investigation

Agency Perspective: The 1980s Writ Small

Although it is not the perspective I employ in this chapter, the agency perspective is consistent with the way in which scholars and the general public understand most cases of organizational wrongdoing (see Mokhiber 1988; Simon 1999; Sutherland 1983). In looking back over cases of wrongdoing or tragedy, the tendency is to view temporally sequential actions as part of an overarching plan of action rather than see that action within its context—that is, as emerging and situational. Because wrongful convictions are only fully recognizable in hindsight, retrospective rationalization may occur: a linear and logical narrative is created to connect temporally sequential events. This narrative structure is very familiar; it serves as the foundation of the classic whodunit, in which all information is evidence and nothing is incidental or superfluous. From this perspective, the wrongful conviction of Dale Johnston was the product of an effort by key decision makers to pursue a knowingly wrongful course of action by framing an innocent but undesirable and "likely" suspect.

In the immediate aftermath of the original conviction, several agency-based narratives were developed to explain Johnston's prosecution and conviction, changing as new evidence was developed. These narratives, advocated most strongly by Johnston's attorneys and journalists who covered the case, are supported by considerable evidence. The issue is the meaningfulness of this evidence in the temporal and behavioral contexts in which it emerged. More specifically, a number of troubling rumors, allegations, substantiated occurrences, and identifiable errors characterize the investigation and prosecution of Dale Johnston. To the extent that these various story elements can be woven together into a coherent and confirmed narrative, one could argue that Dale Johnston was the victim of a malicious prosecution.

Nevertheless, confirming and linking these elements are substantial hurdles.

The evidence offered in support of the agency perspective runs the entire gamut of 1980s cultural politics: satanic ritual sacrifice, drug dealing and corruption, child sexual abuse, child pornography, junk science, refreshed memories, and jailhouse snitches. The general thrust of these different narratives was that local law enforcement was corrupt and that Dale Johnston was targeted by police as a way to direct attention away from the police. In one scenario, Todd and Annette had evidence of this corruption, were reputed to be linked to police involvement in local drug dealing, and were killed as a result. The killer in this case, William Wickline, was a drug dealer and enforcer working with the protection of law enforcement. In another scenario, the chief investigator for the Logan Police Department, James Thompson, was a practicing satanist who was involved in the ritual sacrifice of Todd and Annette. In a third scenario, Todd and Annette were involved in a host of underground activities—drug dealing, pornography, illicit sex—and were killed because of them.

In support of these scenarios, an array of evidence has been offered. Regarding the police, there are reports of evidence tampering, drug use, theft of drug evidence, and other improprieties.[7] In addition, reports surfaced that Thompson, who served for a time as chief of police, was demoted because of his involvement with occult religious practices. Also, police involved in the murder investigation report that Johnston was coerced during his October 1982 confession and that police investigators willingly overlooked evidence by failing to collect physical evidence and pursue leads. Others questioned the FBI profile of the likely offender, arguing that the police shaped the profile by providing leading information to the profilers. Finally, the police engaged in the dubious practice of hypnotizing a witness to refresh his recollections.

The prosecution is implicated in that it hired an expert witness, Louise Robbins, with a reputation for offering scientifically dubious but pro-prosecution evidence.[8] Also, the prosecution withheld requested and exculpatory evidence from the defense.[9] Evidence also suggests that the prosecution engaged in the classic act of creating evidence, relying on a jailhouse informant to whom Johnston reportedly confided his guilt. The judges, the final link in this alleged conspiratorial chain, were led by Hocking County judge Joseph Stilwell, part of the local criminal justice establishment intent on preserving its reputation and illegal activities. The other two judges are portrayed by the defense as pro-prosecution and willing to go along with local wishes.

Structure Perspective: "Throwing Pebbles on a Pond"

The agency perspective offers a compelling narrative: it has easily identifiable good guys and bad guys, neatly ties up loose ends, imposes rationality and linearity on otherwise complex proceedings, and does so with three simple words—"I've been framed." The structure perspective is not amenable to such concise and neat summary. Quite the opposite, it requires an elaborate reconstruction of the many contexts in which the case occurred so as to gain an understanding of the meaning and significance of decisions at the time they were made. Dale Johnston described this complexity aptly. When I asked him to explain his wrongful conviction, he analogized it to "throwing pebbles on a pond" (Johnston 1998). There is no clear starting point or orderly sequence of events; rather, each pebble creates ripples, and the ripples intersect and interact in a manner too complex to anticipate or fully understand.

Although the evidence can be marshaled to suggest that Johnston was framed, a more contextualized reconstruction suggests that he was a viable suspect around whom an adequate case could be constructed and into which evidence could be fitted by straining, but not breaking, credulity, law, science, and standards of practice. Dale Johnston was the most likely suspect in the murders of Todd and Annette. Police attention to him was consistent with the statistical reality that family members or acquaintances perpetrate most homicides. This statistical truth was reinforced by specific exigencies: reports from Annette's associates as well as from Johnston himself of sexual contact between stepfather and stepdaughter, Annette's decision to leave home in the months before her death, conflict between Dale and Todd, Annette and Todd's intentions to marry and possibly leave Logan, and inconsistencies and inaccuracies in Johnston's version of events leading up to the deaths.

Initial police investigation of the murders was compromised—partly for reasons beyond anyone's control, partly due to serious police errors.[10] By the time the bodies were discovered, the crime scene had been trampled by scores of people, destroying important evidence. This was unavoidable: no strong impetus to search for two missing adults existed, and the cornfield was, of course, not recognized as a crime scene until the bodies were discovered. This problem was aggravated by the several-day delay in casting footprints and collecting other evidence. The police also failed to collect and analyze evidence that was available in the cornfield. These latter problems are more troubling. It is important to recognize, however, that the Logan police had little experience in murder or violent crime investigations; the town's most recent previous murder took place in 1976.

Compounding these problems, the lead investigator in the case, Logan police detective James Thompson, was an overzealous, highly moralistic, somewhat unstable figure said to have been adversely affected by his service in Vietnam. Those with whom I spoke portrayed him as a small-town police officer who viewed Logan as beset by big-city crime problems. He believed that the crimes of popular imagination—rampant drug use and trafficking, child sexual abuse, and child pornography—were active threats in Logan. Quite plausibly, once Thompson was persuaded of Johnston's guilt, a result probably easily accomplished through adoption of the sexual abuse narrative of the case, he became single-minded in his focus.

Police and prosecutorial reliance on hypnotically refreshed testimony was not inconsistent with practice at the time.[11] The same can be said for reliance on the testimony of Louise Robbins, a widely used witness, certified by judges as an expert in courts across the country.[12] The FBI profile implicating Johnston, perceived in hindsight as crafted with Johnston's picture and biography in hand, was more likely the product of the sometimes careless and unsystematic manner in which profiles were constructed.[13]

The failure of the police to pursue leads provided by various witnesses, particularly those who saw people resembling Todd and Annette and heard gunshots near the cornfield in the late afternoon of 4 October, is consistent with their comfort level with Dale Johnston as a suspect. Although in hindsight it may appear that the police went to insupportable lengths to discredit these witnesses, within the context of the time, the witnesses were some among many that brought forth evidence evaluated as immaterial. We now know that these witnesses were probably correct in their identifications and supporting versions of events, but at the time their reports were not remarkable. As information retrospectively recognized as exculpatory emerged in the course of the investigation, it was easily and routinely rationalized and realigned, or ignored, particularly as the case against Johnston strengthened.

It is also important to recognize the extent to which existing investigative rules and practices serve as structural advantages to the state, producing a tendency toward wrongful convictions independent of the practices of particular officers. The police function as the de facto investigative arm of the prosecutor's office. Although criminal proceedings are ideally a search for truth by competing parties, the agency empowered to represent the public in investigating crimes has an open relationship with only one party in these proceedings (Fisher 1988, 1993; "Toward a Constitutional Right," 1978).

Efforts to require police and prosecutorial cooperation with the defense have been inadequate. Most notably, the *Brady* rule, created by the Warren Court in *Brady v. Maryland* (1963), requires the prosecution to provide the defense with evidence that is material and exculpatory. Nevertheless, it allows the prosecution the discretion to define these standards, provides few inducements for cooperation, and, as established in a later related case, requires the defense to ask specifically for what it may not know exists.[14] This last requirement is especially problematic because it reinforces the initial problem that evidence collected by police is the property of the prosecution. These rulings are of additional significance in that they occur within a larger legal culture that treats cases as battles to be won or lost and a larger social context that views policing as the central source of public safety and social order.

Police and prosecutorial reliance on Kevin Scudder was routine. Jailhouse snitches serve as a common law enforcement means to strengthen cases by providing what is otherwise lacking: a confession (Winograde 1990). Although this practice is one of the most glaring faults in capital prosecutions and is frequently the subject of calls for reform (Zimmerman 1994), it is a normal feature of prosecutorial practice. As such, it reveals more about prosecutorial culture and the "win at all costs" ethic of prosecutors than it does about the practice of the Hocking County District Attorney's Office in particular.

As for the judges, careful review of the trial transcript and other written records of the case, as well as appellate reviews of the trial, suggests that their rulings were evenhanded and in keeping with existing statutory and case law. Although their decisions regarding hypnotically induced testimony and discovery rules were reversed on appeal, the appellate courts made no suggestion of grievous error. The use of hypnosis in legal proceedings had been an issue for at least fifty years before the Johnston trial (see Diamond 1980; McDonald 1987;

Sies and Wester 1985). While the failure of the judges to scrutinize closely the recordings of hypnotic sessions with Steven Rine was unfortunate, it leaves us no reason to believe it was designed to avoid knowledge of the inadequacies of the hypnosis.[15] Further, my interviews with two of the judges revealed an apparently sincere and continuing belief in Johnston's guilt and in the veracity of hypnotically induced testimony. More notably, in these interviews, the judges appeared genuinely unaware of the numerous controversies relating to alternative theories of the case, suggesting the implausibility of their complicity in any effort to frame Johnston.[16]

Conclusion: Beyond Whodunit

The cultural power of the whodunit framework distorts our understanding of organizational wrongdoing by emphasizing the rationality, linearity, and individuality of wrongdoing within organizational settings characterized by powerful opposing forces: complexity, routines, multiple decision makers, and limitations on individual information and responsibility.

Working within the framework provided by Vaughan (1996), the foregoing analysis has directed attention toward the environments (structural and cultural) within which organizations operate and that mediate macro and micro agency. In this view, individual decision making is nested within organizational structures and cultures, which are themselves nested within larger institutional and societal environments. Carefully reconstructing and closely examining these contexts makes it possible to understand the knowledge and policies that guide decisions and the meaning assigned to decisions by those making them.

Seen from this perspective, the wrongful conviction of Dale Nolan Johnston was the product of the normal, day-to-day, routine operations of decision makers acting free of conspiratorial intent or wrongdoing; the outcome was generated by the structures and routines in which actors act. Such actors are engaged in a kind of "normal science" (Kuhn 1962; Vaughan 1996) in which assumptions of normality and regularity lead actors to follow prescribed practices. Although lacking the drama, linearity, and storytelling power of the agency model, this perspective accords with the mundane nature of daily life and work.

Perhaps most disturbing is the implication that wrongful convictions are essentially unremarkable and much more difficult to guard against than by simply controlling against bias and wrongdoing. More specifically, the foregoing suggests that the occurrence of wrongful convictions is limited first and foremost by the large number of capital murder cases in which the factual involvement of the defendant is not in question. Beyond that, police professionalism, effective capital defense, and independent and investigative media are important sources of protection against wrongful convictions. Conversely, the use of law to improve the implementation of the death penalty may make matters worse (by increasing the complexity of structures as well as our confidence in the process itself). There is little reason to believe that the complex legal framework constructed around the death penalty has reduced the number of wrongful convictions or that further movement in this direction will produce a better result.

NOTES

1. The National Conference on Wrongful Convictions and the Death Penalty was held in Chicago, 13–15 November 1998.
2. The crime and the trial were given substantial coverage by the local paper, the *Logan Daily News,* as well as by several urban papers: the *Columbus Dispatch,* the *Akron Beacon Journal,* and the *Dayton Daily News.* I examined each of these papers.
3. All of the newspapers and legal materials used in reconstructing this case are on file with the author and available on request.
4. This is relevant in that the torsos and limbs were found in different police jurisdictions. The cornfield is in the jurisdiction of the Hocking County Sheriff's Department. The river is in the jurisdiction of the Logan Police Department.
5. It strains credulity to believe that Johnston would abduct Todd and Annette in Logan, return them to his secluded farm to kill them, and then return to more populated Logan to dispose of their bodies. This is particularly true considering the presence of a strip mine on his property, where the bodies could have been disposed of fairly easily.
6. As a measure of the intensity of local interest in the case, this was the first special edition of the *Logan Daily News* since the end of World War II. A special edition was also printed to mark Johnston's conviction.
7. At the center of these allegations is former Hocking County sheriff's deputy James T. Moccabee, who was discharged as a result of marijuana use and subsequently alleged that his superiors ordered him to falsify evidence. He was reinstated on appeal after it was determined that the evidence was insufficient to support his termination (*Moccabee v. Hocking County Auditor* 1982).
8. Dr. Robbins was later a subject of a highly critical *48 Hours* report on unreliable expert witnesses (6 July 1994).
9. In *Brady v. Maryland* (1963), the Supreme Court ruled that the failure of the prosecution to disclose to the defense evidence favorable to the accused was a violation of due process.
10. One well-known consultant to police departments who has direct knowledge of this case described the investigation as the "sloppiest piece of police work" he had ever seen. He rejected the suggestion of a conspiracy against Johnston (Griffis 1997).

11. Only through this case and other contemporaneous higher-profile cases (notably, the Bundy and Spaziano cases in Florida) was hypnotically induced testimony barred.

12. In an interview years after Johnston's conviction was reversed and Robbins's reputation tarnished, Judge Corrigan described her as "very, very impressive" and a central figure in Johnston's conviction (Corrigan 1997).

13. As far as I can determine, the FBI never visited the crime scene or conducted an independent investigation. Rather, their profile was based on materials given to them by local law enforcement and therefore reproduced the bias toward Johnston found in these materials.

14. *United States v. Agurs* (1976) established a high standard for defense efforts to argue that exculpatory material was wrongly withheld by the prosecution.

15. Because capital cases present judges with enormous volumes of material, it would be naïve to deny that much of this material is underscrutinized.

16. It is also interesting, and perhaps significant, to note that Judge Michael Corrigan from Cuyahoga County, who came to the case with the reputation of being hard-nosed and punitive, is the son of Thomas Corrigan, the prosecutor in the infamous Sam Sheppard wrongful conviction case. This raises questions about Corrigan's response to claims of wrongful prosecution and conviction.

REFERENCES

Bedau, Hugo Adam, and Michael L. Radelet. 1987. "Miscarriages of Justice in Potentially Capital Cases." *Stanford Law Review* 40: 21–179.

Corrigan, Michael. 1997. Interview with author, 15 October.

Davies, Nick. 1991. *White Lies: Rape, Murder, and Justice Texas Style*. New York: Pantheon.

Diamond, Bernard L. 1980. "Inherent Problems in the Use of Pretrial Hypnosis on a Prospective Witness." *California Law Review* 68: 313–49.

Dieter, Richard C. 1997. *Innocence and the Death Penalty*. Washington, D.C.: Death Penalty Information Center.

Ermann, M. David. 1991. "Ordinary Deadly Decisions: Why People, Organizations, and Events Cause Hazard Concealment." Manuscript.

Ermann, M. David, and Richard J. Lundman, eds. 1996. *Corporate and Governmental Deviance*. 5th ed. New York: Oxford University Press.

Ermann, M. David, and Gary A. Rabe. 1997. "Organizational Processes (Not Rational Choices) Produce Most Corporate Crimes." In *Debating Corporate Crime: An Interdisciplinary Examination of the Causes and Control of Corporate Misconduct*, edited by William S. Lofquist, Mark A. Cohen, and Gary A. Rabe, 53–67. Cincinnati: Anderson.

Ferguson, Robert A. 1996. "Untold Stories in the Law." In *Law's Stories: Narrative and Rhetoric in the Law*, edited by Peter Brooks and Paul Gewirtz, 84–98. New Haven: Yale University Press.

Fisher, Stanley Z. 1988. "In Search of the Virtuous Prosecutor: A Conceptual Framework." *American Journal of Criminal Law* 15: 197–261.

———. 1993. "'Just the Facts, Ma'am': Lying and the Omission of Exculpatory Evidence in Police Reports." *New England Law Review* 28: 1–62.

Fisse, Brent, and John Braithwaite. 1993. *Corporations, Crime and Accountability*. New York: Cambridge University Press.

Germond, Kate. 1996. "The Reasons for 'Wrong-Man' Cases." In *Convicting the*

Innocent, edited by Donald S. Connery, 114–17. Brookline, Mass.: Brookline Books.

Gershmann, Bennett L. 1993. "Themes of Injustice: Wrongful Convictions, Racial Prejudice, and Lawyer Incompetence." *Criminal Law Bulletin* 29: 502–15.

Gioia, Dennis A. 1992. "Pinto Fires and Personal Ethics: A Script Analysis of Missed Opportunities." *Journal of Business Ethics* 11: 379–89.

Greene, Edith. 1989. "On Juries and Damage Awards: The Process of Decisionmaking." *Law and Contemporary Problems* 52: 225–46.

Griffis, Dale. 1997. Interview with author, 14 October.

Gross, Samuel R. 1996. "The Risks of Death: Why Erroneous Convictions Are Common in Capital Cases." *Buffalo Law Review* 44: 469–500.

Huff, C. Ronald, Arye Rattner, and Edward Sagarin. 1996. *Convicted but Innocent: Wrongful Conviction and Public Policy.* Thousand Oaks, Calif.: Sage.

Johnston, Dale N. 1998. Interview with author, 14 November.

Kelman, Herbert C., and V. Lee Hamilton. 1989. *Crimes of Obedience.* New Haven: Yale University Press.

Kuhn, Thomas S. 1962. *The Structure of Scientific Revolutions.* Chicago: University of Chicago Press.

Lane, Mark. 1970. *Arcadia.* New York: Holt, Rinehart, and Winston.

Lee, Matthew T., and M. David Ermann. 1999. "Pinto 'Madness' As a Flawed Landmark Narrative: An Organizational and Network Analysis." *Social Problems* 46: 30–47.

Lofquist, William S. 1997. "A Framework for Analysis of the Theories and Issues in Corporate Crime." In *Debating Corporate Crime: An Interdisciplinary Examination of the Causes and Control of Corporate Misconduct,* edited by William S. Lofquist, Mark A. Cohen, and Gary A. Rabe, 1–29. Cincinnati: Anderson.

Lofquist, William S., Mark A. Cohen, and Gary A. Rabe, eds. 1997. *Debating Corporate Crime: An Interdisciplinary Examination of the Causes and Control of Corporate Misconduct.* Cincinnati: Anderson.

Markman, Stephen J., and Paul G. Cassell. 1988. "Protecting the Innocent: A Response to the Bedau-Radelet Study." *Stanford Law Review* 41: 121–60.

McDonald, David S. 1987. "The Admissibility of Hypnotically Refreshed Testimony." *Ohio Northern University Law Review* 14: 361–78.

Mokhiber, Russell. 1988. *Corporate Crime and Violence.* San Francisco: Sierra Club Books.

Parloff, Roger. 1996. *Triple Jeopardy.* Boston: Little, Brown.

Pennington, N., and Reid Hastie. 1986. "Evidence Evaluation in Complex Decision Making." *Journal of Personality and Social Psychology* 51: 242–58.

Perrow, Charles. 1984. *Normal Accidents: Living with High-Risk Technologies.* New York: Basic Books.

———. 1986. *Complex Organizations: A Critical Essay.* 3d ed. New York: McGraw-Hill.

Rabe, Gary A., and M. David Ermann. 1995. "Corporate Concealment of Tobacco Hazards: Changing Motives and Historical Contexts." *Deviant Behavior* 16: 223–44.

Radelet, Michael L., Hugo Adam Bedau, and Constance E. Putnam. 1992. *In Spite of Innocence.* Boston: Northeastern University Press.

Radelet, Michael L., Williams S. Lofquist, and Hugo Adam Bedau. 1996. "Prisoners Released from Death Rows Since 1970 Because of Doubts about Their Guilt." *Thomas M. Cooley Law Review* 13: 907–66.

Sies, Dennis Ellsworth, and William C. Wester, II. 1985. "Judicial Approaches to the Question of Admissibility of Hypnotically Refreshed Testimony: A History and Analysis." *DePaul Law Review* 35: 77–124.

Simon, David R. 1999. *Elite Deviance*. 6th ed. Boston: Allyn and Bacon

Sudnow, David. 1965. "Normal Crimes: Sociological Features of the Penal Code in a Public Defender Office." *Social Problems* (Winter): 255–76.

Sutherland, Edwin H. 1983 [1949]. *White Collar Crime*. New Haven: Yale University Press.

"Toward a Constitutional Right to an Adequate Police Investigation: A Step Beyond *Brady*." 1978. *New York University Law Review* 53: 835–74.

Tucker, John C. 1997. *May God Have Mercy*. New York: Norton.

Vaughan, Diane. 1996. *The Challenger Launch Decision*. Chicago: University of Chicago Press.

Winograde, Jana. 1990. "Jailhouse Informants and the Need for Judicial Use Immunity in Habeas Corpus Proceedings." *California Law Review* 78: 755–85.

Yant, Martin. 1991. *Presumed Guilty: When Innocent People Are Wrongly Convicted*. Buffalo, N.Y.: Prometheus.

Yeager, Peter C. 1991. *The Limits of Law: The Public Regulation of Private Pollution*. New York: Cambridge University Press.

Zimmerman, Clifford S. 1994. "Toward a New Vision of Informants: A History of Abuses and Suggestions for Reform." *Hastings Constitutional Law Quarterly* 22: 81–178.

CASES CITED

Brady v. Maryland, 363 U.S. 83 (1963).

Moccabee v. Hocking County Auditor, 82–REM–03–0610 (1982).

State v. Johnston, 83–CR-54 (1984).

State v. Johnston, 529 N.E.2d 898 (1988).

State v. Johnston, 580 N.E.2d 1162 (1990).

State of Ohio v. Dale Johnston, Memorandum opinion, Oct. 25 (1984).

State of Ohio v. Dale Johnston, No. 425, Aug. 6 (1986).

United States v. Agurs, 427 U.S. 97 (1976).

Visions for Change in the Twenty-first Century

CLIFFORD S. ZIMMERMAN

10 Back from the Courthouse

Corrective Measures to Address the Role of Informants in Wrongful Convictions

Discussing the problems that the use of informants poses to our criminal justice system, one former federal prosecutor explained the willingness of informants to corrupt the justice process through "lying, committing perjury, manufacturing evidence, soliciting others to corroborate their lies with more lies, and double-crossing anyone with whom they come into contact" (Trott 1996: 1383). Thus, it should not be surprising that the misuse and misconduct of informants have often been cited as primary causes of wrongful convictions (Zimmerman 1994; see also Armstrong and Mills 2000; Reinhold 1989; Scheck et al. 2000; Trott 1996). Problems that have led to the conviction of innocent individuals include police fabrication of informants, police and prosecutorial shaping and manipulation of informant testimony, active encouragement by police and prosecutors of informants' illegal activity, and prosecutors' intentional reliance on false informant testimony. These problems extend from the informants, through the police and prosecutors who deal with them (known as informant "handlers"), into the judicial doctrines that govern informant and handler behavior.

To address and remedy the numerous flaws connected with the use of informants, this chapter reviews and critiques previously proposed remedies, explores recent suggestions for jailhouse informant reform, and presents a multifaceted plan to address and avoid informant and handler misconduct and abuses. These remedies include the elimination of informant rewards, more stringent rules on the use of informants, ethical guidelines for informant handling, and serious penalties for informant misconduct and mishandling. Unless and until such a plan is implemented, informants will continue to corrupt the justice process and contribute to the conviction of innocent people.

A Review of Previously Proposed and Currently Existing Remedies

For centuries, the use of informants has been criticized, and reforms have been suggested to remedy problems with them. A closer look at recent remedial legislation, jury instructions, academic reform suggestions, and judicial determinations provides a framework for examining a broader solution to the problem of informants.

Statutory Changes

For the most part, statutory reforms have been reactive and ineffectual. Historically, statutory change with respect to informants was, most simply, enactment and repeal of pro-informant legislation (Zimmerman 1994). Legislation in California following the Los Angeles County jailhouse informant crisis in the 1980s is a modern example that mirrors the past. During that decade, numerous instances of informant misuse and misconduct in the jail came to light. Informants admitted to perjury and falsifying confessions and were linked to 225 felony convictions (Reinhold 1989; Trott 1996). Between 1989 and 1994, California enacted a wide range of statutes to address this misconduct. One statute limits in-custody informant rewards to fifty dollars (*California Penal Code* § 4001.1).[1] Nevertheless, the statute has narrow limitations because it only applies to persons "held within a correctional institution" and does not address intangible rewards or rewards to third persons, which were rampant during the crisis. Most telling, the statute does not address the reward of leniency in charging, sentencing, release, or parole.

A second statute requires judges to offer a cautionary jury instruction when an informant testifies (§ 1127a). This instruction, however, merely tells the jury to "consider the extent to which [the testimony] may have been influenced by the receipt of, or expectation of, any benefits" but does not place the informant conduct in a broader context of unreliability, require advance disclosure of benefits information to the court or the defense counsel, or address whether coercion played a role in the witness's willingness to become an informant. It also maintains the alliance between the prosecution and the witness, which, unless explicitly severed, serves to bolster informant credibility.

Another statute modifies the state bribery law regarding payments to fact witnesses in criminal cases (§ 132.5). While this statute criminalizes paying for testimony, it specifically excludes "lawful compensation provided to an informant by a prosecutor or law enforcement agency" and "statutorily authorized rewards" (§ 132.5[e][1] & [4]).[2] First, no statute acknowledges or addresses the inherent conflict between sections 4001.1 (which, as noted, limits rewards to fifty dollars and to informants held in correctional institutions) and 132.5(e). Second, this statute brings about no reform but maintains informants firmly within the criminal justice system.

In a final ironic twist, one piece of the post-crisis legislation now requires prosecutors to notify a crime victim when the suspected perpetrator has become an "in-custody informant" (§ 1191.25). Thus, if an accused enters into an informant arrangement with law enforcement, the victim of the crime that led to the initial contact between the new informant and law enforcement will receive certain information. The victim receives advance notice of any reduction or modification in the informant's sentence or any dismissal of the case or early parole in exchange for information or testimony. Presumably, then, the victim will challenge the reward, effectively shifting the prosecutor's ethical obligations and professional responsibility regarding the informant handling to that victim, a relatively disinterested third party.[3]

This lack of legislative insight and perspective is troublesome. The efforts strongly echo the current judicial doctrines of assumption of risk and informant-handler distancing. "The thrust of the assumption of risk doctrine is the principle that the Constitution will not protect individuals who unknowingly divulge incriminating information to informants or undercover law enforcement officials" (Zimmerman 1994: 105). Here, the burden of responsibility for an encounter with an informant falls on the person speaking with the informant—in the previous scenario, the victim. The doctrine of informant-handler distancing allows handlers to distance themselves from the actions of the informant. Handlers are not held responsible for the misconduct of their informants, even though these handlers often allow, even actively encourage, that very misconduct. Both of these doctrines, as well as the California statutes, fail to address the powerful link between law enforcement and prosecutors, on the one hand, and informants, on the other hand, and instead further insulate handlers from responsibility for abuses.

Likewise, in response to informant crises, new agency regulations have been promulgated, which also reflect little effort at systemic change. For example, while "all of these guidelines state that laws should not be violated and that any criminal conduct should be reported to local law enforcement authorities," they typically permit criminal activity when the informant's role is extremely valuable and allow such decisions to be made by those officials who are involved with the informant (Zimmerman 1994: 134). Thus, the "new protections," when viewed in light of prevailing court doctrines, only serve to further institutionalize and validate past practices.

Jury Instructions

At both the state and federal levels, judges use and rely on jury instructions to advise jurors about informants and correct any imbalances due to their presence. California's new jury instruction, as discussed, is faulty. Similarly, federal-pattern jury instructions addressing informant testimony reflect three common traits, which together do not effectively address the problems with informants.[4]

First, nearly all of these instructions begin by telling jurors to exercise "greater care," "caution," or both when considering informant testimony. Second, in most instructions jurors are asked to determine if the testimony has been affected by the informant's self-interest, the agreement with the government, or any interest the informant has in the outcome. Both of these traits are admirable, but their strength and effectiveness must be evaluated by the instruction as a whole.

Finally, the instructions, universally, contain an additional comment that undermines the caution, care, and critical review embodied in the first two traits and makes it easier for jurors to disregard inconsistencies and accept the informant as offered by the prosecution. Some instructions tell jurors that they should not vote to convict based on informant testimony alone "unless you believe [the] testimony beyond a reasonable doubt" (Committee 1997: 26 [Instruction No. 1.15]). Others state that jurors can give the testimony "such weight as you think it deserves" (Committee 1996: 100 [Instruction No. 4.06]). Still others explicitly validate informant use by describing it as "permissible" and "common" (Devitt et al. 1992: 480 [Instruction No. 7.06A]). In sum, these statements contradict the two previously stated cautions.

To further explore the inability of a jury instruction to affect the prosecution-informant link, consider an instruction given by a Canadian judge regarding an informant:

> I would say to you that he is an unsavoury character in the extreme, and I repeat the other parts in my warning that you can accept his evidence if you wish, but you should in my view look for confirming evidence. In my view, your search will be fruitless in that regard as to the important part of the evidence. I ask you to keep in mind this man's apparent and admitted past in being a liar, a perjurer, and obstructor of justice, a police informer and a bully. I would suggest to you that he has absolutely no regard for the solemnity of an oath. (Kaufman 1998: 596)

Obviously, this instruction raises the question as to why the prosecutor used and the court allowed this informant to testify, given such a past. In fact, the informant, identified only as C, had testified for the Crown in several trials. In one, *Walker,* the Crown attorney disavowed the informant's testimony in closing arguments; in another, *Buric,* the court gave the previously quoted instruction (cases cited in Kaufman 1998). While this instruction adequately conveys the base level of the testimony received, the juries in both cases still convicted the respective defendants (Kaufman 1998). Thus, even this extreme attempt at a curative measure did not adequately reverse the poisoning of the trial by the informant appearance, further indicating that much earlier measures are necessary to prevent such witnesses from testifying and that courtroom personnel must address them differently when they do.

Legal Experts

A review of the legal literature addressing the problem of informants yields six types of proposed remedies, each raised independently of the others and all but one accepting informants. By far the largest amount of attention is given to what is called a rights-based approach (Zimmerman 1994). In this approach, the authors assert that judicial strengthening of a particular constitutional right will result in adequate protection for those who suffer from informant misconduct or mishandling. Thus, stronger concern for and protection of Fourth Amendment (Donovan 1984; Maclin 1996; Stone 1976), Sixth Amendment (Lundstrom 1986; Lurie 1990; Tomkovicz 1988), Due Process (Uviller 1987; White 1979, 1991), or Thirteenth Amendment (Misner and Clough 1977) rights will cure the problem. Each of these arguments suffers the same general faults: failing to question the validity of the underlying conduct; relying on the courts to adequately scrutinize the informant and governmental behavior at issue; and generally failing to understand the nature of the underlying issues, including informant motives, rewards, and the pressures on law enforcement to use informants to facilitate investigations and prosecutions. At best, these are attempts at triage, in which only the most severe cases receive attention while the others, which are just as systemic, go untreated.[5]

Other suggestions suffer similarly. Some scholars suggest that law enforcement officials obtain prior judicial review to use informants, much in the same way that judges review and issue search and arrest warrants ("Judicial Control" 1967; Maclin 1996; Pershetz 1976–77; Pringle 1969). These approaches likewise fail to take into account the nature of the informant-handler relationship and, in particular, the coercive origin of that relationship. Still others suggest greater ability to cross-examine informants at trial (Haglund 1990), better access to post-conviction review (Winograde 1990), and more attention to informant testimony at trial (Mauet 1995). In each of these proposals, the burden remains on the challenger to the informant; there is no shift of any burden to the handler to justify the use of the informant, disclose any greater information about the informant-handler relationship, or question the validity of this type of testimony.[6]

In the end, Judge Trott (1996) provides sound advice when he beseeches prosecutors to use the truth. He urges them not to use criminals as witnesses and vigorously corroborate any and all information received from or related to an informant. Nevertheless, Trott also presents the status quo court-system approach in urging prosecutors to distance themselves from informants. In the context of his presentation, one would hope that prosecutors understand this argument to mean that they should use informants as little as possible. Nevertheless, some law enforcement personnel could read it simply as another reminder that, if they distance themselves from the informant, the courts will likewise distance them from any subsequent misconduct or mishandling.

Recent Corrective Suggestions about the Use of Jailhouse Informants

Recently, the issue of jailhouse informants has been the focus for addressing the need for reform.[7] This is not surprising. Jailhouse informants are the most problematic form of informant (because they frequently provide a prosecutor with a complete case by way of an alleged confession by the suspect) and thus are the easiest to criticize and attempt to address. After two Florida trials, in which the prosecution respectively called twenty-seven and twelve jailhouse informants as witnesses, Boston criminal defense attorney Martin Weinberg developed a list of recommendations, which he then presented to the Ontario Commission investigating the wrongful conviction of Guy Paul Morin (Kaufman 1998: 581–82).[8] In Ontario, the commission, chaired by Judge Fred Kaufman, also proposed new guidelines for the use of jailhouse informants. Finally, in response to a conviction based in large part on suspect jailhouse informant testimony, a panel of the Oklahoma Court of Criminal Appeals recommended new procedures to govern the use of jailhouse informants as witnesses.

Weinberg Testimony

Weinberg (1998) proposed a nine-point plan to address jailhouse informants that included several meaningful suggestions. His plan included several fresh perspectives that imposed burdens on the prosecutors and courts to control jailhouse informants. For example, he proposed that courts initiate investigations into informants who are suspected of lying and that prosecutors terminate any continuing benefits to informants who have lied (Kaufman 1998: 582–83; Weinberg 1998: 64–65). He further suggested that courts instruct juries before and after informant testimony on the "historically . . . unreliable" nature of jailhouse informant testimony (Kaufman 1998: 584; Weinberg 1998: 66). When a court finds that an informant is untruthful, the testimony should be automatically excluded rather than requiring the prosecution to corroborate the informant's testimony. This would eliminate informants who "recruit untruthful corroboration" (Kaufman 1998: 584; Weinberg 1998: 66).

With respect to prosecutors, Weinberg (1998: 66), first and foremost, would require that informants not be placed "in a position (i.e., in the accused's prison cell) where they can receive confessions" (see also Kaufman 1998: 584). Once an informant appears in a criminal case, Weinberg (1998) would require that, before trial, prosecutors provide defense attorneys with information to identify credibility issues, including the identity of the informant and the informant's criminal background—convictions, pending charges, and crimes suspected (which could be affected by benefits conferred). Further, the prosecutor must determine and disclose informant benefits before trial, and these benefits should not be subject to post-trial enhancement. Likewise, at trial, prosecutors should not vouch for informants, which wrongly extends the prosecutor's credibility to the informant (Kaufman 1998: 583; Weinberg 1998: 65). Finally, prosecutors must maintain a registry of informant information and testimony (Kaufman 1998: 584; Weinberg 1998: 66).

This list is impressive in not only its distribution of corrective power but also its depth of understanding of informant problems. For example, the problem of the prosecution's vouching for informants involves both subtle and overt elements. Weinberg (1998) addresses the overt elements by eliminating this practice. He also addresses the subtle elements, in which jurors inherently believe prosecutorial witnesses to be credible and reliable, by having the court place the informant testimony in a broader context as "historically . . . unreliable" (Weinberg 1998: 66). This is critical because it affirmatively addresses the subconscious acceptance of the testimony as credible and reliable.

Like other suggestions, however, this offering maintains and fosters elements of informant acceptance that the criminal justice system and society should not tolerate. In this respect, Weinberg appears to be relying on the very systemic elements, courts and prosecutors, that have perpetuated informant use and abuse to correct themselves. Nevertheless, the criminal justice system in particular and society in general would greatly benefit from the judicial or prosecutorial implementation of any of these suggestions. Further, where implemented, defense counsel should advocate that these changes be extended to the police and prosecutorial use of non-jailhouse informants.

Kaufman Commission on Proceedings Involving Guy Paul Morin

After receiving these suggestions from Weinberg (just discussed) and many other witnesses, the Ontario Commission investigating the informant use against Guy Paul Morin developed and presented its own recommendations for jailhouse informant reform. While the commission refused to propose a ban on the use of all in-custody informants, its recommendations did focus on prosecutorial handling of jailhouse informants, the reliability of informant information, informant benefits, disclosure of informant information to defense counsel, judges' questioning of informants, and the need to educate handlers.

With regard to prosecutorial conduct, the commission recommended that jailhouse, or in-custody, informant use be strictly controlled.[9] Thus, new guidelines should reflect that these jailhouse informants have led to "miscarriages of justice in the past," that they are dangerous and unscrupulous, and that prosecutors should not advance cases based solely on the "unconfirmed evidence of an in-custody informer" (Kaufman 1998: 600–601). Further, a Crown attorney who "rel[ies], in part, on in-custody informer evidence" must bring the case to a supervisor's attention and obtain approval to proceed (602–3).

With respect to the thorny issue of informant reliability, the recommendations permit only "credible" evidence that is "independent" of the informant and "significantly supports" the alleged statements (specifically excluding confirmation by another in-custody informant) (602). In this regard, the commission proposed a laundry list for prosecutors to consider in evaluating informant reliability. This list includes the consistency between multiple informant statements, the level of factual detail offered, a comparison of the information provided with information readily available to the public, the utility of the statements in leading to new evidence, the informant's character (including any psychological profiles), any requests for benefits, the informant's past reliability, the number of occasions the informant has reported statements by others, any prior informant testimony, the existence of any written contemporaneous records of statements received, the timeliness of reporting statements received, the manner in which the statement was taken by the handlers (for example, video- or audiotaped, under oath, nonleading questions, and so on), and any other evidence that may contribute to or diminish the reliability of the statement or credibility of the informant (604–6).

The recommendations also addressed the conferral of benefits on in-custody informants. While the commission refused to propose a ban on informant benefits because it "would run against the grain of existing Canadian jurisprudence," it recommended against benefits conditioned on conviction, benefit enhancement after testimony, and any additional post-testimony benefits (616).[10] Rather than recommend removal of benefits for additional crimes committed by the informant, the commission proposed that such crimes disqualify future use of the informant (Kaufman 1998). Finally, regarding handler-informant inter-action, the commission suggested that the handler-negotiator be some-one other than the prosecutor who will use the information received and that all agreements be reduced to writing.

The commission also addressed the disclosure of informant in-formation to defense counsel. This information should include records addressing the informant's criminal record, prior informant testimony, any offers or promises of benefits or consideration, handler interview notes about the informant, and the custodial nature of the informant's situation at the time he or she first came to the handler's attention. These requirements should be fulfilled even if the informant will not be called as a witness (616–18).[11]

Further recommendations addressed the general obligations of handlers to explore the informant's background and disclose excul-patory information, prosecute informants who give false statements, be wary of non-jailhouse informants, create local and national infor-mant registries with contributions from police and prosecutors, and videotape informant contact with all handlers (Kaufman 1998).

Despite the commission's refusal to ban jailhouse informants, it determined them to be "presumptively inadmissible" (628). Given this finding, the commission recommended that judges question informants to independently determine reliability and balance prosecutorial dis-cretion—an approach similar to how courts determine the acceptabil-ity of expert testimony on novel scientific theories or techniques in which examination focuses on "the reliability of that expert evidence" (628). While the commission did not spell out detailed considerations (as did the Oklahoma Court of Criminal Appeals, discussed later in this chapter), it did state that the testimony would have to be reliable beyond a reasonable doubt.

The commission suggested that the Crown commit resources to educate prosecutors and police about informants and to implement the other recommendations. Further, the commission reinforced that informants should never be placed to obtain information and that wit-nesses should never be placed with or near other witnesses. Where an informant does actively elicit a statement, however, he or she should be treated as a "state agent" (636–37). Finally, if an informant does testify, judges should instruct the jury that "this category of evidence has in the past resulted in unreliable verdicts" (635).

The vast breadth and depth of these recommendations is inspir-ing. The commission addressed many key areas in which reform is necessary and addressed them well below the surface. Nonetheless, the repeated testimony of Crown attorney and police witnesses against the final commission recommendations raises serious concerns about their actual implementation. The commission also repeatedly asserted that the elimination of jailhouse informants was not feasible. Only complete support and full implementation will determine whether the recommended reconfiguration of the Ontario system will correct many of the problems with jailhouse informants or significantly alter their impact on the wrongly accused and convicted.

Oklahoma Court of Criminal Appeals

In an effort to eliminate unreliable jailhouse informants, a panel of the Oklahoma Court of Criminal Appeals proposed new procedures to be followed prospectively by trial courts in that state. The process involved five stages: pretrial disclosure by the prosecutor, pretrial judicial hearing, pretrial judicial determination, jury instruction (if the testimony is admitted), and appellate review (if the defendant is convicted) (*Dodd v. State* 1999).[12]

The pretrial process would require prosecutors to give defense counsel, at least ten days before trial, information about the informant, including his or her criminal history, any "deal, promise, inducement, or benefit" that has been conferred or may be given in the future, information about prior informant testimony in cases (whether or not called to testify), and "any other information relevant to the informant's credibility" (*Dodd v. State* 1999: para. 4).

The judicial hearing would focus on the reliability of the informant. The evidence to be presented would include the informant's testimony, any other relevant witnesses, and any other evidence "bearing on the informant's credibility" (para. 5). The burden of proof would rest on the prosecutor to show "that the informant's testimony is more probably true than not" (para. 6).

In examining the evidence presented and the burden of proof, the trial judge "shall specifically consider" several factors: whether any consideration was received for testimony, whether the informant testified and received benefits for testifying in any other cases, "the specificity of the informant's testimony," how the informant obtained the statements, the existence of independent corroboration of the statement, any changes in the informant's statements, and the informant's criminal history (para. 5).

If the court determined that the prosecution met its burden, the judge would instruct the jury regarding that testimony. In that instruction, the jury would be told to exercise "greater care than the testimony of an ordinary witness"; examine the informant's interests or prejudices; consider "whether the witness has received anything (including pay, immunity from prosecution, leniency in prosecution, personal advantage, or vindication)"; and examine the informant's credibility through prior case testimony, statements, or consideration, changes in informant testimony, prior criminal history, and "any other evidence relevant to the informer's credibility" (para. 6).

Finally, if the informant testimony has been received and the defendant convicted, the appellate court should review the trial court determination to receive the testimony and determine whether an abuse of discretion has occurred (para. 7). While these reforms do not cover the vast realm of informant problems, they constitute a bigger step in the right direction than any other state or state court has made.

Unfortunately, this case was reheard by the Court of Criminal Appeals of Oklahoma which withdrew and vacated the original decision (*Dodd v. State* 2000). The new opinion severely limits the scope and application of its original decision, maintaining only the pretrial disclosure by the prosecutor and the jury instruction (*Dodd v. State* 2000: 784). Thus, in the end, the court refused to establish a pretrial judicial review procedure and automatic review (if the defendant is convicted).

A Multifaceted Solution to Informant Misconduct and Mishandling

Centuries of tinkering, adjustments, and corrections by law enforcement, legislatures, and courts indicate that elimination of informants is clearly the best solution to the problem of informant misconduct and mishandling. Nonetheless, one can hardly imagine that eventuality coming to pass in our society. The hue and cry from law enforcement would be overwhelming, and the political battle for implementation would be monumental. The prospects for such a dramatic, albeit necessary, change in our criminal justice system are dim at best.

Alternative suggestions, with few exceptions, do not address the depth and magnitude of the problems with informants. History teaches that small changes here and there have no impact on the greater system of informants. While a particular suggestion may be good, without a broader scheme, it is ultimately ineffective. Therefore, the solution must extend beyond simple suggestions and changes in perspective to a multifaceted approach that addresses every point in the criminal justice system affected by informants and levies severe penalties for noncompliance.

The solution must supplant the perceptions of informants, ferret out their underlying unreliability, and interject systemic controls designed to prevent abuses from the start in order to control the ways in which handlers approach informant use and enforce penalties for informant misconduct and mishandling so as to deter future problems. Further, each element of this change must be consistent with four key points regarding informants in the criminal justice system:

1. Informants must change from free agents to government agents.
2. Informants must be viewed as risky tools to be handled with care.
3. Courts must presume that informants are not credible.
4. Informants should be the prosecutor's (not the defendant's) problem.

Only by implementing a multifaceted remedy such as the one outlined in this section will the number of wrongful convictions produced through informant abuses be considerably reduced.

The Elimination of All Rewards and Benefits for Information

Rewards and benefits are at the core of the informant problem, providing the incentive for informants to lie, warping law enforcement's ability to evaluate reliability, and refocusing the informant-handler relationship from information receipt to a contractual arrangement. Providing information is not, and should not be seen as, a commercial or a capitalistic enterprise, nor is it a form of plea bargaining. If information is provided without the expectation of compensation, many questions about its veracity and reliability will dissipate or disappear.[13]

To expedite this change, law enforcement budgets for informants must be replaced with incentives for not funding informant use and support for retraining programs to fill the gaps. A nominal reward or recompense for some real and reasonable out-of-pocket expenditure could be acceptable but must be carefully monitored due to the potential for abuse.

To fully eliminate the impact of inducements, charging and sentencing considerations should not be permitted in exchange for information. The removal of such rewards (for example, dropped charges, reduced

sentences, and other leniency related to criminal charges) is necessary given that the coercive situation leads to inherently unreliable
sources and information. Prosecutors should be prepared to prosecute
cases. Although bargaining for a plea in exchange for other information may appear to be a reasonable action, the true plea bargain should
be based on an assessment, by both sides, of the relative merits (and
risks) of their case. Just as the prosecutor can evaluate the case and
make an offer accordingly, an accused can always bargain to avoid a
trial. To overcome past experience with bargaining for information,
prosecutors (and other law enforcement officials) may need additional
training to adequately assess the relative costs of trying the case versus negotiating the plea.

Justification for Informant Use Shifts to Prosecution

With the elimination of some possible informant
motivations, law enforcement handlers will then need to critically examine the existence and role of any other motivations, such as playing detective, fear, or survival. Some informants may try to manipulate
the system. Thus, handlers will have to perform an initial assessment
of informant reliability. The reliability factors to review, which draw
on some factors promoted by the Kaufman Commission, include the
following:

1. The circumstances under which the witness became an informant
2. All informant motivations (including any real or potential benefits
   or considerations that might still persist)
3. All past informant history (including the number of times information was offered, the number of times it was used, prior statements, prior testimony, and past reliability assessments)
4. All criminal history (including past crimes, pending charges, and
   potential or suspected crimes)
5. All statements in the case (for consistency, contemporaneous recording by the informant, contemporaneous reporting to the handler, level of factual detail, the degree to which the content is
   beyond public knowledge, the circumstances under which they
   were taken, how they were recorded by the handler, their potential to lead to new evidence, and potential verification by law enforcement personnel)

Without full use of every one of these criteria, this assessment will be neither sufficiently objective nor sufficiently critical. A second line of defense against informant unreliability must be established.

If an informant is to be used as a source or a witness, the court system must be critical of and critically review that choice. The most effective means is for courts to start with a rebuttable presumption against informant information and testimony based on its historical unreliability. The prosecution must bear a high burden of showing that an informant should be relied on (in the case of a warrant application) or allowed to testify (in the case of a trial). In the case of trial testimony, this review should commence with the prosecution's provision to defense counsel of all information relevant to the reliability factors set forth previously in this section. In the case of a warrant application, there is no opposing counsel to whom the prosecutor or police can give this information. In this circumstance, a new ombudsman-like position should be created to represent the interests of society in ferreting out unreliable informants. Without such a position, the court must fulfill this role and view the evidence presented accordingly.

In the end, the judge's determination should likewise focus on the reliability factors. If the informant testimony is allowed, several additional measures must be taken. First, the burden should fall on the prosecutor to present at trial corroborative, non-informant–based evidence so that any resulting conviction does not result solely from the testimony of an informant. Second, the court needs to sever the natural alliance and transference of credibility from public officials to their witnesses through specific instructions about the historic unreliability of informant testimony and announce that such testimony has led to wrongful convictions in the past. Third, the prosecution should present the jury with all information relevant to the reliability factors so that jurors can fairly assess the witness. Finally, defense counsel should be permitted extensive latitude in questioning the informant witness to sufficiently explore the issue of reliability.

Increased Court Role in Holding Government Accountable for Informant Misconduct or Mishandling

The court system must abandon its present informant jurisprudence, particularly the assumption of risk and informant-handler distancing doctrines. The key focus is accountability:

informants must be held accountable for their actions; and the government must be held accountable for its use of informants, including all consequences that flow from that use. To ensure that this change is effective, courts must adopt a rebuttable presumption: in other words, once an informant-handler relationship exists (whether formalized or not), the informant is a government agent, both in civil and criminal litigation.

Further, courts must be willing to punish informants and handlers when misconduct occurs. Informants can be punished through perjury prosecutions, discrediting, and lack of acceptance. Prosecutors and police can be punished through dismissal of criminal cases in which informant use offends, in any respect, the ethical and procedural guidelines detailed in this section. In addition, the harmless error rule should not be applied in appellate review of cases involving informants. This rule allows an appellate court to review the evidence presented at the original trial and determine that the defendant would have still been found guilty, even with the questionable evidence removed.

The Adoption of Ethical Guidelines and Penalties for Law Enforcement Handling of Informants

Uniform standards that emphasize ethical standards for the handling of informants are essential to changing law enforcement behavior regarding informants.[14] Eliminating rewards and benefits will foreclose much of the preexisting basis for an informant-handler relationship. A presumption against informant use, together with the penalty of dismissal for informant misconduct or mishandling, will caution law enforcement officers in the remaining circumstances. Additional attention must be given to the temptation to coerce future informant service at the time of arrest. Criminal charges and arrests should not be venues for indenturing informants. The penalty for using a criminal charge to create an informant-handler relationship should be dismissal of the criminal charges targeted by that informant information. Thus, if during the course of prosecution, defense counsel or the court becomes aware of any attempts to coerce information from a suspect (regardless of the charge), the charges being prosecuted will be dismissed.

Law enforcement efforts may become more difficult as a result, but this difficulty can and must be overcome through increased training, hard work, and an increase in law enforcement undercover operations. Thus, while informants can be used to gather information (assuming that they did not enter service as a result of a charge, arrest, or conviction), their role should be replaced quickly by law enforcement investigation. This will instantaneously remove the weak link in the system. Further, informant use should be limited to certain types of cases—those in which an informant's work will yield high indicia of reliability—even if this change eliminates many drug cases. Further, informant use should be strictly limited in terms of the number of cases—perhaps even limited to one case.[15]

The Adoption of Procedural Guidelines and Penalties for Law Enforcement Handling of Informants

The earliest and easiest calls for informant reform required strict record keeping of informant use and the establishment of local and national registries. These registries should continue and be modified to correlate the information collected with the reliability factors identified previously. This information must be available nationwide, accompanied by a blacklist of informant perjurers, and accessible by criminal defense attorneys who are confronted by an informant. To be effective, the penalties for failure to maintain proper records and contribute information on a regular basis should result in the loss or diminution of some law enforcement funding.

Further Research on Informant Use

Certainly, much work remains to be done in the study of informants, handlers, and the relationship between them. Additional study of informant motivations, their impact on informant conduct, and the extent to which these motivations are known to and understood by law enforcement will be particularly valuable. Statistical analysis of informant use as shown in local and national informant registries will reveal much about the utility of these records and some about informant use. Nevertheless, these data will be limited by the recent nature of their implementation and may not have the desired degree of reliability.

Obtaining accurate information about police officers' informant use is difficult. Current information comes primarily from dogged journalistic efforts, post-retirement revelations by handlers, and contentious litigation. These efforts will continue to add to the current rich supply of anecdotal information about police use of informants. Unfortunately, efforts to obtain truthful, current data on informant use may be stymied by issues of confidentiality, protection, and the police code of silence.[16] Informant tell-alls continue to surface but also raise issues of veracity. One vital source that has yet to be adequately explored involves surveying prosecutors on their use of informants and collecting numerical rather than anecdotal data. Likewise, surveys of jurors will reveal important information about court and counsel efforts to adequately address informant reliability.

Conclusion

This chapter has offered a beginning framework for accomplishing informant reform and avoiding wrongful convictions based on informant use. Although history teaches that informants have survived serious reconfigurations in the past, legislatures, courts, and law enforcement officials can try to change that situation. Serious and vigorous reform, through the implementation of these suggestions, will address problems with informants, lead to fewer wrongful convictions, and result in a better criminal justice system.

NOTES

Thanks to Richard Leo and Gary Marx for reading and commenting on an earlier draft of this chapter, James F. Tozzi and Julie Livergood for research assistance, and the editors for making this project a wholly satisfying experience.

1. An *in-custody informant* is "a person, other than a codefendant, percipient witness, accomplice, or coconspirator" who receives statements by the defendant "while both the defendant and the informant are held within a correctional institution" (*California Penal Code* § 1127a).
2. Courts have refused to trigger bribery statutes when prosecutors pay witnesses to testify at criminal trials (*United States v. Singleton* 1999, en banc). Nevertheless, if defense counsel offers to pay a fact witness for testimony, that is considered criminal conduct.
3. A more recent statute, enacted in 1998, forbids using minors as informants (twelve years old and under) [*California Penal Code* § 701.5(a)]. The statute, however, allows using minors under age eighteen for tobacco access crimes [§ 701.5(b)]. Further, this statute presumes that the informant-handler relationship will commence when the minor is arrested or charged with an offense, a further recognition of, not a correction to, the previous systemic characteristics of the informant-handler relationship [§ 701.5(c)].
4. Several federal courts of appeals publish pattern (or form) jury instructions to be followed by the federal trial courts within that circuit.
5. For a lengthier discussion of these approaches, see Zimmerman (1994: 129–32).
6. For a lengthier discussion of these approaches, see ibid. (132).
7. The previously discussed legislation from California started with a grand jury inquiry into the Los Angeles County Jail's informant crisis.

8. Weinberg was invited and presented his testimony as a representative of the National Association of Criminal Defense Lawyers. For an extended discussion of the Guy Paul Morin case, see chapter 3.

9. The Kaufman Commission defined an *in-custody informant* as someone who receives statements from an accused while both are in custody and the statements relate to offenses that occurred outside of the custodial institution (Kaufman 1998: 598).

10. These last two categories address distinct post-testimony situations in which the informant seeks benefit enhancement. In the first, the informant requests additional benefits directly following the testimony or conviction. In the latter situation, the informant is later charged with a new crime and seeks prosecutorial assistance in addressing these charges.

11. This finding was conditioned on the "informer's privilege" (Kaufman 1998: 618). In Ontario, this privilege arises when a member of the public provides information to a law enforcement officer. Then, unless a judge finds that "the innocence of an accused is at stake," the police and prosecutors do not have to provide the information or any information that may lead to identifying the informer (*R. v. Thomas* 1998: 186). The commission's conditioning of this requirement on what is termed an "ancient and hallowed protection which plays a vital role in law enforcement" undermines both the effectiveness of its recommendation and the otherwise apparent commitment of the commission to reform (*R. v. Thomas* 1998: 186).

12. The full opinion in *Dodd v. State* (1999) can be found in the *Oklahoma Bar Journal* ("*Dodd v. State*," 1999).

13. An examination of the philosophical and ethical foundations of informing is beyond this chapter. On this matter, current FBI use of informants, termed "assets," relies on societal loyalty in national security and terrorism cases. Further, one can even find judges debating the ethics of judicial ratting. This is an area rich for further discussion.

14. The U.S. Department of Justice (1980: 602) decided not to adopt a rule such as this one because it would "undoubtedly lead to continuing vexatious litigation, confrontation between the Department [of Justice] and certain courts, and nettlesome actions by state bar associations." Current "ethical" guidelines are vague and amorphous. American Bar Association Disciplinary Rule 7–104 prohibits an attorney from contacting an opposing party without consent from that party's attorney. Courts are hesitant to apply this ethical standard in the absence of a more serious constitutional violation of the defendant's Sixth Amendment rights (*United States v. Hammad* 1994; prosecutor interfered with defendant's attorney-client relationship but suppression of recordings inappropriate).

15. This is to address the commonly asserted law enforcement fear of "burning" informants at trial. Much effort is placed on protecting informants' anonymity because, once revealed, they are no longer of any use to law enforcement.

16. The code of silence typically arises in scenarios in which police refuse to identify the misconduct of another officer. The most common example is when one officer witnesses another using excessive force against a suspect. If an informant comes under greater scrutiny, however, and the penalties proposed are enforced, the code may well play a role in an officer's refusal to identify the mishandling of an informant.

REFERENCES

Armstrong, Ken, and Steve Mills. 2000. "Ryan: 'Until I Can Be Sure' Illinois Is First State to Suspend Death Penalty." *Chicago Tribune,* 1 February. [Internet]

California Penal Code. 1999. St. Paul, Minn.: West.

Committee on Model Criminal Jury Instructions within the Eighth Circuit. 1996. *Manual of Model Criminal Jury Instructions for the District Courts of the Eighth Circuit.* St. Paul, Minn.: West.

Committee on Pattern Jury Instructions, District Judges Association Fifth Circuit. 1997. *Pattern Jury Instructions (Criminal Cases).* St. Paul, Minn.: West.

Devitt, Edward J., Charles B. Blackmar, Michael A. Wolff, and Kevin F. O'Malley. 1992. *Federal Jury Practice and Instructions Civil and Criminal.* St. Paul, Minn.: West.

"Dodd v. State." 1999. *Oklahoma Bar Journal.* 70 (4 September): 2382–89.

Donovan, Dolores A. 1984. "Informers Revisited: Government Surveillance of Domestic Political Organizations and the Fourth and First Amendments." *Buffalo Law Review* 33: 333–88.

Haglund, Evan. 1990. "Impeaching the Underworld Informant." *Southern California Law Review* 63: 1405–47.

"Judicial Control of Secret Agents." 1967. *Yale Law Journal* 76: 994–1019.

Kaufman, Fred. 1998. *The Report of the Commission on Proceedings Involving Guy Paul Morin.* Toronto: Publications Ontario.

Lundstrom, Bruce D. 1986. "Sixth Amendment—Right to Counsel: Limited Postindictment Use of Jailhouse Informants Is Permissible." *Journal of Criminal Law and Criminology* 77: 743–74.

Lurie, David R. 1990. "Sixth Amendment Implications of Informant Participation in Defense Meetings." *Fordham Law Review* 58: 795–822.

Maclin, Tracey. 1996. "Informants and the Fourth Amendment: A Reconsideration." *Washington University Law Quarterly* 74: 573–635.

Mauet, Thomas. 1995. "Informant Disclosure and Production: A Second Look at Paid Informants." *Arizona Law Review* 37: 563–76.

Misner, Robert L., and John H. Clough. 1977. "Arrestees As Informants: A Thirteenth Amendment Analysis." *Stanford Law Review* 29: 713–46.

Pershetz, Martin L. 1976–77. "Domestic Intelligence Informants, The First Amendment and the Need for Prior Judicial Review." *Buffalo Law Review* 26: 173–208.

Pringle, Bruce D. 1969. "Present and Suggested Limitations on the Use of Secret Agents and Informers in Law Enforcement." *Colorado Law Review* 41: 261–84.

Reinhold, Robert. 1989. "California Shaken over an Informer." *New York Times,* 17 February, p. A1.

Scheck, Barry, Peter Neufeld, and Jim Dwyer. 2000. *Actual Innocence.* New York: Doubleday.

Stone, Geoffrey R. 1976. "The Scope of the Fourth Amendment: Privacy and the Police Use of Spies, Secret Agents and Informers." *American Bar Foundation Research Journal*: 1195–1271.

Tomkovicz, James J. 1988. "An Adversary System Defense of the Right to Counsel Against Informants: Truth, Fair Play, and the Massiah Doctrine." *University of California Davis Law Review* 22: 1–92.

Trott, Stephen S. 1996. "Words of Warning for Prosecutors Using Criminals As Witnesses." *Hastings Law Journal* 47: 1381–1431.

U.S. Department of Justice, Office of Legal Counsel. 1980. "Ethical Restraints of the ABA Code of Professional Responsibility on Federal Criminal Investigations." *United States Opinions Office of Legal Counsel* 4B (18 April): 576–602.

Uviller, H. Richard. 1987. "Evidence from the Mind of the Criminal Suspect: A Reconsideration of the Current Rules of Access and Restraint." *Columbia Law Review* 87: 1137–1212.

Weinberg, Martin G. 1998. "Excerpts from: The Commission Report." *Champion* 22 (August): 60–66.

White, Welsh S. 1979. "Police Trickery in Inducing Confessions." *University of Pennsylvania Law Review* 127: 581–629.

———. 1991. "Regulating Prison Informers under the Due Process Clause." *Supreme Court Review*: 103–42.

Winograde, Jana. 1990. "Jailhouse Informants and the Need for Judicial Use Immunity in Habeas Corpus Proceedings." *California Law Review* 78: 755–85.

Zimmerman, Clifford S. 1994. "Toward a New Vision of Informants: A History of Abuses and Suggestions for Reform." *Hastings Constitutional Law Quarterly* 22: 81–178.

CASES CITED

Dodd v. State, No. F-97–26 Okla.Ct.Crim.App., slip op. (1999).

Dodd v. State, 993 P.2d 778 (Okla.Crim. 2000).

R. v. Thomas, 124 C.C.C. 3d 178 (1998).

United States v. Hammad, 858 F.2d 834 (1994).

United States v. Singleton, 165 F.3d 1297 (1999).

ADELE BERNHARD

11 | Effective Assistance of Counsel

The adversarial system is the foundation of our judicial branch of government. When one of the adversaries is substantially weaker than the other or unfairly handicapped, just outcomes are less likely. As the Supreme Court has stated,

> the right to be heard would be, in many cases, of little avail if it did not comprehend the right to be heard by counsel. Even the intelligent and educated lawman has small and sometimes no skill in the science of the law. . . . He requires the guiding hand of counsel at every step in the proceedings against him. Without it, though he be not guilty, he faces the danger of conviction because he does not know how to establish his innocence. If that be true of men of intelligence, how much more true is it of the ignorant and illiterate, or those of feeble intellect. (*Powell v. Alabama* 1932: 68–69)

Far too frequently, lawyers hired or appointed to represent the accused provide woefully ineffective assistance of counsel. In every study of wrongful convictions, investigators inevitably conclude that ineffective assistance of counsel—bad lawyering—is an important factor in unjust convictions.[1] Of the thirteen men originally sentenced to death in Illinois who have been exonerated since 1987, "four were represented at trial by an attorney who had been disbarred or suspended" (Armstrong and Mills 1999). Twenty-six men, once sentenced to death, have received a new trial or a new sentencing hearing because reviewing courts determined that their trial counsel was ineffective (Armstrong and Mills 1999). This chapter reviews the systemic factors that disadvantage defense counsel and excuse poor lawyering, discusses the impediments to improving systems that provide counsel to the poor, and proposes reforms. It begins, however, with a case study that illustrates the relationship between ineffective assistance of counsel and wrongful conviction.

The People of the State of New York v. Luis Rojas (1995) is a typical appellate court decision that tells the story of a state court murder prosecution. The mistakes made by the witnesses, police, prosecution, and defense counsel are commonplace. Although defense counsel was hired, not appointed to the case, the deficiencies in his work are representative of mistakes made every day, even by attorneys who specialize in criminal defense. Even the most diligent and competent attorney cannot prevent a false accusation or misidentification or ensure an honest police investigation or a fair prosecution. What an attorney *can* do—and what the public has a right to expect that an attorney *will* do—is protect the accused from the mistakes, corruption, or overreaching of others.

The People of the State of New York v. Luis Rojas

One Saturday night in November 1990, Luis Rojas and a friend took the PATH train from New Jersey to Greenwich Village. The pair walked around Washington Square Park and the surrounding streets, enjoying the evening. Early in the morning, they ate a late dinner at the always crowded barbecue spot on Eighth Street and University Place.

Unbeknown to Luis, a tragedy was unfolding several blocks away. A pair of young men—one wearing a puffy orange jacket, the other in green—bumped into a group of boys walking in the opposite direction on the cool side of lower Broadway. The slight physical contact evolved into a full-scale argument, and soon the youth with the orange jacket drew a revolver and fired shots into the air. The weapon was passed to his companion in green, who fired at the now fleeing boys. Two were hit; one lived, and the other died three weeks later.

The shooters fled up Broadway, turning west on Eighth Street, as one of the group that had been fired on called the police and accompanied them in a search for the perpetrators. Meanwhile, an alarm was broadcast to all squad cars in the area and to police stationed in the nearby subway platforms. As the officers fanned out, Luis was heading home wearing a maroon jacket lined in bright orange. He entered the nearby PATH station with half a mind to jump the turnstile and beat the fare home. On the steps of the station, Luis turned his jacket inside out, to the orange side, so that the cameras he thought might be watching would record an orange-jacketed fare beater, not one in a maroon coat. Just as he was ready to jump, he noticed police in plain clothes hiding in the station and bought a token.

The PATH police watched all this activity in secret, hoping that Luis would be their next arrest. The officers saw Luis and Carlos board the PATH train as it pulled into the station. When they received the all-points alarm, "Looking for one in orange," the officers held the train. Moments later, a friend of the slain youth arrived with the police and identified Luis as "orange jacket." The same witness identified Luis's friend, Carlos, as one of the crowd on Broadway and identified another PATH rider, sitting further back in the train with shopping bags and a school backpack, as "green jacket"—the shooter. The PATH officers turned the three youths over to the New York Police Department and relinquished involvement in the case.

The three suspects, in handcuffs, were taken to the scene of the shooting so that more witnesses could view them. The following morning, before the district attorney formally charged the suspects, the three were identified once again in what were later called confirmatory lineups. But before the trip to 100 Centre Street, where the criminal courts process people twenty-four hours a day, the boy identified as "green jacket" was released when the train conductor called the investigating detective to verify that she had seen her passenger, with his Macy's bags, board the train much farther uptown. The witness had confused an innocent stranger on the train with the perpetrator simply because each was wearing a green jacket. The witness's misidentification should have caused the prosecution to worry about whether he had the capacity to accurately distinguish among individuals. Nevertheless, despite the previous mistake, the witness was permitted to testify at trial that he was sure Luis was the perpetrator in orange.

Carlos's case was dismissed because he had only been identified as someone in the crowd, not as a participant in the crime. "Green jacket" was never charged because of his verifiable alibi. Luis alone was tried (and convicted)—even though he, too, was innocent.

To investigate the allegations and handle the trial, Luis's family hired a New Jersey lawyer recommended by friends. Rojas family members are working people who earn too much to qualify for a public defender but do not have the means to hire one of the handful of exceptional local criminal defense attorneys. Moreover, the family may have been afraid to rely on the local public defender, who is too often considered an expert in plea bargaining only. Tragically, the attorney's pretrial investigation was perfunctory, and his performance at trial was confused, unskilled, and unconvincing. To begin, the New Jersey attorney was unfamiliar with the variety of trains that stopped close to Washington Square Park. He subpoenaed Metropolitan Transit Authority (MTA) records to document the time when Luis entered the station. But because Luis's stop was on the PATH line, the subpoena went unanswered. PATH trains run from New York to New Jersey and are supervised by the New York/New Jersey Port Authority. Because the MTA is a completely separate New York City system, it had no information about the incident. Counsel did not bother to ascertain why his subpoena was ignored. As a result, he did not discover the officers who had been watching for fare beaters and who would have testified, as they later told defense investigators working on Luis's appeal, that Luis was already in the station when the shots rang out on lower Broadway. The alarm that prompted them to hold the train did not specify the exact time of the shooting; so the officers simply assumed, because of Luis's subsequent identification, that the murder had happened much earlier. Post-conviction, when the officers learned when the shooting had really occurred, they swore that Luis could never have been the shooter. The officers had not realized that they were actually alibi witnesses for the defense. Defense counsel did not know either.

Defense counsel did not obtain from the prosecution the tape recordings of emergency 911 telephone calls made by witnesses to the shooting. The descriptions on the tapes were more detailed than were those contained in the police reports. On the tapes, witnesses reported that the orange-jacketed perpetrator had long hair worn in a pony tail. Luis did not.

Luis was arrested and convicted because police focused their investigation on him too quickly and neglected to track any other leads. Moreover, the police were so sure they had a killer in custody that they conducted sloppy, suggestive identification procedures that failed to protect him from mistaken identifications. If Luis's attorney had conducted a complete, thorough, and diligent investigation, he would have been able to discredit the police work at trial and establish Luis's innocence. He accomplished neither goal.

The attorney expended little time conferring with his client. Counsel never traveled to Rikers Island, where Luis was held awaiting trial, and spent a total of only thirty minutes with him in the jail cells behind the courtroom where incarcerated defendants wait for their cases to be called. Counsel's lack of empathy, energy, or commitment had terrible results at trial. Apparently unconvinced of Luis's innocence as well as unprepared to establish it in the courtroom, the attorney failed to present a consistent defense to the charges at trial. For some portion of the trial, he argued that Luis was the innocent victim of a mistaken identification, while at other times he suggested that Luis was present at the scene of the shooting but did not fire the gun. These hypotheses are inconsistent and cannot be harmonized. If one is true, the other simply cannot be. Arguing both undercut each.

Of course, Luis Rojas was not present at the shooting. The witnesses had simply mistaken him for one of the perpetrators. Instead of building an alibi and establishing innocence, Luis's own lawyer's questions undercut the best and true defense. The following excerpt from the trial illustrates how defense counsel's questions placed Luis on lower Broadway just before the shooting.

> Q: *[defense counsel]* Now, at the time the [bumping] occurred, your testimony was that some word [*sic*] were exchanged. Is that correct?
> A; *[witness]* Correct.
> Q: And those words were between Anthony Oquendo and Mr. Rojas. Isn't that right?
> A: That is correct.
> Q: You saw Mr. Rojas or the man in the orange jacket at that point, isn't that right, somebody in an orange jacket like this one, right?
> A: Correct. (*People v. Rojas* 1995: 66)

Luis Rojas's attorney failed to pursue leads, neglected to visit the scene, failed to interview either the PATH officers or the waitress in the barbecue restaurant, overlooked the New York State discovery statute that requires the prosecution to relinquish tape recordings related to a criminal prosecution (but only on request), ignored the basic rules of cross-examination, and delivered a closing argument that was not only incoherent but also placed Luis at the scene of the shooting—

contrary to Luis's version of the events. Rather than protecting Luis, defense counsel actually compounded the mistakes made by the police and prosecutors.

The Inadequacy of Criminal Defense Services

For the past thirty years, U.S. law has affirmed that people charged with serious crimes are entitled to be represented by an attorney free of charge (*Gideon v. Wainwright* 1963). Although courts interpret the right to counsel to mean the right to effective, meaningful assistance of counsel (*Evitts v. Lucey* 1985; *McMann v. Richardson* 1970), they have done little to ensure such effective or meaningful assistance.

As our nation's population has expanded, so have the number of people arrested each year.[2] Even though serious crime has been diminishing since the second half of the 1990s, after climbing for two decades, incarceration continues to increase—more than tripling since 1980 (U.S. Department of Justice 1998: 162). "The United States is building prisons at a record pace. If the current trend continues, the number of Americans behind bars will soon surpass the number of students enrolled full-time in four year colleges and universities" (Smith and Montross 1999: 443).[3] As a result of the increase in the rate of crime (Stunz 1997) and society's preference for incarceration to solve intractable social problems (Schlosser 1998), the industry of providing criminal defense services has expanded.[4] In many jurisdictions, indigent defense systems represent the overwhelming majority— as much as 90 percent—of those arrested (Spangenberg and Beeman 1995: 31–32).

Naturally, the cost of providing constitutionally required defense services has become a pressing concern for counties and states, while the adequacy of the services has been less of a worry for the public. There is a widening gap between the states' obligation to provide services and their resolve to do so.[5]

Jurists, bar associations, journalists, and academics readily agree that poor people are too often badly represented in criminal court. Former chief judge David Bazelon of the Washington, D.C., Circuit Court of Appeals put it this way: "The battle for equal justice is being lost in the trenches of the criminal courts where the promise of *Gideon* and *Argersinger* goes unfulfilled. The casualties of those defeats are easy to identify. . . . The prime casualties are defendants accused of street crimes, virtually all of whom are poor, uneducated, and unemployed . . . represented all too often by 'walking violations of the Sixth Amendment'" (Klein 1986: 656, quoting Bazelon [1976]).

In 1986, the American Bar Association's Special Committee on Criminal Justice in a Free Society reported that defense representation "is too often inadequate because of underfunded and overburdened public defender offices" (Klein 1993: 390). Michael McConville and Chester L. Mirsky's exhaustive study (1986–87) of criminal defense services in New York City criticizes both The Legal Aid Society, the nation's largest public defense law firm, as well as the city's assigned counsel plan for failing to investigate cases, consult with clients, file motions, or even appear in court on cases.

Stephen Bright, director of the Southern Center for Human Rights and a visiting lecturer at both the Yale and Harvard law schools, has collected innumerable stories of lawyers, assigned to represent poor people charged with capital offenses, who slept through the presentation of evidence, arrived at the courthouse intoxicated with alcohol or narcotics, were unable to recall a single relevant case, failed to conduct any investigation, or failed to present any evidence "in mitigation of their clients' sentences because they did not know what to offer or how to offer it, or had not read the state's sentencing statute" (Bright 1997b: 791–92).[6]

Professor Vivian Berger (1986: 60–62) of Columbia Law School concludes that the crisis in criminal defense is serious enough to "call into question the 'legal and moral foundations of the criminal process.'"[7] She grounds her verdict on a study of the literature, the increasing complexities of the criminal procedure laws, the youth and inexperience of those who generally volunteer for service in the public defender offices, and the increasing numbers of claims of ineffective assistance of counsel. The more challenging the laws become and the more inexperienced, overworked, and embattled the defenders, the more likely it is that unjust convictions will result.

The Structure of Defense Systems

To fulfill their constitutional obligation, counties and states have developed various mechanisms for providing counsel to those who cannot afford to hire an attorney, including assigned counsel programs, contract attorney plans, and full-time public defender offices (Spangenberg and Beeman 1995). Although no one way of organizing services fully protects against malpractice, a well-managed, supervised, and financed provider system minimizes the likelihood that a client will be wrongfully convicted.

Assigned counsel plans can be either informal or organized. In rural counties, where both population and crime are low, the plan may be no more than local judges' appointment of available attorneys to handle criminal matters as necessary. In fact, thousands of poor people in this country are represented by attorneys who are picked by the judge who will preside over their case and to whom they must petition for fees and permission to hire an investigator or expert. Assigned counsel plans are notoriously underadministered, unsupervised, and unregulated. Lawyers simply ask to join. Neither experience nor qualifications are reviewed, and participation in training programs is not required. Membership lasts forever. Attorneys stop taking assignments when they no longer need or want to. Their capacity to provide a competent defense is never reviewed.

In organized assigned counsel plans, attorneys must meet specific criteria to be assigned cases. Administrators screen candidates, rotate assignments, and try to insulate attorneys from judicial influence and pressure. Nevertheless, even in well-administered plans, attorneys must seek court approval for expert and investigative services as well as their own fees.

The second and most worrisome of the three delivery models involve contract attorney programs, especially fixed-price contracts in which a contracting firm agrees to handle all assignments in a given jurisdiction over a set period of time for a set price. Attractive to governments concerned about containing costs and accurately predicting expenditures, fixed-price contracts risk reducing the quality of services, especially when contracts are awarded through competitive bidding.

A public defender office is a public or private nonprofit organization staffed by attorneys who usually work for the defense office full time and whose exclusive responsibility is to handle criminal cases. Public defender programs have the best chance at delivering adequate services. "When adequately funded and staffed, defender organizations employing full-time personnel are capable of providing excellent defense services" (American Bar Association 1992b, commentary to 5–1.2). Unfortunately, defender organizations are not always adequately funded, supported, or supervised. When the organization is compromised, the work of the individuals is affected.

The Major Contributors to Ineffective Assistance of Counsel

Inadequate Funding

Commentators agree that inadequate funding leads to bad lawyering. Richard Klein (1993: 363) believes that "inadequate funding has created a situation wherein overburdened defense counsel cannot possibly provide competent representation to all of the clients they are assigned to represent." Inadequate funding adversely affects all defense systems (Spangenberg and Beeman 1995). Assigned counsel plan lawyers are frequently paid at rates so low that only lawyers who are beginning practice or have been unsuccessful in business will agree to take assignments. In New York City, lawyers who accept court-appointed, noncapital criminal cases in the state courts are paid $25 an hour out of court and $40 an hour in court—less than they would be paid in Alabama for the same work. The rates force those attorneys who make their living through assigned cases to accept a large volume of cases, limit out-of-court time (preparing motions, conducting investigations, and researching the law), and minimize expenses—responses antithetical to effective representation. The fee cap of $1,500 can be exceeded only in extraordinary circumstances and only if the trial judge agrees, a requirement that has the potential to impinge on counsel's independence and zealous advocacy.

In addition to low hourly rates, many state- or county-assigned counsel systems limit reimbursement to a maximum number of hours, even on capital cases. The Texas Court of Criminal Appeals, for example, limits lawyers to fifty hours on a capital case despite the fact that a local state bar association committee found that it takes between four hundred and nine hundred hours of time to prepare adequately (Bright 1997b: 806–7).

"Many jurisdictions process the maximum number of cases at the lowest possible cost without regard to justice" (788). For example, Bright reports that the county commission in McDuffie County, Georgia, hired Bill Wheeler, whose $25,000 bid for the year was almost $20,000 lower than that of the next-closest contenders, to handle all local criminal cases in the county. After four years of contract attorney service, Wheeler had tried only three contract cases and filed only three motions but had entered 313 guilty pleas (788–89).

Although public defender offices are best equipped to provide quality services, even a dedicated and focused work force cannot do its job without adequate funding. Typically, a public defender organization provides representation to everyone in its designated area who is arrested and in need of a lawyer. The budget for the office is negotiated in the local legislative body, where it competes with more popular public expenditures such as schools, hospitals, and police. It is hardly surprising that prosecutors and public safety officers receive more funds than do the public defenders whose nonvoting clients are universally disliked and feared (Taylor-Thompson 1999: 201–2).

A funding disparity between the prosecutorial and the defense function is expected and accepted, if not always explicitly acknowledged (Luban 1993). Moreover, any budget-line comparison will underestimate the size of the discrepancy. A public defender office rarely receives any supplements to its budget from other agencies or funding sources. The office must provide all essential services—including investigation and social work support services—from its legislative grant. An expenditure in one budget line necessitates a cut in another. Prosecutors, on the other hand, are provided with an array of services from other public agencies, free of charge. The police investigate crime, make arrests, and turn the results of their efforts over for prosecution. The police collect evidence, contact and interview witnesses, and generally assist with the preparation of the trial. In short, prosecutors do not pay to prepare their cases (Luban 1993). Defender organizations do.

When budgets are tight, public defenders make hard decisions about where to spend their funds. Staff vacancies are not filled, and caseloads rise. Social workers and investigators shoulder too many assignments and spend insufficient time working with individual clients. Everyone on staff selects among individuals represented by the office and compromises on services. Lawyers are compelled to spend more time in court, answering calendar calls on behalf of their greater number of clients, and less time in the field or in the library (Bernhard 1998).

Increasingly, urban defender organizations have been disadvantaged by "zero tolerance" or "broken windows" crime-fighting techniques characterized by numerous arrests for low-level violations, such as jumping onto a subway without paying the fare or carrying an open beer bottle on the street, which give police a pretext to search for weapons or drugs or to check for outstanding warrants. These approaches pump a huge number of cases through local criminal justice systems. If the public defender or contracting law office has not been included in planning for the flood of minor cases, staff members will find themselves responsible for more cases than anticipated or budgeted (Indigent

Defense Organization Oversight Committee 1998: 6–7).[8] Jurisdictions that depend on assigned counsel plans will quickly run short of lawyers to send to court, and those lawyers who are available will be stretched to their limit. Naturally, mistakes will be more likely as lawyers devote less time to each case and skimp on preparation, investigation, and research.

Absence of Quality Control

Underfunding is not the sole impediment to quality lawyering in the criminal courts. The absence of mechanisms designed to ensure quality adversely affects the caliber of the work, the public's appreciation of defense services, clients' trust in the services provided, and the support of local legislatures. Part of the explanation for the almost total lack of monitoring or evaluation can be attributed to the difficulty of defining quality legal work, especially when the work is criminal defense. Outcomes (acquittals or reduced sentences) do not accurately reflect excellent effort. Client satisfaction is irrelevant in a system in which market forces play no role.[9] And although standards exist that purport to identify the components of quality lawyering, such as the American Bar Association's (1992b) *Standards for Criminal Justice,* those standards are purposely vague so as to be generally applicable to a variety of cases.[10]

Although "lawyers have a duty to report unprofessional conduct to appropriate authorities" (American Bar Association 1994: 101/201), they report some types of unprofessional conduct more than others. Complaints about attorney competency are reported to disciplinary committees almost exclusively by clients despite the existence of rules that define incompetent lawyering as unprofessional or unethical. The Model Code of Professional Responsibility, for example, states: "A lawyer shall not . . . 1) handle a legal matter which he knows or should know that he is not competent to handle, without associating with him a lawyer who is competent to handle it. 2) Handle a legal matter without preparation adequate in the circumstances. 3) Neglect a legal matter entrusted to him" (American Bar Association 1969: disciplinary rule 6–101[A]).

Perhaps because attorneys discount lay opinions on lawyering competency, such complaints are rarely treated seriously. An American Bar Association study of professionalism in Illinois found that, although more than 50 percent of the complaints filed with the disciplinary commission were from clients claiming that their cases had been neglected or their lawyers had failed to communicate with them, these complaints were generally not investigated or pursued. Most attorneys were disciplined only for mishandling client funds and dishonesty, not for incompetence (Grosberg 1987: 658, note 337). "A 1996 national survey by [the National Association of Criminal Defense Lawyers] of bar discipline counsel revealed only one clear-cut example of acknowledgment of the problem and concern by bar officials" ("Low-Bid Criminal Defense," 1997: 26).[11]

Further insulating ineffective assistance of counsel, more than a few recent court decisions grant public defenders immunity from personal liability for malpractice, a trend that protects attorneys at the expense of their clients (*Coyazo v. State* 1995; *Dziubak v. Mott* 1993; *Scott v. City of Niagara Falls* 1978). Ironically, in at least one jurisdiction, the court was persuaded to grant immunity by the difficult conditions of the defenders' employment. In other words, while the court recognized that some poor defendants would be badly represented because the defense provider was overburdened and understaffed, it nonetheless opted to protect the attorneys from liability for potential malfeasance rather than design a remedy to reduce the chances that malfeasance would occur (*Dziubak v. Mott* 1993).

Lack of Motivation

Lack of oversight is doubly dangerous in the world of criminal court, where little independent motivation to perform well exists. No one receives a salary increase for winning a case or creating a new legal theory. Promotions within a public defender office are rare and not always awarded on merit. Clients are notoriously dissatisfied, and gratitude is scarce. Because courts and prosecutors often view zealous defense work as a waste of precious time, lawyers who grease the wheels of justice become more popular than those who put on the brakes with their fervent representation (Bernhard 1998). Outside the courthouse doors, the public variously views defenders as incompetent at their job or immoral for doing it (Ogletree 1995; see also Casper 1971 and Kunen 1983). Quality control would not only improve services but also communicate the profession's commitment to justice.

The Presumption of Guilt and the Strickland *Standard*

Another reason for the poor quality of criminal defense services is the unacknowledged but pervasive belief of all participants in the criminal justice system—even criminal defense attorneys—that anyone who has been arrested is guilty. The presumption of guilt is a "core belief shared by virtually all personnel who work within the criminal justice system" (Givelber 1997: 1329) and a major hindrance to improving criminal defense services. The presumption of guilt affects everyone in the criminal justice system, from jurors to judges. Lawyers are discouraged from diligent efforts on behalf of individual clients by the broad-based institutional climate that brands all suspects as guilty.

The presumption of guilt can be ascribed to the attractive, although frequently misguided, conviction that police only arrest guilty people. Even though the public will happily speculate about the accuracy of a police investigation in a particular case, especially when the details of the case are highly publicized and familiar, people generally believe that police arrest the guilty. This "predisposition can be ascribed to several . . . causes: the basic feeling that where there's smoke there's fire . . . ; [gratitude to the police for protection against crime]; obedience to authority and a 'belief in a just world'" (Luban 1993: 1741).

The presumption of guilt helps to explain why the Supreme Court has formulated an almost insurmountable standard of review for ineffective assistance claims on appeal. In *Strickland v. Washington* (1984: 686), the Court held that "the benchmark for judging any claim of ineffectiveness must be whether counsel's conduct so undermined the proper functioning of the adversarial process that the trial cannot be relied on as having produced a just result." In other words, egregiously negligent work will be excused if the reviewing court is not convinced that a better effort would have produced a different result. If the *Strickland* standard for ineffective assistance of counsel were to be applied to the medical realm, it would forgive a doctor's malpractice in the belief—impossible to validate—that the patient would have died anyway.

The problem with the *Strickland* standard was captured by Justice Marshall in dissent:

> It is often very difficult to tell whether a defendant convicted after a trial in which he was ineffectively represented would have fared better if his lawyer had been competent. Seemingly impregnable cases can sometimes be dismantled by good defense counsel. On the basis of a cold record, it may be im-

possible for a reviewing court confidently to ascertain how the government's evidence and arguments would have stood up against rebuttal and cross-examination by a shrewd, well-prepared lawyer. (*Strickland v. Washington* 1984: 710)

The majority opinion in *Strickland* overlooks the simple fact that the prosecutor's evidence will always appear unassailable when counsel for the accused neglects to conduct an investigation or fails to challenge the state's version of the case. The decision deprives persons against whom the prosecution has collected persuasive evidence—even if that evidence is misleading—of the right to effective assistance of counsel (Geimer 1995).

The Future: Strategies for Change

In the last decade of the twentieth century, lawyers, students, and journalists succeeded in exonerating a staggering number of individuals who were wrongly convicted.[12] These stories have attracted media attention, fostered debate among academics, interested the U.S. Department of Justice (Connors et al. 1996), and are increasingly becoming part of the national debate over the death penalty. The compelling evidence that people on death row and in prisons across the country have been mistakenly arrested, prosecuted, and convicted will undermine the powerful presumption of guilt. Even a slight change in that sentiment could have far-reaching consequences on the willingness of courts to use their inherent powers to improve indigent defense systems, the desire of local governments to more adequately fund defense systems, and the professionalism and morale of defenders. Capitalizing on this shift in attitude, advocates for a fairer criminal justice system are developing a variety of strategies to improve the quality of criminal defense services, including litigation, mechanisms to increase accountability, and education.

Litigation

Although courts shy away from prophylactic solutions (Berger 1986: 155), judges can be pushed to use their inherent administrative powers when presented with injustices that cannot be remedied otherwise and are particularly within the expertise of the judicial branch of government (Feeley and Rubin 1998). Thus, litigation can force change. Already, courts in states as diverse as Connecticut and Louisiana, among many others, have forced their state legislatures to invest funds in indigent defense. The cases have arisen in a variety of ways.

In Louisiana, for example, a single public defender, Rick Tessier, was assigned to represent Leonard Peart on a number of violent crimes. At the time, Tessier was also responsible for seventy other active felony cases. Unable to turn to his overburdened office for help, he petitioned the court for relief, claiming that because he was assigned to represent so many individuals, he was actually providing ineffective assistance of counsel to all. After a hearing, the Criminal District Court ordered substantial reductions in the caseload of Tessier's parish office and ordered the legislature to provide funds to pay for additional facilities. The Louisiana State Supreme Court reversed, limiting relief, but warned the legislature that it would not hesitate to "employ more intrusive and specific measures" if conditions did not improve (*State v. Peart* 1993: 784).

In an alternative approach, the Connecticut Civil Liberties Union successfully sued the state of Connecticut on behalf of indigent defendants. The lawsuit was settled in 1999, with the state agreeing to raise the rates of assigned counsel. The litigation was particularly significant because it required more than an infusion of cash. The settlement required the adoption of specific performance standards for attorneys representing poor people in criminal court.[13]

Accountability: Oversight and Monitoring

Litigation is not the only way for courts to improve the quality of defense services. Institutional defense service providers can be monitored and evaluated in the same way as schools, hospitals, and other public establishments are. The monitoring can be provided by citizen groups, bar associations, or even the courts. For example, the First Department Appellate Division, an intermediate appeals court that presides over the trial bench in Manhattan and the Bronx, has worked with private bar associations to monitor the provision of defense services. The court established a committee that drafted detailed, specific standards for defense organizations, covering attorney qualifications, training, supervision, workloads, evaluation of attorney performance, support services, case management and quality control, compliance with standards of professional responsibility, and reporting obligations. The standards serve multiple purposes, from educating a skeptical public about the value of quality defense services to engendering support for increased spending and providing notice to the organization itself of what is expected of a publicly funded defense office (Bernhard 1998: 27–28). Applying the committee's standards to the operation of the defense offices revealed problems in the management and delivery of services and alerted the courts and the public to dangerous trends in the operation of the local criminal justice system.

Private attorneys who are not part of an institution, such as the man who represented Luis, can also be held accountable for their actions or omissions. Lawyers traditionally fail to report the malpractice they see. Judges excuse the failings of counsel appearing before them. Loyalty to the profession trumps loyalty to the accused or to the abstract idea of justice. But the collegiality of the bar cannot justify the profession's failure to police itself. Reporting and punishing malpractice and neglect of clients might make a difference in services.

Education and Outreach

Before it will support increased spending on defense services, the public needs more information about the importance of defense work. Guarded about discussing advocacy on behalf of clients, some of whom have committed violent and antisocial acts, and inhibited by rules of confidentiality and ethical prohibitions against public commentary on pending cases, defenders shy away from public conversation about criminal defense. Significantly, many of the essential components of everyday defense work—counseling clients, diverting appropriate cases away from the criminal justice system, monitoring the police, challenging unreliable forensic techniques—are not publicly recognized or appreciated. The public understands and values the work of the prosecutor's office. Public defenders must teach their communities the benefit of a strong and dedicated defender program to reducing recidivism and protecting the innocent accused (Taylor-Thompson 1999). Outreach is not inconsistent with the work of a public defender office. In the South Bronx, a new small defense provider, the Bronx Defenders, has since 1995 worked to educate its community about the job of a defender (Rovella 2000). Staff members travel to schools, invite the parents and siblings of their clients to the office, and join the district attorney at press conferences. So far, the results have been impressive. The office is proving that when defense attorneys are less isolated from the communities they serve, they are less likely to shirk their responsibilities to those communities.

Conclusion

Luis Rojas's conviction illustrates just how easily an innocent person can be convicted when his or her attorney fails to actively engage in the tough, mundane job of building a defense by interviewing witnesses, visiting the scene, and tracking down evidence. Hindsight illuminates mistakes made by the witnesses, the police, and the prosecution at Luis Rojas's first trial. All of these participants contributed to the miscarriage of justice—but it was defense counsel's responsibility to protect Luis from the mistakes of others: from witnesses' misidentifications, police officers' rush to judgment, and prosecution's reluctance to reveal potentially exculpatory material. Instead, the attorney's failures actually contributed to the battery of problems that led to Luis's conviction. Unfortunately, his case is not an anomaly. A study in Maricopa County, Arizona (which includes the Phoenix metropolitan area), showed that only about 55 percent of defense attorneys assigned visited the crime scene before the final felony trial (Steiner 1981). Only 31 percent interviewed all of the prosecution witnesses (approximately 15 percent interviewed none of the prosecution witnesses), while 30 percent entered plea agreements without interviewing any defense witnesses (Lieberman 1981). In New York City, McConville and Mirsky (1986–87: 763) found that only 20 percent of assigned counsel panel attorneys used investigative or expert services regularly, 70 percent used them occasionally, and 11 percent never used them at all.

After Luis Rojas was convicted, his high school photography teacher, shocked by the conviction, began writing letters to local newspapers. He believed that Luis had been unjustly convicted and collected the signatures of two hundred of Luis's fellow high school students, who agreed. The story caught the attention of a local attorney who had never tried a criminal case. This volunteer lawyer, spending her own retirement funds, convinced a retired New York City police detective to investigate and persuaded a young attorney to write and file a motion to set aside the verdict. Together the team found the witnesses, the tapes, and the reports to convince the appeals court that Luis had not been adequately represented.

Luis Rojas served seven and a half years in prison before the appellate division set aside his conviction for ineffective assistance of counsel. When the case was tried a second time, his new trial attorney introduced all of the evidence that had been uncovered post-conviction. This time the jury's verdict was "not guilty."[14]

NOTES

1. In their ground-breaking law review article, Bedau and Radelet (1987) document 350 cases in which individuals were convicted of capital crimes they did not commit. Bedau and Radelet estimate that in 2.8 percent of the cases the incompetence of defense counsel was the primary cause of the unjust conviction, although counsel's incompetence contributed to many others.
2. In 1961, the American population was close to 184 million; by 1997, it had grown nearly to 267 million (U.S. Department of Commerce 1998: 8).
3. Smith and Montross (1999) are quoting here from Butterfield (1997: D1).
4. William Stunz (1997) is relying on the FBI's *Uniform Crime Report* (U.S. Department of Justice 1974, 1981, 1992) for the United States for 1973, 1980, and 1991 as well as on information from the Bureau of Justice Statistics. See also the U.S. Department of Justice's *Sourcebook of Criminal Justice Statistics* (1998: 260) which shows a drop in the rate of crime between 1991 and 1997 after thirty years of steady growth.

   Presently, the United States incarcerates a greater percentage of its population than does any other country in the world. Thirty-eight states provide for the death penalty, and more than fifty federal crimes are punishable by death. More people were executed in the United States in 1999 than in any year since the reinstatement of capital punishment in 1976. The United States is one of only five countries in the world that has executed children in the past six years (Bright 1997a). "No matter what the question has been in American criminal justice over the last generation, prison has been the answer" (Schlosser 1998: 51).
5. Berger (1986: 26) uses the term *widening gap* slightly differently: "There is a widening gap between the heavy responsibilities increasingly being laid on counsel to safeguard the defendant's rights and her perceived ability to do so."
6. Bright is quoting Chief Justice Thurgood Marshall (1986).
7. Here, Berger is quoting from Cover and Aleinikoff (1977).
8. Spangenberg (1995) discusses the advantages to public defenders of establishing commissions to anticipate the effect on all participants in the criminal justice system of new initiatives.
9. Clients could and perhaps should be surveyed and asked to describe the conduct of their lawyers, but I do not know of any jurisdiction that has tried such an approach to monitoring lawyer quality.
10. Although the American Bar Association Section of Legal Education and Admissions to the Bar (American Bar Association 1992a) has formulated a comprehensive statement of fundamental lawyering skills and professional values (commonly known as the MacCrate Report), those skills and values do not appear to guide practice outside the law schools.
11. "In case No. 96–PDB-012, the Disciplinary Board of the Louisiana Bar Association concluded that inmate Vincent Singleton's right to appeal had been neglected for over two years due to excessive case loads. It directed the Office of Disciplinary Counsel to 'investigate the matter further to ascertain if the system is as the lawyer describes it and if the system needs to be altered to meet the requirements of the Rules of Professional Conduct'" ("Low-Bid Criminal Defense," 1997: 26).
12. As of November 1999, sixty-seven individuals have been exonerated with the use of post-conviction DNA testing. The Innocence Project of the

Cardozo School of Law has succeeded in exonerating thirty-six of the total number (Conversation between the author and Jane Siegel Greene, executive director of the Innocence Project, 30 November 1999).

13. See a letter from the Connecticut Civil Liberties Union to the author, September 1999, on file with the author.

14. Many individuals worked to free Luis Rojas. An NBC television news magazine, *Dateline,* produced a one-hour show on the story entitled "Eyewitness," which aired on 11 October 1999. The show identified Priscilla
Chenoweth as the volunteer lawyer who believed in Luis and hired the
retired police detective who reinvestigated the shooting and found the crucial evidence. The *Dateline* story does not identify Tina Mazza as the appellate attorney who authored the post-conviction motion on Luis's behalf
that resulted in the eventual appellate division ruling setting aside the
guilty verdict. Jed Eisenstein volunteered to retry Luis Rojas's case. A second trial was necessary because the prosecution refused to dismiss the
charges, even after the reversal. The case was tried for a second time, and
the second jury acquitted.

REFERENCES

American Bar Association. 1969, as amended. *Model Code of Professional Responsibility.* Washington, D.C.: American Bar Association.
———. 1992a. *Legal Education and Professional Development—An Educational
Continuum.* Chicago: American Bar Association, Legal Education and Admissions to the Bar Section..
———. 1992b. *Standards for Criminal Justice: Providing Defense Services.*
3d ed. Chicago: American Bar Association, Criminal Justice Standards
Committee.
———. 1994. *Lawyers' Manual on Professional Conduct.* Washington, D.C.:
American Bar Association, Bureau of National Affairs.
Armstrong, Ken, and Steve Mills. 1999. "Inept Defense Clouds Verdict." *Chi-
cago Tribune,* 15 November, metro section.
Bazelon, David. 1976. "The Realities of *Gideon* and *Argersinger.*" *Georgetown
Law Journal* 64: 811–35.
Bedau, Hugo Adam, and Michael L. Radelet. 1987. "Miscarriages of Justice in
Potentially Capital Cases." *Stanford Law Review* 40: 21–179.
Berger, Vivian. 1986. "The Supreme Court and Defense Counsel: Old Roads,
New Paths—A Dead End?" *Columbia Law Review* 86: 9–116.
Bernhard, Adele. 1998. "Private Bar Monitors Public Defense." *ABA Criminal
Justice* (Spring): 25–30.
Bright, Stephen B. 1997a. "Casualties of the War on Crime: Fairness, Reliabil-
ity and the Credibility of Criminal Justice Systems." *University of Miami
Law Review* 51: 413–24.
———. 1997b. "Neither Equal nor Just: the Rationing and Denial of Legal Ser-
vices to the Poor When Life and Liberty Are at Stake." *Annual Survey of
American Law* 4: 783–836.
Butterfield, Fox. 1997. "Crime Keeps on Falling but Prisons Keep on Filling."
New York Times, 28 September, p. D1.
Casper, Jonathan. 1971. "Did You Have a Lawyer When You Went to Court?
No, I Had a Public Defender." *Yale Review of Law and Social Action* 1: 4–9.
Connors, Edward, Thomas Lundregan, Neal Miller, and Tom McEwan. 1996.
Convicted by Juries, Exonerated by Science: Case Studies in the Use of DNA

Evidence to Establish Innocence after Trial. Washington, D.C.: National Institute of Justice.

Cover, Robert M., and T. Alexander Aleinikoff. 1977. "Dialectical Federalism: Habeas Corpus and the Court." *Yale Law Journal* 86: 1035–1102.

Feeley, Malcom M., and Edward Rubin. 1998. *Judicial Policy Making and the Modern State: How the Courts Reformed America's Prisons.* Cambridge: Cambridge University Press.

Geimer, William. 1995. "A Decade of *Strickland*'s Tin Horn: Doctrinal and Practical Undermining of the Right to Counsel." *William and Mary Bill of Rights Journal* 4: 91–178.

Givelber, Daniel. 1997. "Meaningless Acquittals, Meaningful Convictions: Do We Reliably Acquit the Innocent?" *Rutgers Law Review* 49: 1317–96.

Grosberg, Lawrence M. 1987. "Illusion and Reality in Regulating Lawyer Performance: Rethinking Rule 11." *Villanova Law Review* 32: 575–690.

Indigent Defense Organization Oversight Committee. 1998. "Report for 1998." New York: Supreme Court of New York Appellate Division, First Department.

Klein, Richard. 1986. "The Emperor *Gideon* has No Clothes: The Empty Promise of the Constitutional Right to Effective Assistance of Counsel." *Hastings Constitutional Law Quarterly* 13: 625–93.

———. 1993. "The Eleventh Commandment: Thou Shalt not Be Compelled to Render the Ineffective Assistance of Counsel." *Indiana Law Journal* 68: 363–432.

Kunen, James. 1983. *How Can You Defend Those People? The Making of a Criminal Lawyer.* New York: Random House.

Lieberman, Marty. 1981. "Investigation of Facts in Preparation for Plea Bargaining." *Arizona State Law Journal* 2: 557–83.

"Low-Bid Criminal Defense Contracting: Justice in Retreat." 1997. *Champion* 22 (21 November): 26–28.

Luban, David. 1993. "Are Criminal Defenders Different?" *Michigan Law Review* 91:1729–66.

Marshall, Thurgood. 1986. "Remarks on the Death Penalty Made at the Judicial Conference of the 2nd Circuit." *Columbia Law Review* 86, part 1: 1–8.

McConville, Michael, and Chester L. Mirsky. 1986–87. "Criminal Defense of the Poor in New York City." *New York University Review of Law and Social Change* 15.

Ogletree, Charles J., Jr. 1995. "An Essay on the New Public Defender for the 21st Century." *Law and Contemporary Problems* 58: 81–93.

Rovella, David E. 2000. "The Best Defense . . . Rebuilding Clients' Lives to Keep Them from Coming Back." *National Law Journal,* 31 January, p. A1.

Schlosser, Eric. 1998. "The Prison Industrial Complex." *Atlantic Monthly* (December): 51–77.

Smith, Abbe, and William Montross. 1999. "The Calling of Criminal Defense." *Mercer Law Review* 50: 443–535.

Spangenberg, Robert L. 1995. "Criminal Justice Planning Commissions: Improving the System through Coordination, Cooperation and Communication." *Spangenberg Report* 2: 1–5.

Spangenberg, Robert L., and Marea L. Beeman. 1995. "Indigent Defense Systems in the United States." *Law and Contemporary Problems* 58: 31–48.

Steiner, Margaret L. 1981. "Adequacy of Fact Investigation in Criminal Defense Lawyers' Trial Preparation." *Arizona State Law Journal* 2: 523–56.

Stunz, William. 1997. "The Uneasy Relationship between Criminal Procedure and Criminal Justice." *Yale Law Journal* 107: 1–76.

Taylor-Thompson, Kim. 1999. "Effective Assistance: Reconceiving the Role of the Chief Public Defender." *Journal of the Institute for the Study of Legal Ethics* 2: 199–230.

U.S. Department of Commerce, Bureau of the Census. 1998. *Statistical Abstract of the United States.* Washington, D.C.: U.S. Department of Commerce.

U.S. Department of Justice, Federal Bureau of Investigation. 1974. *Uniform Crime Report.* Washington, D.C.: U.S. Department of Justice.

———. 1981. *Uniform Crime Report.* Washington, D.C.: U.S. Department of Justice.

———. 1992. *Uniform Crime Report.* Washington, D.C.: U.S. Department of Justice.

U.S. Department of Justice, Office of Justice Programs, Bureau of Justice Statistics. 1998. *Sourcebook of Criminal Justice Statistics.* Washington, D.C.: U.S. Department of Justice.

CASES CITED

Coyazo v. State, 897 P.2d 234 (Ct. App. N.M. 1995).

Dziubak v. Mott, 503 N.W.2d 771 (Sup. Ct. Minn. 1993).

Evitts v. Lucey, 469 U.S. 387, 105 S.Ct. 830 (1985).

Gideon v. Wainwright, 372 U.S. 335, 83 S.Ct.792 (1963).

McMann v. Richardson, 397 U.S. 759, 90 S.Ct. 1441 (1970).

People v. Rojas, 213 A.D.2d 56, 630 N.Y.S.2d 28 (N.Y. 1st Dept. 1995).

Powell v. Alabama, 287 U.S. 45, 53 S.Ct. 55 (1932).

Scott v. City of Niagara Falls, 407 N.Y.S.2d 103 (Sup. Ct. Niagara Cty. 1978).

State v. Peart, 621 So.2d 780 (Sup. Ct. La. 1993).

Strickland v. Washington, 466 U.S. 668, 104 S.Ct. 2052 (1984).

BARRY SCHECK

PETER NEUFELD

12 | DNA and Innocence Scholarship

At the time of this writing (October 2000), there have been eighty-two post-conviction DNA exonerations in North America: seventy-six in the United States and six in Canada. When the U.S. Department of Justice issued a monograph cataloguing post-conviction exonerations as of June 1996 (Connors et al. 1996), it reported twenty-eight exonerations since the advent of forensic DNA testing in 1989. Thus, the rate of exonerations has accelerated in the past four years (fifty-four in four years versus twenty-eight in seven years), and there is every reason to believe we have not yet reached the apogee of this phenomenon.

Nothing comparable has ever happened in the history of American jurisprudence; indeed, nothing like it has happened to any judicial system anywhere. The significance of these DNA exonerations does not lie simply in the extraordinary number of documented miscarriages of justice but in the unique certainty of the innocence determinations and the concomitant utility such certainty brings to revealing and studying the strengths and weaknesses of the criminal justice system.

This chapter briefly addresses some issues arising from post-conviction DNA exonerations that will outline innocence scholarship in the coming years. How many post-conviction DNA exonerations will there be? What does DNA testing tell us about the true number of wrongful convictions? Why are DNA exonerations different in terms of certainty? What directions can innocence scholarship take from the

DNA exonerations, and how can a network of innocence projects at various law schools facilitate such studies?

How Many Post-conviction DNA Exonerations Will There Be?

Naturally, it is impossible to answer this question precisely, but one can confidently identify certain trends. When the U.S. Department of Justice published its monograph in June 1996—*Convicted by Juries, Exonerated by Science: Case Studies in the Use of DNA Evidence to Establish Innocence after Trial* (Connors et al. 1996)—it reported on twenty-eight post-conviction DNA exonerations. In little more than four years, fifty-four more have come to light. The pace of exonerations is accelerating for a number of reasons.

The Technology Has Improved

The first generation of forensic DNA tests used the restriction fragment length polymorphism (RFLP) technique. Starting in 1989, this was the method used by the principal government laboratory (the FBI) and the private laboratories (Lifecodes and Cellmark). Putting aside the considerable start-up problems these laboratories encountered transferring RFLP technology from medical clinical uses to forensic applications (such as the need for matching rules, band shifting, and controversy among population geneticists over statistical calculations), the RFLP method had a significant strength and a serious weakness. The strength was its power of discrimination. If a valid RFLP match at a number of DNA markers on a definitive piece of biological evidence existed, such as on a vaginal swab in a rape case involving one perpetrator, there was an excellent chance an innocent person would be excluded and a guilty person incriminated by some hefty statistics. On the other hand, RFLP testing was not very sensitive; that is, it took a comparatively large amount of high-molecular-weight DNA in a crime scene sample to get a result.

A second generation of forensic DNA testing—DQ alpha polymarker—relied on the polymerase chain reaction (PCR) method, a technique that can be analogized to molecular Xeroxing. Through PCR, the DQ alpha and polymarker DNA markers could be analyzed from a biological sample containing very little DNA. Since it was based on the PCR technique, the DQ alpha polymarker test was extremely sensitive; it could get results from small or old, degraded samples. Often, a DQ alpha polymarker test would exonerate an inmate who claimed innocence after an RFLP test of insufficient DNA had failed to get a result. The problem, however, with DQ alpha testing is that it is not very discriminating. At best, it can yield frequencies on the order of 1 in 5,000. With mixed samples (contributions from two or more persons to a blood, saliva, or semen stain), the limited discriminatory power of DQ alpha testing becomes a significant problem.

In the past four years, a new PCR-based forensic DNA test has been developed—short tandem repeats (STRs)—which has both the discriminating power of RFLP and the sensitivity of DQ alpha. The STR test employs as many as thirteen DNA markers and also has a marker that sex-types samples. The STR test is the foundation of DNA data banks in the United States and the United Kingdom. Although U.S. data banks are at an embryonic stage, especially compared with those in the United Kingdom, it is becoming increasingly possible not only to test an old sample in a case in which an inmate claims innocence to see if he or she can be excluded but to take the resulting STR DNA profile and plug it into the data bank to see if it "hits" a convicted offender or a profile from an unsolved case. So far, the real perpetrator has been identified in fifteen of the seventy post-conviction DNA exonerations. Unfortunately, prosecutors in many of the cases have not seen fit to retest samples from situations in which the exonerations arose from RFLP or DQ alpha testing with the STR technique so that a DNA profile of the real perpetrator can be logged into the national data bank.

Finally, another technological advance, mitochondrial DNA testing, will contribute to exonerating more wrongfully convicted inmates. Mitochondrial DNA testing employs the PCR technique but has greater sensitivity than do previous tests because its molecular Xeroxing is directed at sequences of mitochondrial DNA found in a cell. Prior RFLP and PCR tests analyzed DNA from a cell's nucleus: the twenty-three pairs of chromosomes we inherit from both our parents. While nuclear DNA contains only two copies of each gene, mitochondrial DNA, which is spread throughout a cell, is copied many thousands of times. Consequently, since mitochondrial DNA is ordinarily much more available in a small degraded biological sample than is nuclear DNA, mitochondrial DNA testing is much more sensitive. In the past, even with an STR test, one would need to find a fleshy root, with a nucleus, on a hair left at a crime scene to perform a DNA test. Using a mitochondrial test, however, forensic scientists can now extract mitochondrial DNA directly from the shaft of a rootless hair. Therefore, old convictions based on the inferior science of microscopic comparisons of shed hairs can now be successfully challenged with mitochondrial typing.

The major disadvantage of mitochondrial testing is its comparative lack of discriminatory power. Mitochondrial DNA is inherited maternally. Unless something strange is occurring within a family, brothers and sisters and maternal cousins will have the same mitochondrial patterns as each other and their mothers; they should not match their fathers! Thus, mitochondrial testing has limited value in distinguishing among family members and statistically is not as powerful as STR or RFLP testing. Nonetheless, it is a useful tool in some old and new cases.

Undoubtedly, more technological advances will soon be available that enhance an investigator's ability to resolve old cases through DNA testing. Already new tests are being developed directed at the y chromosome, which can help differentiate among males in mixture cases, as well as plant and animal DNA.

Access to the Evidence Is Slowly Expanding

The primary impediment to exonerating wrongfully convicted inmates through the use of DNA testing has been legal and practical roadblocks thrown in the path of those who seek access to the evidence to perform a test that can prove innocence.

The principal legal roadblock is that thirty-three states have statutes of limitations of six months or less on motions to present newly discovered evidence of innocence. Worse still, even when an inmate seeks access to the evidence to perform a DNA test, vowing to present the exculpatory results to a governor for a pardon rather than a state court, the state courts have repeatedly deemed the access motions to be newly discovered evidence applications and have ruled them time-barred. Similarly, federal habeas corpus applications (used by inmates to obtain a judicial review after all avenues of appeal are exhausted) have a six-month statute of limitations in capital cases and a one-year statute in all other matters. The Innocence Project at Cardozo Law School (the leading organization in the United States in securing post-conviction DNA exonerations, co-founded by the chapter authors) takes the position that statutes of limitation should not, as a federal or state constitutional matter, preclude an inmate from either getting access to the evidence for a DNA test that could prove actual innocence or presenting such evidence in a state or federal court. Nevertheless, this issue is being fiercely litigated across the country with mixed results.

One new approach for raising the claim is a federal civil rights action for injunctive relief against the state agency, requiring the DNA evidence being withheld to be made available to the inmate.

Recently, some progress in gaining access to the evidence was made with the publication of *Postconviction DNA Testing: Recommendations for Handling Requests,* a report by the National Commission on the Future of DNA Evidence (1999), a Justice Department panel made up predominantly of law enforcement officials. These recommendations urge prosecutors to consent to DNA testing, even if state laws allow them to preclude the application on procedural grounds, if the case was one in which a reasonable argument could be made that exculpatory DNA results would raise a reasonable probability that the inmate would not have been convicted at the original trial.

Initially, only two states, Illinois and New York, had statutes that authorized DNA tests for inmates without statute-of-limitation restrictions and also provided payment for the testing if the inmate could not afford it. It is no accident that these two states have the most postconviction DNA exonerations—fourteen and eight, respectively. A few states recently joined Illinois and New York. If efforts currently underway in Congress and state legislatures are successful in getting statutes passed, the number of exonerations is bound to increase appreciably.

The practical roadblock faced by inmates seeking to prove their innocence is finding the evidence. In 75 percent of Innocence Project cases, matters in which it has been established that a favorable DNA result would be sufficient to vacate the inmate's conviction, the relevant biological evidence has either been destroyed or lost. Interestingly, it does not seem to matter too much whether state law permits the destruction of the evidence while the inmate is still incarcerated; indeed, in many jurisdictions, most actors within the system are not even aware of the rules that govern evidence preservation. Local evidence storage practices are of greatest importance. For example, it is virtually impossible, due to storage facility problems, to find samples more than five years old in New York City, where the law does not permit destruction unless notice is given to the parties. On the other hand, in the state of Virginia, where the law permits the destruction of samples soon after conviction, local courthouses routinely save samples for decades in a comparatively traceable fashion.

Frequently, evidence samples reported lost have been found if a vigorous, in-person search is conducted. Therefore, if more investigative resources can be focused on finding these valuable biological samples, the greater the chance more wrongfully convicted people will be exonerated by DNA testing.

The Realistic Universe of Possible Post-conviction DNA Exonerations

All considered, it is realistic to expect a finite class of cases, with the bulk starting between 1983 and 1994 (when discriminating PCR-based DNA testing of relevant biological evidence became common in new cases), in which it will be possible to attain post-conviction DNA exonerations. The matter is simply a race to see how many people can be proven innocent before the evidence samples are lost or destroyed. The faster that statutes are passed authorizing such testing, the more resources that are devoted to finding the evidence in appropriate cases, and the more law schools and lawyer groups that provide the long hours necessary to screen inmate requests and litigate claims, the greater the number of wrongfully convicted prisoners who will walk out of their cells to freedom.

What Does DNA Testing Tell Us about the True Number of Wrongful Convictions?

Very simply, DNA testing has demonstrated that far more wrongful convictions occur than even the most cynical and jaded scholars had suspected.

Probably the most provocative data on this issue come from the FBI itself. The FBI began doing DNA testing in 1989 on sexual assault and sexual assault homicide cases. In general, the bureau received biological samples from state and local police agencies after they had already arrested or indicted someone in these cases. The purpose of the testing was to confirm or exclude the person(s) who had been apprehended, usually as a result of eyewitness identifications.

In June 1996, the FBI reported that it had excluded the primary suspect in 25 percent of these sexual assault cases in which DNA results could be obtained (Connors et al. 1996). By that time, the FBI had done DNA testing in more than 10,000 cases. A Justice Department survey of private and public laboratories revealed a 33 percent exclusion rate, although these numbers were admittedly estimates, not the hard count offered by the FBI. Indeed, it is worth noting that the FBI counted as a single exclusion a case in which four individuals charged in the sexual assault of one victim were excluded as semen donors by a DNA test.

It is, of course, possible that some of the individuals excluded by the FBI were, in fact, guilty and falsely excluded. It could be that the suspect did not ejaculate or wore a condom and the victim did not report a prior consensual partner within twenty-four to forty-eight hours. If there had been a concealed consensual partner and the suspect had ejaculated, the suspect would not be excluded because his DNA would show up in a mixture. Also possible is a false exclusion because of sample-handling errors. But neither of these scenarios could conceivably account for a 25 percent exclusion rate.

It is hardly a bold inference to conclude that, if not for the DNA testing in sexual assault cases by the FBI and other laboratories, thousands of individuals would have been wrongfully convicted in the United States since 1989. It seems equally safe to conclude that thousands of similarly situated inmates, convicted when DNA testing did not exist, could prove their innocence if they could get testing of critical biological evidence.

Another safe inference from the extraordinary rate of DNA exclusions offered by the FBI and other laboratories in sexual assault cases is that most of these errors arise from mistaken eyewitness identification since DNA testing, a scarce resource, was rarely, if ever, performed in cases when the parties knew each other and the issue was consent. Mistaken eyewitnesses have long been known as a major cause of wrongful convictions, but the DNA data serve as an important reminder that their impact may be underestimated. For example, in what might be the most exhaustive study of wrongful convictions due to mistaken identifications, Professor Samuel Gross (1987) expressed surprise at finding so few of them. First, he conducted an impressive review of the literature of social science experiments in the area of eyewitness identification and rightly concluded that it predicted that a comparatively substantial error rate should be found in identification cases. Next, Gross surveyed all of the mistaken identification cases he could find, relying primarily on the only records available—press reports. He found the number of wrongful convictions due to mistaken eyewitnesses to be remarkably low. He consequently hypothesized that there were fewer wrongful convictions due to mistaken identification than expected because police and prosecutors informally declined to prosecute in cases in which the identification testimony was weak.

The DNA exclusion data reported by the FBI and others strongly support a more disturbing hypothesis. The unexpectedly low number of reported wrongful convictions from mistaken identification is not a function of law enforcement's effectiveness at preventing weak cases from going to trial but the system's abject failure to uncover and correct anything close to the true number of wrongful mistaken identification convictions. Indeed, there is no reason to believe that the extraordinarily high rate of mistaken identifications in stranger sexual assault cases exposed by pretrial DNA testing is due to something unique in the nature of sexual assault cases. Eyewitness mistakes are likely to be as high in robbery cases and other crimes; the extent of those errors is simply not as well known because there are no biological samples on which DNA testing can be performed to resolve the issue of identity definitively.

Plainly, much more work needs to be done in studying the extent to which DNA testing is showing more wrongful convictions than anyone had suspected. In particular, the FBI's DNA data in post-arrest cases, as well as the large number of post-arrest exclusions now being generated by state and local DNA laboratories, should be systematically counted and analyzed. They can be a rich source of information about the true incidence of eyewitness errors and the overall error rate of the system.

Why Are DNA Exonerations Different in Terms of Certainty?

In the past, innocence scholarship was plagued by debates over whether exonerated inmates were, in fact, innocent (compare Markman and Cassell 1988 to Radelet et al. 1992). Other than cases in which individuals were convicted of murdering someone whose body was not found, and then the "dead" person miraculously reappeared, few post-conviction exonerations reached the level of scientific certainty achieved by the DNA exonerations. Witness recantations, the appearance of new witnesses, or even the discovery of some persuasive exculpatory evidence suppressed by law enforcement (the usual sources of newly discovered proof that brings about exonerations) are often subject to debate and controversy long after a case has been overturned.

DNA exonerations are different. Unlike witnesses who disappear or whose recollections fade over time, DNA in biological samples can be reliably extracted decades after the commission of the crime. The results of such testing have invariably been found to have a scientific certainty that easily outweighs the eyewitness identification testimony or other direct or circumstantial proof that led to the original conviction. To our knowledge, no post-conviction DNA exoneration has ever been successfully opposed on the grounds that the DNA evidence was not reliable.

This is not to say that DNA testing is foolproof. Only a fool would make that claim. The underlying theory and methods used for forensic DNA testing are surely sound; yet like any scientific technique, it can, and has been, applied incorrectly. Many of the concerns include errors in sample handling, interpretation of results, and collection and preservation of samples. Nonetheless, there is little doubt that DNA testing has been the most reliable and revolutionary tool of forensic scientists since the invention of fingerprinting.

Most important, one aspect of post-conviction DNA exonerations makes them particularly reliable: the evidence samples in question most frequently have been sperm deposited by a perpetrator. When the biological sample is sperm on a vaginal swab or in a stain on a victim's clothing, certain important built-in protections make sample-handling errors unlikely, even in very old cases in which the chain of custody is hard to reconstruct. First, the DNA tests involve differential extractions. This means that DNA from sperm can be separately extracted from DNA from the victim's epithelial (skin) cells. The victim's DNA profile serves as a built-in control: if the DNA from the epithelial cells correctly matches the victim, one has greater confidence that the swab or the stain has not been switched. Even more important, since the critical DNA comes from the perpetrator's sperm, the only way evidence handlers could cross-contaminate the sample is by removing sperm DNA from the real assailant and then depositing someone else's sperm on the swab or piece of clothing. Once prosecutors understand this point, usually after hearing it from their own experts, objections to DNA results from such samples cease.

A final and increasingly important aspect to the DNA exonerations is that the test results can lead to the apprehension of the real perpetrator, especially through the use of DNA data banks that contain profiles from convicted offenders and unsolved cases. To date, in the eighty-two DNA exonerations, the real perpetrator has been linked to the crime by DNA testing fifteen times, and that number is bound to grow as data banks eliminate their backloads and STR DNA testing becomes standard operating procedure.

What Directions Can Innocence Scholarship Take from DNA Exonerations? How Can a Network of Innocence Projects Facilitate Such Studies?

In our book *Actual Innocence*, co-authored with Jim Dwyer (Scheck et al. 2000), we make an effort at studying the first seventy post-conviction DNA exonerations to see why the innocent were convicted and what simple reforms of the criminal justice system could be undertaken to minimize future miscarriages of justice. We focus on mistaken eyewitness identification, false confessions, jailhouse informants, junk forensic science, fraudulent forensic science, ineffective and underfunded defense lawyers, and prosecutorial and law enforcement misconduct. Much more can be learned from these cases and the new exonerations that will undoubtedly occur in the coming decade. The challenge is to collect the data systematically and study the cases with great care.

We and others engaged in innocence work are trying to organize a network of law schools, journalism schools, and graduate schools (psychology, criminology, and so on) devoted to studying and researching the causes of and remedies for wrongful convictions as well as working with members of the private bar and public defenders' offices to investigate and litigate cases in which there have been miscarriages of justice. We believe these institutions have a critical role to play as well as a special responsibility.

Unfortunately, law schools have devoted limited time to the study of what causes wrongful convictions. The primary orientation of the legal academy in the criminal law area has been toward teaching substantive doctrine and procedure. Nothing is wrong with this orientation per se; indeed, it is a necessary first step. But to gain a deeper understanding of the strengths and weaknesses of our criminal justice system, one needs to adopt an interdisciplinary approach. Psychologists provide a rich literature and high level of expertise with respect to the phenomenon of eyewitness identification and confessions. It must be integrated into the legal academy, just as the input of legal academics can greatly benefit the social scientists. Similarly, forensic science now involves knowledge of the hard sciences (molecular biology, neurology, biophysics, pathology, neuropathology, chemistry, and computer sciences, to name just a few) along with the procedures and approaches of traditional criminalistics. These disciplines are increasingly crucial parts of the process of criminal investigation and trial. Unfortunately, legal academics are no different from lawyers generally—if we had natural gifts in the hard sciences, many of us would be doctors! But that is no excuse for failing to pursue serious, interdisciplinary study of the way in which the system really functions. The idea behind the innocence network is to stimulate this kind of research and teaching within the academy, with the goal of not only training better lawyers but making constructive, institutional changes in forensic science.

To this end, we make one more proposal to close this chapter: the formation of innocence commissions. When an airplane falls from the sky, a train derails, or a person dies unexpectedly at a hospital, a postmortem usually takes place as a matter of course. Was the problem a system error, human error, or no one's fault? Was there unethical conduct? And, most important, what can be done to prevent these failures from happening again? Independent experts conduct serious investigations and write reports. In short, major public and private institutions that are entrusted with the life and liberty of citizens take their errors—particularly systemic failures—seriously and issue reports on what happened. The criminal justice system is a remarkable exception. When inmates are released from death row or from long terms of imprisonment on newly discovered evidence of innocence, an opinion is rarely even written to mark the event. Ordinarily, judges simply issue orders vacating the convictions, and at best there are detailed press accounts covering the occasion. Scholars and students years later will find nothing in the official reports except opinions affirming convictions of those later proven innocent, opinions finding that the trial was fair and the evidence overwhelming, opinions that give no hint that something terribly wrong could have transpired during the investigation or trial of the matter. In short, no independent body performs a systematic analysis of what went wrong and how to prevent it from happening again.

Such institutions must be created; and this remarkable, albeit limited, run of post-conviction DNA exonerations provides the perfect opportunity to do so. Already in Canada, after the well-publicized DNA exoneration of Guy Paul Morin, a detailed commission of inquiry issued comprehensive recommendations for reform in the forensic sciences (laboratory procedures and microscopic hair comparisons were pointedly criticized) as well as the way in which police rely on jailhouse informants and investigate alibi defenses (Kaufman 1998). In the United Kingdom, after the infamous miscarriages of justice in the Guilford Four and the Birmingham Six cases, the Home Office set up the Criminal Cases Review Commission, an independent institution with a staff of more than forty investigators (many of them former police officials), subpoena power, and a blue-ribbon panel of commissioners who were former prosecutors, defenders, and judges. In the United States, such an innocence commission would necessarily take a somewhat different form than the Canadian or United Kingdom approaches, but there is little doubt that we need one and that the movement to make this happen should come from the legal academy itself.

REFERENCES

Connors, Edward, Thomas Lundregan, Neal Miller, and Tom McEwan. 1996. *Convicted by Juries, Exonerated by Science: Case Studies in the Use of DNA Evidence to Establish Innocence after Trial.* Washington, D.C.: National Institute of Justice.

Gross, Samuel R. 1987. "Loss of Innocence: Eyewitness Identification and Proof of Guilt." *Journal of Legal Studies* 16: 395–405.

Kaufman, Fred. 1998. *The Report of the Commission on Proceedings Involving Guy Paul Morin.* Toronto: Publications Ontario.

Markman, Stephen J., and Paul G. Cassell. 1988. "Protecting the Innocent: A Response to the Bedau-Radelet Study." *Stanford Law Review* 41: 121–60.

National Commission on the Future of DNA Evidence, Office of Justice Programs. 1999. *Postconviction DNA Testing: Recommendations for Handling Requests.* Washington, D.C.: National Institute of Justice.

Radelet, Michael L., Hugo Adam Bedau, and Constance E. Putnam. 1992. *In Spite of Innocence.* Boston: Northeastern University Press.

Scheck, Barry, Peter Neufeld, and Jim Dwyer. 2000. *Actual Innocence.* New York: Doubleday.

DANIEL GIVELBER

13 The Adversary System and Historical Accuracy
Can We Do Better?

Studies of the causes of wrongful convictions tend to focus on the mistakes (intentional or not) made during the investigation and adjudication of a case by police and prosecutors. These studies examine the importance of mistaken eyewitness testimony, biased police lineups, false confessions, prosecutorial misconduct, and jailhouse informants, just to name a few. (For an overview of the numerous factors leading to wrongful convictions, see Huff et al. 1996; Radelet et al. 1992; Scheck et al. 2000). In addition, however, it is also essential to understand that wrongful convictions originate from the very nature of the process that is at the core of our criminal justice system: the adversary system. Some of the reasons that we convict the innocent flow from choices we have made as a society about the process we use to determine guilt.

By employing the adversary system, with its reliance on the parties to frame the evidentiary and legal dispute for resolution by a neutral decision maker (that is, a fact finder—either a judge or jury), we have treated criminal adjudication as if its goal were to resolve disputes rather than determine the historical facts of a case. This means that some innocents will be convicted because a neutral decision maker who is comparing the state's case for guilt against the defendant's case of non-guilt (if any) will conclude rationally that the state's case leaves no room for a reasonable doubt about the defendant's guilt. The same decision maker, operating under the same set of rules, might arrive at a very different conclusion about the defendant's guilt if it had been provided with more information about the event in question. This difference in outcomes is tolerable, we persuade ourselves, because the parties themselves control the amount and quality of evidence submitted for adjudication.

This chapter focuses on three related problems for the innocent generated by our use of the adversary system: the theoretical goals of adversary justice, the reality of our criminal adversarial justice system, and the incongruity of relying on one adversary (the prosecution) to ensure that the other adversary (the defense) is provided with information that would undermine the prosecutor's case. The chapter then considers what might be done to ameliorate features of our adversary system that compromise historical accuracy.

The Supreme Court has interpreted the U.S. Constitution as embracing central features of the adversary system: for example, the accused's right to confront witnesses against him or her (*Davis v. Alaska* 1974), call witnesses in his or her favor (*Washington v. Texas* 1967), or remain silent throughout the proceeding (*Wilson v. United States* 1893). Other constitutional guarantees, such as the right to a jury (*Duncan v. Louisiana* 1968) and to proof beyond a reasonable doubt (*In re Winship* 1970), have been interpreted and implemented in a manner that supports the adversarial approach. Given the extent to which we have come to believe that our Constitution embodies this approach, the most feasible strategy for reform centers on ameliorating rather than replacing the adversary system. Thus, the suggestions in this chapter, while important, are considerably less sweeping than a critique of the adversarial system might suggest is appropriate.

The Criminal Justice Filter: Protecting the Innocent?

Acquitting the innocent purports to be a central concern of our system of criminal adjudication. Better that ten guilty go free, it is said, than that one innocent be convicted (Volokh 1997). In theory, we ensure that only the guilty are punished by putting criminal charges through a series of filters, which, taken together, guarantee that all of the innocent have been spared the possibility of criminal punishment.

The process of filtering out the innocent occurs at every stage from arrest through trial. We start with the assumption that an individual will not be arrested in the first instance unless the police have serious grounds to believe that he or she is guilty of a crime. Even if the police err in that judgment, we assume that prosecutors will exercise their discretion in not proceeding with formal charges when the accused person is perceived as probably innocent. Even if the prosecutor charges the person, a grand jury in many states has to conclude that probable cause supports the prosecutor's decision before a formal felony charge can be entered against the accused. Even among those so charged, prosecutors dismiss a significant percentage of the cases for a variety of reasons, including doubts about the individual's actual guilt.

What of those who remain after all this filtration? The overwhelming majority plead guilty to some crime, even if not the one with which they are originally charged. A distinct minority go to trial. With respect to street crime, at least, the conviction rate following trial appears to be in the 75 to 85 percent range. Since all of the apparently innocent people have been filtered out long before the trial stage, and since the defendant can only be convicted by proof beyond a reasonable doubt at trial, and since some 15 to 25 percent of defendants in state felony cases are acquitted, it seems apparent that this process will necessarily exonerate all of those who are in fact innocent (see Givelber 1997).

Reality belies theory. This system does not reliably protect the innocent. The filtration system stops working when the prosecutor decides to proceed to trial against an accused. Once prosecutors believe in good faith that a defendant has probably committed the crime with which he or she has been charged, they assume the role of an advocate in an adversary system (Melilli 1992). From this point forward, the fate of the innocent depends on the extent to which our adversary system either can or does express a particular concern for assuring the innocent will be acquitted. There is no reason to believe that the American system of adversarial justice places the acquittal of the innocent on a higher footing than either convicting the guilty or simply disposing of cases as efficiently as possible (Stacy 1991).

The Adversary System: Theory

The central precept of the adversary process is that out of the sharp clash of proofs presented by adversaries in a highly structured forensic setting is most likely to come the information upon which a neutral and passive decision maker can base the resolution of a litigated dispute acceptable to both the parties and to society. This formulation is advantageous not only because it expresses the overarching adversarial concept, but also because it identifies the method to be utilized in adjudication (the sharp clash of proofs in a highly structured setting), the actors essential to the process (two adversaries and a decision maker), the nature of their functions (presentation of proofs and adjudication of disputes, respectively), and the goal of the entire endeavor (the resolution of disputes in a manner acceptable to the parties and to society). (Landsman 1984: 2)

As this summary from a leading proponent of the adversary system clarifies, the fundamental goal of the process is to resolve disputes in a structured and socially acceptable manner. This system is not primarily designed to do a superior job of ascertaining the truth about historical events.[1] There are those who argue that this should be the primary focus of lawyers working within the adversary system (Schwartz 1983), but no one who suggests that it *is* their focus. Those who believe that the adversary system is either a good system (Landsman 1984) or at least as good as any alternative one (Luban 1988) build their argument on how the system responds to civil disputes. Since we work out much of the relationship between the individual and the state through the rights we grant the accused in our system of criminal adjudication, these supporters suggest that the criminal system does not provide a fair measure of the efficacy of the adversary system as a mode of ascertaining historical truth (Luban 1988). The right of the defendant to withhold testimony and the right of his or her lawyer to cast doubt on the state's case without being required to present the defendant's case are viewed as particularly problematic for the goal of achieving historical accuracy (Schwartz 1983). While not stated in so many words, the assumption running through all of these discussions is that the defendant is, in fact, guilty; therefore, it is the defendant, not the state, who has the vested interest in a system that does not place truth as the paramount adjudicatory goal. With respect to the falsely accused innocent, of course, this assumption is invalid.

The adversary system embraces dispute resolution by a neutral decision maker who is responding to the information provided by the parties themselves. The quality of the information presented to the decision maker limits its ability to determine accurately what happened. If the parties, for whatever reason, provide the decision maker with less than a complete picture of the potentially available evidence relating to the facts in dispute, the decision maker will make its decision based on that incomplete evidence. While it may be possible for a decision maker to draw generally reasonable conclusions about what the missing evidence might have demonstrated, these conclusions will be less reliable than conclusions based on actual evidence. Moreover, the ability to draw conclusions about what the missing evidence might have demonstrated assumes that the fact finder knows that evidence is missing.

If the goal of the system is to resolve disputes, there may be considerable justification for permitting the parties to control what the decision maker knows. After all, it is the parties' dispute; and if they are prepared to live with a decision based on incomplete information, we are simply respecting the wishes of autonomous individuals. The parties can decide for themselves whether the desirability of a more accurate determination of historical fact justifies any costs associated with acquiring or disclosing the information. These costs can range from the expense of doing an investigation to acquire additional information, to the lawyers' fees involved in presenting the information to the decision maker, to the potential embarrassment inherent in disclosing it. If a party is unwilling to pay these costs, it is appropriate for the decision to be made without the missing information. As long as the decision maker is aware that the parties have not put before it all the potentially available information, the decision maker may be able to compensate for the missing information by making reasonable guesses about what the undisclosed information might reveal. Indeed, juries are told that they may infer that undisclosed information would have been unfavorable to the party who chose not to produce it (Devitt et al. 1987).

While the decision maker might not be in a position to make these guesses if it is not aware that available information has not been revealed, theoretically that is a deficiency that the parties are apparently willing to live with as well. The adversary system produces satisfactory results, then, as long as we assume that the parties have had the opportunity to present whatever proofs they deem appropriate to the triers of fact. In theory at least, the parties receive qualitatively accurate final judgments in reasonably direct relation to the care they take to provide the fact finder with all of the information necessary for an informed decision.

This discussion assumes that the parties are free to give the fact finder any information they deem significant. This is not true of the American system, which denies the neutral decision maker whole categories of apparently relevant information. For example, our rules of evidence preclude the jury from receiving information in the form of hearsay; considering prior bad acts for their predictive power; or hearing what someone told his or her lawyer, therapist, or priest. Our Constitution gives everyone the right to withhold testimony that would be self-incriminatory and gives the criminal defendant the right to refuse to answer any questions at all under oath.

Perhaps these rules operate in a way that is equally disadvantageous to both sides in a criminal prosecution. If so, the result is fortuitous, not designed. More likely, however, these rules—which exclude relevant evidence—operate primarily to the disadvantage of the state, which has the burden of proof in criminal cases. Nevertheless, even if we can agree that rules excluding relevant evidence aid the general run of defendants, this does not mean that they operate necessarily to the advantage of innocent defendants. This class of individuals needs accuracy, not noblesse oblige. The notion that criminal trials are designed to affirm our commitment to the rights of the individual confronting the might of the state suggests that the trial is about whether the government, playing by the rules, can convict a guilty person. The trial may not be a deeply serious inquiry into whether the defendant did or did not commit a crime. Anomalous as it may appear, once a case proceeds to trial, rules that benefit the general run of defendants may disserve the actually innocent. Evidence that is typically excluded may be the very evidence needed to demonstrate a defendant's innocence. Thus, the Fifth Amendment right to remain silent means that a falsely accused innocent cannot compel the actually guilty person to testify at the innocent's trial. In some jurisdictions, the hearsay rule means that a falsely accused innocent cannot introduce at trial a third party's out-of-court confession to the crime because the statement is considered hearsay.

The Adversary System: Reality
Unequal Distribution of Resources

The abstract theoretical difficulties with our adversary system pale in comparison with the practical challenges that the system poses for the falsely accused innocent. In the overwhelming majority of criminal cases, the state has an enormous advantage in terms of the resources it brings to bear in a given case. Its investigative resources are vastly superior in size and authority, and the state has the capacity to decide for and by itself how much to expend in an investigation and for what (Luban 1993).

The typical criminal defendant, on the other hand, has no resources. The defendant has to ask the court for funds to pay for whatever investigation the defendant (or, more likely, the defendant's lawyer) wants to be conducted. In many jurisdictions, the defendant's lawyer is appointed by a judge pursuant to a compensation plan that encourages the lawyer to minimize the time spent on a particular case, so the lawyer's financial incentive to pursue an investigation vigorously may be quite limited. While the court should theoretically be open to a defendant's request for funds for an investigation, as a practical matter courts share the pervasive assumption that those who are charged are guilty. Thus, many judges perceive the expenditure of public funds to aid a criminal defendant's investigation as wasteful at best and possibly aiding the perversion of justice at worst. Even if the court were truly neutral, however, the fact remains that the defendant can pay only for those investigations that a court can be persuaded to support, whereas the prosecution can conduct any investigations it deems appropriate.

The prosecution is able to secure testimony that a defendant, no matter how wealthy, cannot match: by bartering a witness's—an informant's—freedom for his or her testimony. For needed testimony, the state can trade indulgences ranging from dropping charges against the witness to recommending a reduced sentence to assuring that the witness receives better accommodations in prison. The state also has the power to grant immunity and thus force a witness to testify even if that testimony would be self-incriminatory. The defendant, on the other hand, is not in a position to offer such incentives and rewards.

Treatment of Exculpatory Information

In addition to limitations inherent in the adversary system and the profound imbalance in resources between the accused and the defense, our system employs a strikingly asymmetrical process for sharing pretrial information. The prosecutor is required to provide the defendant with exculpatory information, while the defendant has no obligation to disclose self-incriminatory information to the prosecutor. While this asymmetry would appear to work entirely to the benefit of the accused (and therefore protect the innocent), paradoxically it appears to have the opposite effect. Prosecutors may point to this asymmetry as a justification for the limited pretrial discovery typical of criminal cases. Given that the defense is not required to disclose incriminating information to the prosecution, the prosecutor may argue that, in fairness, he or she need not provide the defense with helpful information.

This system may achieve reasonable results when the accused actually committed the crime. In that circumstance, the defendant knows more about the crime than the state. Providing the defendant with a great deal of information about the state's case may only aid the defendant in obscuring the truth in a variety of ways both legitimate (through cross-examination) and illegitimate (through the intimidation of witnesses). But if the defendant had nothing whatsoever to do with the crime, the state has an overwhelming advantage in terms of information about the crime. If exculpatory evidence exists, the police and prosecutor are far more likely to have it than the defendant is. Information in the hands of the prosecution may represent the defendant's best chance of escaping conviction.[2]

All participants in the criminal justice system—police, prosecutors, judges, and jurors—assume that those who are formally charged are guilty. Procedural rules are developed in light of this presumption of guilt rather than the presumption of innocence. Thus, based on this assumption, rules limiting the right of this obviously guilty (and knowledgeable and unscrupulous) defendant to learn the state's case before trial make sense. The accused, after all, has an absolute right to remain silent and to insist that the government prove its case beyond a reasonable doubt without any assistance from the defense. If we assume that all defendants are guilty, it also makes sense to discourage perjury by permitting courts to sentence those defendants who take the stand and deny guilt to a longer term than those who do not. Again, given this assumption, what does not make sense is that the prosecutor must turn over to the obviously guilty defendant information that might help him or her persuade the jury to acquit. But if we admit the possibility that an accused may be innocent and view the trial as a search for truth as opposed to a mechanism for resolving a dispute, it does make sense to provide exculpatory information to the defense because this may be the only way the judge or jury can determine the innocence of the defendant.

Prosecutors are supposed to be capable of rising above their role as advocate to assure that justice is done (*Berger v. United States* 1935).

While defense counsel can seek ethically to exonerate someone whom he or she knows to be guilty, prosecutors are barred ethically from seeking to convict someone whom they know to be innocent.

Overwhelmingly, prosecutors honor this ethical mandate. But prosecutors' obligations theoretically go further; they are supposed to provide exculpatory evidence to people whom they believe to a point of certainty to be guilty. The justice they are supposed to pursue is rather more complex than simply assuring that the guilty are punished and the innocent go free. They are assigned the role of preserving adversarial justice by providing the opponent with information that may cast doubt on the guilt of the accused.

This is no easy task. Unlike the tennis player who refuses to take advantage of the umpire's error and graciously acknowledges that an opponent's ball was in rather than out, prosecutors are asked to provide opponents with information that might lead the umpire to call the opponents' ball in when prosecutors believe the ball is out. At a minimum, considerable tension exists between the prosecutor's obligation to play fair by providing the defendant with helpful evidence and the psychological reality that the prosecutor, operating within the adversary system, inevitably comes to embrace the virtue of his or her own position.

A number of considerations push prosecutors to resolve this tension by withholding exculpatory information from the defendant. First, a prosecutor's failure to turn over exculpatory material rarely jeopardizes a conviction. While the prosecutor may have an ethical obligation to turn over information that "tends to negate guilt" (Rosen 1987: 7), legally adverse consequences attach only when the information not revealed "undermines confidence in the outcome" of the trial (*Bagley v. United States* 1985: 678). In other words, a reviewing court will not overturn a conviction because the prosecutor failed to provide exculpatory evidence to an accused unless the exculpatory evidence would have likely led to a different result (*Strickler v. Greene* 1999). Since, by definition, the prosecutor believes in good faith that the defendant is guilty, the prosecutor is also likely to believe in good faith that any potentially exculpatory evidence in his or her possession does not really undermine the reliability of the case. If it did, the ethical prosecutor would not be proceeding against the defendant in the first instance.

Other factors support the prosecutor in the belief that potentially exculpatory information is not really material to the defendant's guilt. Defendants rarely learn of information that was withheld from them.

The only way that a defendant learns that the state was in possession of undisclosed exculpatory evidence is if the defendant seeks collateral, post-conviction relief and is permitted to examine the state's entire file. Realistically, the only defendants who can do this are those who are represented by a lawyer. The Constitution does not require the state to provide a lawyer for such proceedings (*Pennsylvania v. Finley* 1987), and in the vast majority of states, the only prisoners who receive such lawyers are those under a sentence of death. Thus, the overwhelming number of cases in which evidence is withheld go undetected.

In addition, the ethical as opposed to legal obligation to provide exculpatory evidence is rarely enforced. Even blatant acts of prosecutorial dishonesty rarely if ever lead to official inquiry, much less sanctions, by those in charge of enforcing ethical standards (Rosen 1987). Finally, even a conscientious prosecutor committed to providing exculpatory evidence to the accused, despite the seeming futility of doing so, can only provide the information in his or her possession. It is a fair guess, although impossible to know for certain, that the vast majority of potentially exculpatory evidence never makes it to the prosecutor's file. The police have either not turned it over or destroyed it (Fisher 1993). Again, this does not mean that the police are venal. What it means is that they have solved the crime to their satisfaction and provided the prosecutor with the information he or she needs to prosecute successfully.

To summarize, our commitment to the adversary system combined with the radical disparity between the adversaries in terms of resources and credibility compromises the reliability of the fact-finding process. The defense advantages that are thought to balance the struggle—the state's burden to prove guilt beyond a reasonable doubt, the defendant's right to force the state to prove the case without the defendant's own testimony—are of greatest assistance to the guilty, not the innocent. But the very existence of these advantages combined with the tendency of advocates to believe in the integrity of their case may lead prosecutors to be restrained in providing exculpatory evidence to the accused.

Possible Reforms

Curing these difficulties poses a greater challenge than identifying them. Although wrongful convictions occur with a much greater frequency than is officially acknowledged (Givelber 1997), the system, in the main, does work to convict the guilty and filter out the innocent. We must therefore be cautious that a proposed solution does not result in throwing out the baby with the bathwater. This does not mean that we should not consider radical reform of our process of criminal adjudication. It does mean, however, that such reform should not be undertaken solely in the name of assuring that we never convict the innocent.

The discussion to this point has pointed out that the argument for the adversary system assumes that the parties have the resources and the will to put before the fact finder the most reliable evidence of what occurred. If we are going to rely upon adjudication to identify the innocent, we need to begin by insisting on more complete and better-quality evidence than the parties in fact offer and courts currently accept. If we are to place a higher value on accuracy, the judiciary must take a more activist stance.

The current arrangement leaves it to the state to determine whether potentially helpful evidence should be provided to the accused. Ideally, this decision ought to be made by a more neutral party—for example, the court. And the court should have before it the entire file compiled by the state: police records as well as those in the possession of the prosecutor. Given the legitimate, if overused, fear of witness intimidation by the defendant who learns the details of the state's case, we need to consider mechanisms that would reduce this danger. One possibility is to limit complete disclosure of all potentially exculpatory material to those defendants who reciprocate by providing the judge with a binding statement of their account of their innocence.[3]

This proposal is not without its difficulties. One would need a vigorous enforcement mechanism to ensure that the prosecutor and, in particular, the police keep and turn over to the court the records of their investigation of the crime. This would represent a considerable change in current practice (Fisher 1993). Appellate courts would need to support the new approach by signaling to the police and prosecutors that their failure to search for, identify, and disclose exculpatory information would not be tolerated. Since the most obvious remedy— reversal of the conviction—is one that appellate courts have traditionally been reluctant to employ, appellate judges need to change their approach to such cases by consistently reversing convictions in which nontrivial exculpatory material is withheld. Otherwise, enforcement will be left to the very agencies—the police and prosecutors—that have fallen short of their obligations in the first instance.

The conduct of defense counsel might be equally difficult to change. Like other courthouse regulars, defense lawyers tend to believe that their clients are guilty. They also tend to believe (and their experience probably confirms) that they are far more likely to win a case because of the weakness of the state's evidence than because of the strength of their own case. Defense counsel may be reluctant to surrender their ability to deny the state any insight into the defendant's position before trial in return for something as uncertain as the benefits flowing from a judge's comprehensive review of the state's case to determine whether there is any meaningful exculpatory evidence.

Despite these difficulties, there is no way out of the conundrum other than the judiciary's more active role in ensuring that exculpatory evidence is identified, revealed, and evaluated. A prominent critic of our criminal justice system has called for the creation of the role of investigating magistrate (a judicial official with the power to direct and control the investigation of a crime) as indispensable to any effort to improve the quality of the investigation of crime and the processing of the criminally accused (Weinreb 1977). Should that suggestion ever bear fruit, such an official would be well situated to perform the role I suggest. Failing such a development, however, the responsibility should be undertaken by the trial judge.[4]

A second suggestion again requires a more active role for the judiciary. One might improve the quality of justice accorded the innocent if the court had the power to refuse to permit a case to be tried on what is patently second-best evidence. For instance, the state should not be able to prosecute a case involving violence against a stranger by relying primarily on eyewitness testimony when biological material exists, which, if analyzed appropriately, could be highly relevant to the defendant's guilt or innocence. Trial courts might also require that, if the prosecution proposes to use the testimony of a jailhouse informant, it make full disclosure of any deal it has made with the witness to secure the testimony. If the prosecution insists that no such deal has been made, the prosecutor ought to be required to make a statement, under oath, detailing the investigation that he or she has conducted to ensure that no promises have been made to the witness.

Here, too, the judge needs to take a much more active role than is traditional. Given our current rules of discovery in criminal cases, the second-best nature of the evidence may not become evident until the trial itself. Our present understanding of a criminal trial is that once begun it should be completed without significant interruption. There are many reasons for this approach, such as efficiency, minimizing the inconvenience of lay jurors, and assuring that the defendant is tried only once. This view of the criminal trial needs to change: minimally, the defendant ought to be permitted to waive his or her right to protection against double jeopardy and insist that the state investigate further before proceeding with the trial when it becomes apparent that the state's evidence is something less than the most reliable evidence available.

Although not related to the adversary system per se, another feature of our criminal justice system is that those who deny guilt and insist on trial can be and are sentenced more harshly than those who do not. Moreover, those who take the stand at trial and are convicted can be and frequently are punished more severely than those who stand silent at trial (Givelber 2000). This occurs when the trial judge determines that the defendant committed perjury when testifying as to his or her innocence and increases the sentence accordingly (*United States v. Dunnigan* 1993). The federal sentencing guidelines explicitly authorize both practices (Hutchinson et al. 1998: 786–806, 835–52).[5] The wrongly accused innocent will feel most intensely the sting of these conventions: if the defendant insists on trial and testifies to his or her innocence, the person will suffer greater punishment than if he or she either pled or stood silent at trial. These conventions serve as disincentives to defendants to insist on a trial and proclaim their innocence while testifying. Whatever the justifications for these rules as applied to the guilty, their impact on the innocent is perverse.

Although solutions are cumbersome, we might attempt to apply these disincentives so that they are most likely to punish only the guilty. Although the Constitution requires us to protect the meanest and most apparently guilty as avidly as the powerful and most improbably guilty, it does not require us to treat individuals identically for purposes of sentencing. We know that the overwhelming majority of crimes are solved because they are either committed in the presence of the police or because the victim or witnesses know the perpetrator. We know also that those cases that are solved through lengthy investigation are the ones that create the greatest danger of error. While the lines of demarcation between the two kinds of cases blur, justice might well be served if we restricted the possibility of punishment for insisting on trial and testifying to those cases in which the police observed the crime or the victim or a witness identified the culprit immediately. While this suggestion removes a disincentive to testify for many guilty people (for example, those accurately identified as the result of a criminal investigation), that should be a price we are willing to pay to assure that we do not convict the innocent.

These suggestions are hardly panaceas. All create new problems even as they respond to existing ones. They assume that the Constitution commits us to the adversary system. And even a perfect system of adjudication could not eliminate the problems caused by human limitations and venality. Nonetheless, if we ever hope to bring reality somewhat in line with our rhetorical commitment to protecting the innocent, we need to reconsider our belief that the criminal adversary system of adjudication adequately protects the falsely accused.

NOTES

1. This does not mean that courts do not pay considerable lip service to the need to arrive at the truth. "We have elected to employ an adversary system of criminal justice in which the parties contest all issues before a court of law. The need to develop all relevant facts in the adversary system is both fundamental and comprehensive. The ends of criminal justice would be defeated if judgments were to be founded on a partial or speculative presentation of the facts. The very integrity of the judicial system and public confidence in the system depend on full disclosure of all the facts, within the framework of the rules of evidence" (*United States v. Nixon* 1974: 709).
2. The defendant will have an opportunity to put on a defense, but, by definition, the defendant's story has failed to persuade the police and prosecutor to drop the charges. The jury may still acquit; but the state is proceeding on the good-faith assumption that the defendant did it, that the defendant's insistence that he or she did not is a lie, and that the jury will so conclude.
3. A plea of not guilty does not have the same meaning as the claim "I am innocent." A not guilty plea means the defendant insists on a trial. It is as consistent with the position that the government will be unable to prove that the defendant committed the crime as it is with the position that the defendant did not commit the crime. A defendant who pleads not guilty is not required to offer any evidence of any kind or provide any explanation of his or her behavior. The proposal here is to limit the requirement of complete disclosure of exculpatory material to those defendants who insist that they are innocent and are willing to tell their story in advance.
4. It may appear a small step from this proposal to a more general requirement of full disclosure from the prosecution and defense cases before trial. Unfortunately, it is not. The proposal advanced in the chapter takes an obligation that already exists—making exculpatory evidence available to the defense—and attempts to put real teeth into the requirement, particularly when the defendant claims he or she is innocent. No consensus exists on requiring a more general exchange of information before trial; indeed, the practice is quite the opposite (Sarokin and Zuckerman 1991).
5. As a formal matter, the guidelines do not increase the sentence of some-

one who insists on going to trial. Instead, section 3E1.1 calls for a reduction in the sentence that someone would otherwise serve for defendants who are "accepting responsibility." Since nine out of ten federal defendants plead guilty, and since trial judges overwhelmingly consider this group as having "accepted responsibility" (O'Hear 1997), the tiny minority of all defendants who actually insist on trial are the people most likely to receive the full sentence for a particular crime. On the other hand, in section 3C1.1, the guidelines do call for an increase in the sentence of those whom the trial judge decides "obstructed justice" by, among other things, committing perjury when they testify at trial and deny guilt.

REFERENCES

Devitt, Edward J., Charles B. Blackmar, and Michael A. Wolff. 1987. *Federal Jury Practice and Instructions*. St. Paul, Minn.: West.

Fisher, Stanley Z. 1993. "'Just the Facts, Ma'am': Lying and the Omission of Exculpatory Evidence in Police Reports." *New England Law Review* 28: 1–62.

Givelber, Daniel. 1997. "Meaningless Acquittals, Meaningful Convictions: Do We Reliably Acquit the Innocent?" *Rutgers Law Review* 49: 1317–96.

———. 2000. "Punishing Protestations of Innocence: Denying Responsibility and Its Consequences." *American Criminal Law Review*. 37: 1363–1408.

Huff, C. Ronald, Arye Rattner, and Edward Sagarin. 1996. *Convicted but Innocent: Wrongful Conviction and Public Policy*. Thousand Oaks, Calif.: Sage.

Hutchinson, Thomas, David Yellen, Peter Hoffman, and Deborah Young. 1998. *Federal Sentencing Law and Practice*. St. Paul, Minn.: West.

Landsman, Stephan. 1984. *The Adversary System: A Description and Defense*. Washington, D.C.: American Enterprise Institute.

Luban, David. 1988. *Lawyers and Justice: An Ethical Study*. Princeton, N.J.: Princeton University Press.

———. 1993. "Are Criminal Defenders Different?" *Michigan Law Review* 91: 1729–66.

Melilli, Kenneth J. 1992. "Prosecutorial Discretion in an Adversary System." *Brigham Young University Law Review*: 669–704.

O'Hear, Michael. 1997. "Remorse, Cooperation and 'Acceptance of Responsibility': The Structure, Implementation, and Reform of Section 3E1.1 of the Federal Sentencing Guidelines." *Northwestern University Law Review* 91: 1507–73.

Radelet, Michael L., Hugo Adam Bedau, and Constance E. Putnam. 1992. *In Spite of Innocence*. Boston: Northeastern University Press.

Rosen, Richard A. 1987. "Disciplinary Sanctions against Prosecutors for *Brady* Violations: A Paper Tiger." *North Carolina Law Review* 65: 693–744.

Sarokin, H. Lee, and William Zuckerman. 1991. "Presumed Innocent? Restrictions on Criminal Discovery in Federal Court Belies This Presumption." *Rutgers Law Review* 43: 1089–1111.

Scheck, Barry, Peter Neufeld, and Jim Dwyer. 2000. *Actual Innocence*. New York: Doubleday.

Schwartz, Murray L. 1983. "The Zeal of the Civil Advocate." *American Bar Foundation Research Journal*: 543–63.

Stacy, Tom. 1991. "The Search for Truth in Constitutional Criminal Procedure." *Columbia Law Review* 91: 1369–1451.

Volokh, Alexander. 1997. "N Guilty Men." *University of Pennsylvania Law Review* 146: 173–212.
Weinreb, Lloyd L. 1977. *Denial of Justice*. New York: Free Press.

CASES CITED

Bagley v. United States, 473 U.S. 667 (1985).
Berger v. United States, 295 U.S. 78 (1935).
Davis v. Alaska, 415 U.S. 308 (1974).
Duncan v. Louisiana, 391 U.S. 145 (1968).
In re Winship, 397 U.S. 358 (1970).
Pennsylvania v. Finley, 481 U.S. 551 (1987).
Strickler v. Greene, 119 S.Ct. 1936 (1999).
United States v. Dunnigan, 597 U.S. 87 (1993).
United States v. Nixon, 418 U.S. 683 (1974).
Washington v. Texas, 388 U.S. 14 (1967).
Wilson v. United States, 149 U.S. 60 (1893).

MICHAEL L. RADELET

HUGO ADAM BEDAU

14 Erroneous Convictions and the Death Penalty

Luck can work in mysterious ways. On 21 September 1998, we received a phone call from University of New Mexico law professor James Ellis, a leading authority on issues surrounding the execution of mentally retarded prisoners. A past president of the American Association on Mental Retardation, Ellis was working on the appeal and clemency petition of Illinois death row inmate Anthony Porter. He asked us for assistance in identifying other twentieth-century cases in which executive clemency had been granted to mentally retarded prisoners on death row. Since we have both published studies on clemency issues in capital cases (Bedau 1990–91; Radelet and Zsembik 1993) as well as other death penalty work, the call was not unusual; we receive similar calls or letters asking for help in death penalty cases virtually every week. We spent a couple of hours doing some research, faxed Ellis some information, and wished him and his client good luck.

And good luck later became the distinguishing characteristic of the case. An African American with an IQ of 51, Porter had been on death row in Illinois for sixteen years, convicted of killing two teenagers in Chicago in 1982. When we received the phone call, he was scheduled to be executed in forty-eight hours. But luckily for him, just as we were beginning our research on the clemency issue, the Illinois Supreme Court granted a temporary stay in the case so that lower courts could more closely explore the issue of whether a death row prisoner with an IQ of 51 can be constitutionally executed (Parsons 1998).

We heard nothing more about the case for four months. Then in February 1999, we were shocked to see in our local newspapers a picture of Porter walking out of prison, a free man (Belluck 1999). In the short time since we had last heard of the case, Porter's defense team had been able to prove that he was totally innocent of the crime that had sent him to death row.

Despite sixteen years on death row for a crime he did not commit, Anthony Porter is an incredibly lucky man. His luck included his low IQ: had he not been mentally retarded, the September stay that saved his life would never have been issued, and he would have been executed. His luck included securing the volunteer efforts of Jim Ellis, the very best in the business, as well as other volunteer attorneys and investigators. More luck came after the September stay, when his case was "adopted" by a class in investigative journalism taught by Professor David Protess at Northwestern University. Students reinvestigating the crimes were initially troubled by the fact that Porter is right-handed, while a witness claimed the killer had used his left hand. The students then interviewed the main prosecution witness, who stated that his incrimination of Porter had been false and was given only after prolonged police pressure. The students interviewed relatives of another suspect, who confirmed that this suspect had indeed admitted to the killings. And finally they located that suspect— alive and well and living in Milwaukee—who promptly admitted his guilt in a videotaped confession.

So Porter was lucky not only because of his mental retardation. He was lucky that a college course in investigative journalism was being offered and that the class had adopted his case. He was lucky that the lead witness recanted and lucky that the true killer had bragged about the crime, was still alive and could be found, and was willing to confess. And the citizens and authorities in Illinois were lucky that they did not send an innocent man to the executioner.

Nonetheless, Illinois authorities initially refused to gloat about their luck or to take any blame for their (and Porter's) need for luck. "The system worked," said the governor's press secretary, Dave Urbanek. "The process did work. Sure it took 17 years, but it also took 17 years for that journalism professor to sic his kids on that case" (Belluck 1999: 17). Urbanek, in our view, fails to see that a class of journalism students is not part of the criminal justice system and is not the type of group that a state government ought to rely on to detect its worst blunders. Had the system worked, Anthony Porter would be dead.

In an unprecedented move and in response to Porter's exoneration and those of twelve other Illinois death row inmates in the past two decades (Bienen 1998; "Last Chance Class," 1999), the governor of Illinois declared a moratorium on executions in early 2000 (Armstrong and Mills 2000).

The Scope of the Problem

According to the Death Penalty Information Center, between 1972 and mid-2000 some seven dozen inmates have been released from U.S. death rows because of serious questions about their guilt.[1] Thirty of these death row survivors gathered in November 1998 on a stage at Northwestern University School of Law in Chicago, united by their distrust of the criminal justice system and antipathy for the death penalty. There (with 1,500 others) to attend a conference on erroneous convictions, one after another they moved forward and introduced themselves, as this man did: "My name is Joseph Green Brown. Had the state of Florida gotten its way, I'd be dead today" (Bendavid 1998; Terry 1998: A12).

Hundreds of other defendants have been erroneously convicted of homicide in American jurisdictions, often escaping a death sentence or the execution chamber with a degree of luck not altogether different from Anthony Porter's (Radelet et al. 1992). This gives rise to a question frequently posed by journalists: what proportion of those convicted of homicide or sentenced to death are likely to be innocent?

Aside from the simple response, "too many," the question is impossible to answer. In part this is because of different ways in which innocence can be conceptualized. In its narrowest sense (the sense we have used in the bulk of our research), the term includes only those who had nothing to do with the criminal homicide of which they were convicted. But additional categories of innocent defendants sentenced to death need to remain in the spotlight. Undoubtedly, a number of prisoners on death row today and in the past in reality killed by accident or in self-defense; thus, they ought to be considered innocent of the capital murder charge on which they were convicted. Many on death row, given proper representation and proper access to mental health professionals, would have been found not guilty by reason of insanity; these prisoners, too, can be considered in this sense to be innocent of the capital charge. Hundreds and hundreds of prisoners on U.S. death rows, given a more perfect justice system, would have been convicted of second-degree murder or some other type of noncapital criminal homicide; these prisoners, too, can be thought of as innocent of capital murder. All of these types of convicted murderers can be seen as victims of wrongful conviction and miscarriages of justice, even if not totally innocent of the homicide (Black 1981; Radelet and Bedau. 1998a, 1998b).

Even if researchers endeavored to make an accurate count of people released from death rows who were totally uninvolved in the homicide for which they were convicted, precise counting quickly becomes impossible. We have been very careful to label our inventory "people released from death row because of doubts about their guilt," not "innocent people released from death row," because absolute, definitive innocence is all but impossible to prove. Even in cases with DNA exoneration, one can argue that the lack of a DNA match could be explained by the mishandling of the evidence, for example, rather than the prisoner's innocence. Like guilt, where the standard for conviction is "beyond a reasonable doubt," not "100 percent certainty," the determination of innocence is a question of where to draw the line on a continuum of probabilities of innocence.

Under the label "released from death row because of doubts about guilt," we include Joe Spaziano, who spent nineteen years on death row in Florida before his conviction was thrown out in 1996. In November 1998, rather than risk even a slight chance of reconviction, Spaziano executed a no-contest plea to second-degree murder in exchange for time served (Griffin and Leusner 1998). Because of this plea, he will forever stand as a convicted murderer, even though most observers—and certainly those of us who know Spaziano and worked on the case—realize that, given the deal, his plea tells us absolutely nothing about his guilt. It is a sad commentary that public officials who have committed a horrendous blunder—sending a person to death row despite sizable doubts about guilt—can extract from their victim a guilty plea as their price for release.

Should Spaziano be included on the Death Penalty Information Center's list of individuals who have been released from death row because of their innocence? Right now, he is not. Given our criterion "released from death row because of doubts about guilt," we have included similar cases in our work on this issue; but that still leaves open the question of whether he (and similar others) should be called innocent. Our answer to this dilemma is that it really does not matter. To publicly insist that the facts definitively prove Spaziano's innocence forces us into battles about trees, which only deflects attention from the forest. We need to find common ground, and more will agree that there are substantial doubts about Spaziano's guilt than will agree that the evidence absolutely (or "almost certainly" or "probably") proves his innocence. Furthermore, if the lessons of human fallibility are not clear after reviewing the stories narrated in our research of eighty others who were released from death rows because of doubts about guilt or even the stories of the four hundred defendants erroneously convicted in the twentieth century (Radelet et al. 1992), adding several cases in which prisoners were forced to plead guilty to secure their release from prison will not change any additional minds.

How Do We Know That Innocent People Have Been Executed?

One of the main reasons that England abolished the death penalty was incontrovertible evidence that it had executed an innocent person. This miscarriage of justice led Queen Elizabeth to issue a posthumous pardon to Timothy John Evans, who had been hanged in 1950 (Kennedy 1961; Lewis 1966). But in the United States, government officials probably will not admit that an innocent person has been executed unless the homicide victim shows up alive. The last time a government official admitted that an innocent person had been executed was in 1893, when Governor John Altgeld pardoned three of the surviving Haymarket defendants in Chicago (Avrich 1984: 42 1). The pardons were issued because the three men as well as four codefendants who had been hanged six years previously and an eighth codefendant who committed suicide on the eve of his scheduled execution were totally innocent. Altgeld made it clear that he was freeing the three "not as an act of simply mercy, not because they had suffered enough, but because they had been wrongfully convicted and were innocent of the crime for which they had been imprisoned" (423).

There are, indeed, good examples of executions in the past twenty years where we believe reasonable and informed people would find the person "probably" or "almost certainly" innocent (see, for instance, the cases of Jesse Tafero [Radelet et al. 1996: 941–43] or James Adams [Bedau and Radelet 1987: 91]). There are reasonable doubts about several others recently executed (such as Roger Keith Coleman [Tucker 1997]), but no published work to date has compiled a list and description of all these cases. But because no government (state or federal) has admitted carrying out an erroneous execution in the twentieth century, critics claim that no errors have occurred. For example, University of Utah Law School professor Paul Cassell, the nation's leading apologist for judicial errors, states, "My view is that no innocent person has been executed in the past 50 years. It is interesting that the organizers [of the Northwestern University conference] . . . cannot name one innocent person who has been executed" (Bendavid 1998). Cassell's complaint is misleading; what he means is that he remains unconvinced that any executed prisoner was innocent. So do most state government officials, to judge from their evasions and silence on the issue. But the view of one ultra-conservative law professor who has never done any original research on the subject certainly does not settle the issue. States have been less than cooperative in investigating claims of innocence by supporters of inmates who have been executed. For example, in the case of Joseph O'Dell, executed in Virginia in 1997 despite strong protests of innocence, the commonwealth of Virginia refuses to release evidence from the crime to O'Dell's family so DNA tests that might exonerate him can be performed ("A Sister's Plea," 1999). By releasing the DNA, of course, the government has everything to lose and nothing to win.

Another way to realize that innocent people have been executed is to look at the case summaries of the eighty-seven men and women who have been released from death rows in the past thirty years and examine the type and quality of evidence on which their convictions were based. In case after case, any unbiased reader will find that many of these defendants, and many other inmates who were executed, were convicted on extremely precarious testimony. Our research shows that the main cause of erroneous convictions in homicide cases is perjury by prosecution witnesses—often prisoners or individuals facing criminal charges (including, in some cases, charges for the homicide that the witness is pinning on someone else) who hope to use their false testimony to curry favor with the prosecution. To highlight the inadequacy of such evidence, we propose what we call "the babysitter test" for future prosecution witnesses in death penalty cases. We suggest that, to send someone to the gurney or the electric chair on the word of one witness, the prosecutor must agree to hire that witness as a babysitter for her or his kids for one evening. Again and again, we see capital convictions based on the word of people whose credibility is so highly questionable that we would not let them near our own children. These witnesses are far too unreliable to provide testimony on which to base life-and-death decisions.

Another clear conclusion from our work is that people are not released from death row because the system works. Most of those released were vindicated only because they were incredibly lucky. They had extraordinarily committed attorneys, family, friends, and often sympathetic journalists (or journalism professors such as David Protess) who helped to reinvestigate the case or put it in the public spotlight.[2] They were lucky that a previously silent witness stepped forward or that a prosecution witness admitted perjury. In the Bloodsworth case (Radelet et al. 1996: 926–27), the defendant was lucky that the victim was both raped and murdered because the rape evidence could later be reanalyzed to prove his innocence. All of the cases of the vindicated prisoners teach us that the criminal justice system goes to great lengths to hide its mistakes. People released from death rows today are not released because of the system; they are released in spite of it. If the main ingredient in a successful exoneration is luck, one can only wonder how many executed prisoners were not only unlucky but also innocent.

Thus, we need to keep in mind that, until a dozen years ago, defenders of the death penalty rarely if ever acknowledged the inevitability of executing the innocent. Today, proponents and opponents of the death penalty have found common ground; both sides realize that innocent people can be and are being executed. For example, on the television show *Nightline* (14 July 1997), Congressman Bill McCollum, a staunch death penalty supporter, made a remarkable admission: "I think the system actually is working quite well in terms of trying to protect the innocent. . . . [But] I don't think there's any question that some day, somebody who is innocent will be executed in this country again. It's happened before."

The Significance of Erroneous Convictions in the Death Penalty Debate

Those who support the death penalty take the position that, while erroneous executions may be inevitable, the risk is justified by the net benefits this penalty offers over and above long imprisonment. Former solicitor general and Supreme Court nominee Robert Bork admitted that even one innocent person wrongly executed is terrible. "But, the question is," he asked, "if you do away with it, have you condemned other people to death?" (Associated Press 1998). Bork seems to be insinuating that the death penalty has a special deterrent effect, regardless of whether the executed inmate is guilty or innocent. In response, those who oppose the death penalty would jump at the chance to move the debate back to the deterrence issue, which in most informed minds has been all but settled (Bailey and Peterson 1997). Virtually all criminologists and the vast majority of police chiefs and sheriffs today agree that the data clearly show that the death penalty never has been, is not, and never could exert stronger deterrent effects than long imprisonment (Radelet and Akers 1996).

One could also approach this cost-benefit assessment by arguing that no matter what the benefits of the death penalty (and we vehemently argue there are none), the cost of even one erroneous execution is simply not a cost that democratic societies should be willing to bear. Few readers of this chapter might be able to imagine themselves convicted of murder (whether innocent or guilty) and on death row, but those who have experienced this or seen family or friends endure the ordeal are unanimous in their stand that this is a power that governments should not have.

For many Americans, the inevitability of erroneous executions is the single most important reason for doing away with the death penalty. In his comprehensive review of recent opinion polls on this issue, Gross (1998) finds the issue of special importance because it is not simply cited by those who already oppose the death penalty but also appeals to those who are inclined to support capital punishment. In fact, a 1993 poll found that some 58 percent of respondents—both supporters and foes of the death penalty—felt the issue of innocence raised "serious" or "some" doubts in their minds about its propriety. Similarly, 73 percent of those responding in a 1997 *Newsweek* poll found that innocence was "among the best reasons" for opposing the death penalty (Gross 1998: 1463).

For jurors, lingering doubt about guilt is often translated into votes for prison sentences rather than death. In South Carolina, for example, lingering doubt about the defendant's guilt is the single most important reason why jurors select prison sentences over death sentences (Garvey 1998: 1559, 1562–64). Overall, "lingering doubt, when it is present, is an integral element in forming a reasoned moral judgment about punishment. Indisputably, lingering doubt plays a central role in jurors' thinking about what punishment the defendant deserves" (Bowers et al. 1998: 1536).

Unlike the general public and jurors, neither elected legislators (with rare exceptions) nor the highest courts seem to be concerned about the possibility of executing the innocent. In the United States, both Congress and the Supreme Court are increasingly restricting access to federal courts by inmates contesting their death sentences (Freedman 1998; Yackle 1998). This has provoked some important calls for moratoria on death sentencing and executions. In 1999, for the third consecutive year, the U.N. Commission on Human Rights, headquartered in Geneva, passed a resolution calling for a moratorium on executions in the United States, with an eye toward its eventual total abolition (Amnesty International 1999). In May 1999, the Nebraska legislature passed a resolution calling for a two-year moratorium on executions because of questions of equity in the administration of their state's death penalty (Tysyer 1999). This resolution was vetoed by the governor, but later the legislature unanimously overrode the governor's veto of the part of the legislation that allocated some $165,000 to study the issue. Finally, in February 1997 the normally conservative House of Delegates of the American Bar Association, on behalf of its 400,000 members, called for a moratorium on the death penalty. It cited four principal reasons: the lack of adequate defense counsel, the erosion of state post-conviction and federal habeas corpus review, the continuing problem of racial bias in the administration of the death penalty, and the refusal of states and the courts to take action to prevent the execution of juveniles and the mentally retarded.[3] While the association did not oppose the death penalty per se, it did strive to bring these problems to the attention of legislators and the American public.

In light of this growing division between those calling for the reevaluation of the death penalty and state and federal authorities who appear committed to its use, the moratorium enacted in Illinois seems all the more remarkable. The governor has declared that no execution will take place in his state until he can be sure that only the guilty will be subject to it (Armstrong and Mills 2000), a move that signals the centrality of the wrongful conviction issue to the current death penalty controversy.

Conclusion

We argue that people should not be executed, regardless of the person's guilt or innocence. Nevertheless, guilt or innocence, standing alone, is not the issue. The problem of wrongful convictions is important because it is part of a much larger issue: once we decide that some of our citizens will be executed, all the evidence shows that our government officials do a positively horrible job in selecting who should live and who should die. Some are selected because of their race or class (or the race or class of the victim); some because of pure arbitrariness; some because they are not like we are. Above all, the quality of the defense counsel at trial matters; many today end up on death row not because of the brutality of their crime but because of the incompetence of their defense (Bright 1997). As Marvin Wolfgang (1996) argued in his last major paper before his death, the issue is less about who deserves to die and more about who deserves to kill.

NOTES

1. This count was originally based on our work but for the last two years has been maintained and updated regularly on a website by the Death Penalty Information Center at http://www.deathpenaltyinfo.org. For a description of sixty-eight of these cases, see Bedau and Radelet (1987) and Radelet et al. (1996). The center uses slightly different criteria for defining *innocence* than we have.
2. Protess's work (and that of his students) has also helped release several other innocent men from death row in Illinois (see, for example, Protess and Warden 1998).
3. For an elaboration of this resolution and the reasons behind it, see the series of papers published in a special issue of *Law and Contemporary Problems* (Autumn 1998).

REFERENCES

Amnesty International. 1999. "Press Release—1999 Commission on Human Rights." AI Index: IOR 42/05/99 (29 April), News Service 082/99.

Armstrong, Ken, and Steve Mills. 2000. "Ryan: 'Until I Can Be Sure' Illinois Is First State to Suspend Death Penalty." *Chicago Tribune*, 1 February, p. 1.

Associated Press. 1998. "Wrongfully Convicted Present Big Challenge to Death Penalty." *Gainesville Sun*, 8 November, p. 3A.

Avrich, Paul. 1984. *The Haymarket Tragedy*. Princeton, N.J.: Princeton University Press.

Bailey, William C., and Ruth D. Peterson. 1997. "Murder, Capital Punishment, and Deterrence: A Review of the Literature." *In The Death Penalty in America: Current Controversies*, edited by Hugo Adam Bedau, 135–61. New York: Oxford University Press.

Bedau, Hugo Adam. 1990–91. "The Decline of Executive Clemency in Capital Cases." *New York University Review of Law and Social Change* 18: 255–72.

Bedau, Hugo Adam, and Michael L. Radelet. 1987. "Miscarriages of Justice in Potentially Capital Cases." *Stanford Law Review* 40: 21–179.

Belluck, Pam. 1999. "Convict Freed after 16 Years on Death Row." *New York Times*, 6 February, p. A7.

Bendavid, Naftali. 1998. "Escaping Execution." *Chicago Tribune*, 13 November, p. 3.

Bienen, Leigh B. 1998. "The Quality of Justice in Capital Cases: Illinois As a Case Study." *Law and Contemporary Problems* 61: 193–217.

Black, Charles L., Jr. 1981. *Capital Punishment: The Inevitability of Caprice and Mistake*. 2d ed. New York: Norton.

Bowers, William J., Marla Sandys, and Benjamin D. Steiner. 1998. "Foreclosed Impartiality in Capital Sentencing: Jurors' Predispositions, Guilt-Trial Experience, and Premature Decision Making." *Cornell Law Review* 83: 1476–1556.

Bright, Stephen B. 1997. "Counsel for the Poor: The Death Sentence Not for the Worst Crime but for the Worst Lawyer." *In The Death Penalty in America: Current Controversies*, edited by Hugo Adam Bedau, 275–309. New York: Oxford University Press.

Freedman, Eric. 1998. "Federal Habeas Corpus in Capital Cases." In *America's Experiment with Capital Punishment*, edited by James R. Acker, Robert M. Bohm, and Charles S. Lanier, 417–36. Durham, N.C.: Carolina Academic Press.

Garvey, Stephen P. 1998. "Aggravation and Mitigation in Capital Cases: What Do Jurors Think?" *Columbia Law Review* 98: 1538–76.

Griffin, Michael, and Jim Leusner. 1998. "Spaziano's No-Contest Plea Deal Keeps Him out of Electric Chair." *Orlando Sentinel*, 7 November, p. 1.

Gross, Samuel R. 1998. "Update: American Public Opinion on the Death Penalty—It's Getting Personal." *Cornell Law Review* 83: 1448–75.

Kennedy, Ludovic. 1961. *Ten Rillington Place*. New York: Simon and Schuster.

"Last Chance Class." 1999. *Newsweek*, 31 May, pp. 32–34.

Lewis, Anthony. 1966. "Britain Pardons a Man Hanged in 1950 for Murder of Daughter." *New York Times*, 19 October, p. 19.

Parsons, Christi. 1998. "Court Stalls Execution, Asks If Killer Is Smart Enough to Die." *Chicago Tribune*, 22 September, p. 1.

Protess, David, and Rob Warden. 1998. *A Promise of Justice*. New York: Hyperion.

Radelet, Michael L., and Ronald L. Akers. 1996. "Deterrence and the Death Penalty: The Views of the Experts." *Journal of Criminal Law and Criminology* 87: 1–16.

Radelet, Michael L., and Hugo Adam Bedau. 1998a. "The Execution of the Innocent." *Law and Contemporary Problems* 61: 105–24.

———. 1998b. "The Execution of the Innocent." In *America's Experiment with Capital Punishment*, edited by James R. Acker, Robert M. Bohm, and Charles S. Lanier, 223–42. Durham, N.C.: Carolina Academic Press.

Radelet, Michael L., and Barbara A. Zsembik. 1993. "Executive Clemency in Post-*Furman* Capital Cases." *University of Richmond Law Review* 27: 289–314.

Radelet, Michael L., Hugo Adam Bedau, and Constance E. Putnam. 1992. *In Spite of Innocence*. Boston: Northeastern University Press.

Radelet, Michael L., William S. Lofquist, and Hugo Adam Bedau. 1996. "Prisoners Released from Death Rows Since 1970 because of Doubts about Their Guilt." *Thomas M. Cooley Law Review* 13: 907–66.

"A Sister's Plea: Test the DNA." 1999. *Time*, 28 June, p. 8.

Terry, Don. 1998. "Survivors Make the Case against Death Row." *New York Times*, 16 November, p. A12.

Tucker, John C. 1997. *May God Have Mercy.* New York: Norton.

Tysyer, Robynn. 1999. "Execution Suspension Approved." *Omaha World Herald*, 20 May, p. 1.

Wolfgang, Marvin E. 1996. "We Do Not Deserve to Kill." *Thomas M. Cooley Law Review* 13: 977–90.

Yackle, Larry W. 1998. "The American Bar Association and Federal Habeas Corpus." *Law and Contemporary Problems* 61: 171–92.

About the Editors
and Contributors

SAUNDRA D. WESTERVELT is an assistant professor of sociology at The University of North Carolina at Greensboro. Her first book, *Shifting the Blame: How Victimization Became a Criminal Defense* (Rutgers University Press 1998), documents and explains the development and expansion of the victimization defense strategy—commonly called the "abuse excuse"—beginning with the success of the battered women's self-defense strategy in the late 1970s. *Shifting the Blame* was recognized by *Choice Magazine* as one of their "Outstanding Academic Titles" for 1998. In addition to her current focus on wrongful convictions, her other research interests include the development and use of parental liability laws and the proliferation of the family court movement.

JOHN A. HUMPHREY is a professor of sociology at The University of North Carolina at Greensboro. His research interests include sociocultural analyses of criminal homicide, physical and sexual assault, self-destructive behavior, and substance abuse. He is co-author of three books and numerous journal articles with colleagues in anthropology, medicine, psychology, and sociology. His research has been funded by the National Institute of Mental Health, the National Institute of Justice, the Bureau of Justice Assistance, and the Centers for Disease Control and Prevention.

JAMES R. ACKER has written extensively on capital punishment. His numerous articles about the death penalty have reviewed the history of capital punishment in New York, analyzed New York's contemporary death penalty legislation, and covered a wide range of other issues. He is co-editor of *America's Experiment with Capital Punishment: Reflections on the Past, Present, and Future of the Ultimate Penal Sanction* (Carolina Academic Press 1998). He earned his J.D. at Duke Law School and was awarded his Ph.D. from the University of Albany, State University of New York. He is a professor in the School of Criminal Justice at the University of Albany. His chapter in this book is the result of a collaborative research effort begun in a graduate seminar on capital punishment in which all co-authors participated. Thomas Brewer, Eamonn Cunningham, Jamie Flexon, Barbara Ryn, and Bivette Stodghill are Ph.D. students at the School of Criminal Justice at the University of Albany. Allison Fitzgerald was awarded her M.A. in criminal justice in 1999, and Julie Lombard is pursuing her M.A. at the University of Albany.

HUGO ADAM BEDAU received his Ph.D. from Harvard University in 1961 and taught at Dartmouth, Princeton, and Reed before joining the Tufts faculty in 1966, where he is Austin Fletcher Professor of Philosophy Emeritus. He is the author, editor, co-author, or co-editor of several books, including *The Death Penalty in America* (Oxford University Press 1964, 1982, 1997), *Death Is Different* (Northeastern University Press 1987), *In Spite of Innocence* (Northeastern University Press 1992), *Capital Punishment in the United States* (AMS Press 1976), and *Making Mortal Choices* (Oxford University Press 1997), as well as many articles and reviews, notably "Miscarriages of Justice in Potentially Capital Cases," co-authored with Michael Radelet and published in the *Stanford Law Review* (1987).

ADELE BERNHARD is an associate professor of law at Pace University Law School, where she directs a criminal defense clinic and externship. She began practicing law as a public defender with the Legal Aid Society in the South Bronx and has concentrated on criminal law for most of her career. She has managed an experimental grant-funded project that provided training, continuing legal education, and resources for private court-appointed counsel assigned to represent poor people in criminal court. She is currently a member of the First Department Appellate Division Indigent Defense Organization Oversight

Committee, which monitors the provision of defense services in the Bronx and Manhattan. Her most recent publication is "When Justice Fails: Compensation for the Unjustly Convicted," published in the University of Chicago *Roundtable* (Fall 1999).

GEORGE CASTELLE is the chief public defender in Charleston, West Virginia. He represented the interests of all West Virginia prisoners in both the 1993 and 1999–2000 investigations into fraud in the West Virginia State Police Crime Lab. He also represented many of those same prisoners in their subsequent efforts to overturn their convictions based on the false forensic science, including William Harris, whose case is discussed in Castelle and Loftus's chapter in this book. In 1997 he received the National Legal Aid and Defender Association's Reginald Heber Smith Award for exposing crime lab fraud and freeing prisoners wrongly convicted by false scientific data.

MARI A. DEWEES is a doctoral student in the Department of Sociology at the University of Florida. Her current research interests include cross-cultural comparisons of homicide as well as the effect of race and gender on urban homicide.

DANIEL GIVELBER is a professor of law and dean emeritus at the Northeastern University School of Law. A graduate of Harvard College and Law School, he was an assistant U.S. attorney before beginning his career at Northeastern. His most recent practice experience has been in the area of death penalty defense work. His recent scholarship and teaching have focused on criminal law, with particular emphasis on capital punishment, post-conviction relief, and the accuracy of our criminal process.

WILLIAM M. HOLMES is a visiting associate professor at the University of Massachusetts at Boston in the College of Public and Community Services, Criminal Justice Center. He is the former director of the Statistical Analysis Center for Massachusetts. He has conducted research funded by the Bureau of Justice Statistics, the National Institute of Justice, the National Institute of Mental Health, and the National Center on Child Abuse and Neglect. His co-authored book *Portrait of Divorce* (Guilford Press 1992) won the William Goode Award from the family section of the American Sociological Association for contributions to family research. He received the G. Paul Sylvester

Award from the U.S. Bureau of Justice Statistics for contributions to criminal justice statistics. He is also former president of the Justice Research and Statistics Association.

RICHARD A. LEO, PH.D., J.D., is an assistant professor of criminology, law, and society and an assistant professor of psychology and social behavior at the University of California at Irvine. He is one of the leading experts in the world on American police interrogation practices, coercive influence techniques, false confessions, and miscarriages of justice. He has published numerous academic articles on these subjects, and his research has been profiled by national and international media, including the *New York Times*, the *Los Angeles Times*, the *Washington Post*, *U.S. News & World Report*, the *Nation*, National Public Radio, and the *American Bar Association Journal*. He has consulted with attorneys in more than two hundred fifty cases involving disputed interrogations or confessions and has testified numerous times on these topics in state, federal, and military courts across the United States. He is the 1999 recipient of the Ruth Shonle Cavan Award for outstanding scholarship from the American Society of Criminology.

WILLIAM S. LOFQUIST is an associate professor of sociology at the State University of New York College at Geneseo. His recent research focuses on documenting and theorizing wrongful convictions in death penalty cases. By emphasizing the organizational causes and control of wrongful convictions, this research extends his earlier work on the causes and control of corporate crime. He has published articles in *Law and Society Review, Justice Quarterly, Studies in Law, Politics, and Society,* and other journals on a variety of topics relating to the legal control of organizational misconduct and co-edited *Debating Corporate Crime* with Mark Cohen and Gary Rabe (Anderson 1997).

ELIZABETH F. LOFTUS is a professor of psychology and adjunct professor of law at the University of Washington, Seattle. She has published twenty books and more than three hundred scientific articles. Her fourth book, *Eyewitness Testimony* (Harvard University Press 1996), won a National Media Award (Distinguished Contribution) from the American Psychological Foundation. One of her most widely read books, *The Myth of Repressed Memory* (co-authored with Katherine Ketcham), was published by St. Martin's Press (1996) and has been translated into Dutch, Taiwanese, French, German, Japanese, and other languages. In addition, Loftus has been an expert witness or consultant in hundreds of cases, including the McMartin PreSchool Molestation case, the Hillside Strangler case, the Abscam cases, the trial of Oliver North, the trial of the officers accused in the Rodney King beating, the Menendez brothers' case, the Michael Jackson case, the Bosnian War trials in the Hague, the Oklahoma bombing case, and the trial of the Marines accused of culpable negligence when they severed the cables of a ski lift while flying in the Italian Alps.

DIANNE L. MARTIN is an associate professor at Osgoode Hall Law School at York University. She cofounded and is the current director of the Innocence Project at Osgoode, a clinical program devoted to reversing wrongful convictions, and teaches at both York University and the Centre of Criminology at the University of Toronto. Her research interests are criminal law, policing, and feminist analysis. She is co-editor, with Clayton Ruby, of the *Criminal Sentencing Digest* (Butterworths 1994) and, with Christine Boyle and Marilyn Mac-Crimmon, is co-author of the textbook *The Law of Evidence: Fact Finding, Fairness and Advocacy* (Emond-Montgomery 1999). Martin is a founding director of the Association in Defense of the Wrongly Convicted and the author of a study on the causes of wrongful conviction presented at the Inquiry into Proceedings against Guy Paul Morin (the Kaufman Inquiry) in 1997.

PETER NEUFELD co-founded and directs the Innocence Project at the Benjamin N. Cardozo School of Law in New York City, which currently represents more than two hundred inmates seeking postconviction release through DNA testing. In its five years of existence, the Innocence Project has been responsible in whole or part for exonerating more than forty clients. He is in private practice, specializing in criminal defense, civil rights, and constitutional litigation. He has litigated and taught extensively in both the "hard" and behavioral forensic sciences. His trials frequently redefine and expand the parameters of forensic psychiatry, laboratory science, and civil rights. Most of his work is pro bono and of public interest. His cases often result in enhancing public awareness of systemic problems, improving the criminal justice system, and legislative reform.

KAREN F. PARKER is an assistant professor of sociology at the Center for Studies in Criminology and Law at the University of Florida. Her current research interests include examining the effects of racial competition and labor market factors on racial patterns in homicide, exploring drug-related violence in Miami communities, and evaluating recidivism patterns among Florida inmates. Her most recent publications appear in *Criminology, Social Forces, Social Science Quarterly,* and *Crime and Delinquency.*

MICHAEL L. RADELET is a professor in the Department of Sociology at the University of Colorado–Boulder. During the past two decades, he has testified in sixty capital cases and worked with most of the last forty men and women executed in Florida. His specific interests include race and death sentencing, innocence, and the execution of the mentally ill.

BARRY SCHECK is a professor of law at the Benjamin N. Cardozo School of Law in New York City, where he has served for twenty-one years as the director of Clinical Education, Trial Advocacy Programs, and the Jacob Burns Center for the Study of Law and Ethics. In 1992, Scheck and his colleague Peter Neufeld established the Innocence Project at the Cardozo School of Law, which has either represented or assisted in the representation of more than forty men who were exonerated through post-conviction DNA testing and freed from lengthy prison sentences or the death penalty. Scheck serves on the Board of Directors of the National Association of Criminal Defense Lawyers and was recently appointed to the National Institute of Justice's Commission on the Future of DNA Evidence. He also serves as a member of New York State's Commission on Forensic Science, a body that regulates all crime and forensic DNA laboratories in the state, pursuant to legislation he and Neufeld helped to draft.

MARGARET VANDIVER is an associate professor in the Department of Criminology and Criminal Justice at the University of Memphis and holds M.A. and Ph.D. degrees in criminology from Florida State University. Her principal research interest is state violence in its various forms, including the death penalty, genocide, and human rights violations.

CLIFFORD S. ZIMMERMAN is a clinical associate professor of law at the Northwestern University School of Law. He has written and spoken widely on the issue of government responsibility, including the handling of informants. His scholarship in these areas and others includes articles in the *Hastings Constitutional Law Quarterly,* the *DePaul University Law Review,* and the *Arizona State University Law Journal.* He is also an editor of and contributor to the *Police Misconduct and Civil Rights Law Report,* a bimonthly journal focusing on legal developments affecting civil rights litigation.

Index